Please return/renew this item by the last date shown.

To renew this item, call **0845 0020777** (automated)
or visit **www.librarieswest.org.uk**

Borrower number and PIN required.

To Michael

SUD DE FRANCE

The food and cooking of Languedoc

Caroline Conran

PROSPECT BOOKS
2012

First published in Great Britain in 2012 by Prospect Books, Allaleigh House, Blackawton, Totnes, Devon TQ9 7DL.

British Library Cataloguing in Publication Data:
A catalogue entry for this book is available from the British Library.

ISBN 978-1-903018-90-3

Set in Cochin and Adobe Jenson by Lemuel Dix and Tom Jaine.
Printed and bound by Gutenberg Press Ltd., Malta.

Contents

CHAPTER SIX
Poultry and Other Birds

CHAPTER SEVEN
Meat   215

Foreword

The writing of a cookery book involves considerably more than just writing. Literary authors may think that their job is hard, but it is a straightforward mingling of creativity and intellectual effort, as they gather and then tease out their research or pound away at the computer, like Rumpelstiltskin.

But a cookery book adds physical labour to the writing and research; the early-morning shopping bag weighing as much as a sack of potatoes, which it may contain. You imagine or translate and write down and then cook the recipes, every single one at least twice, which takes months, years.

After the daily four-hours-worth of measuring and chopping and then measuring and chopping again, you are waxy from the raging heat of the cooker and the kitchen sink is blocked with graters and whisks and clotted pans. There is a scuffled track on the floor from the cooker to the computer and the table-space gets smaller and smaller. The balcony is a larder now, full of casseroles and baskets of pumpkins and cabbages.

My friends Beth Coventry and Richard Ehrlich shared this job with me, and I cannot thank them enough, for all the fun and expertise they brought along with their knives and aprons.

Finding the right tone (profound, historical, amusing, accessible were all possible), the apt title, ('Big Flavours', 'Wild Winds' and 'Garlic' all had a chance) and, most importantly, the conviction to go ahead, these are every would-be author's preoccupation. All of them were resolved or made so much easier for me by consummate editor, writer and friend, Carmen Callil, who convinced me it was all possible, and came up with the final title. I was always encouraged by my friends Fay Maschler and Dee Macquillan, by my partner Michael Seifert, who risked his health trying out all the dishes, and by my dear Languedoc companion, journalist and former editor at the *Sunday Times* (with me), *Observer* and *Telegraph*, Suzanne Lowry, whose knowledge of France is legendary.

I was supported by Lyn Roe, who manages to keep my head from kaleidoscoping. And I fondly thank book-maker and graphic designer Stafford Cliff, one of my oldest friends from Habitat days, who has helped me so many times, for his input on the drawings and the cover. I thank also the many writers whose books I have used as inspiration, all listed, I hope, in the bibliography.

And I thank my publisher, Tom Jaine, for making the book happen.

Caroline Conran
Saint-Chinian and London, August 2012

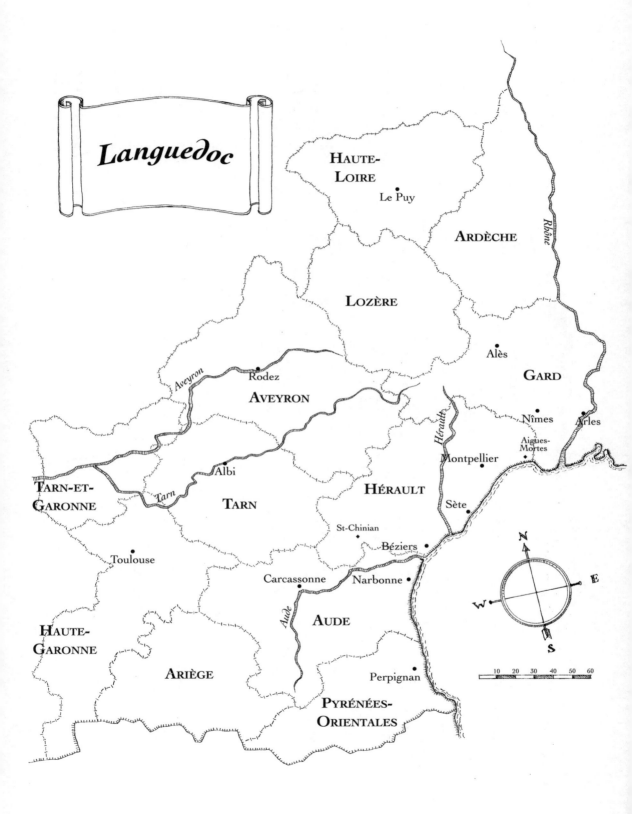

Languedoc

HAUTE-LOIRE
Le Puy

ARDÈCHE

Rhône

LOZÈRE

Alès

GARD

Aveyron   Rodez

AVEYRON

Nîmes   Arles

Hérault

Aigues-Mortes

Montpellier

TARN-ET-GARONNE

Albi

Tarn

TARN

HÉRAULT

Sète

St-Chinian

Béziers

Toulouse

N

Carcassonne   Narbonne

E

Aude

AUDE

W

HAUTE-GARONNE

S

ARIÈGE

Perpignan

10 20 30 40 50 60

PYRÉNÉES-ORIENTALES

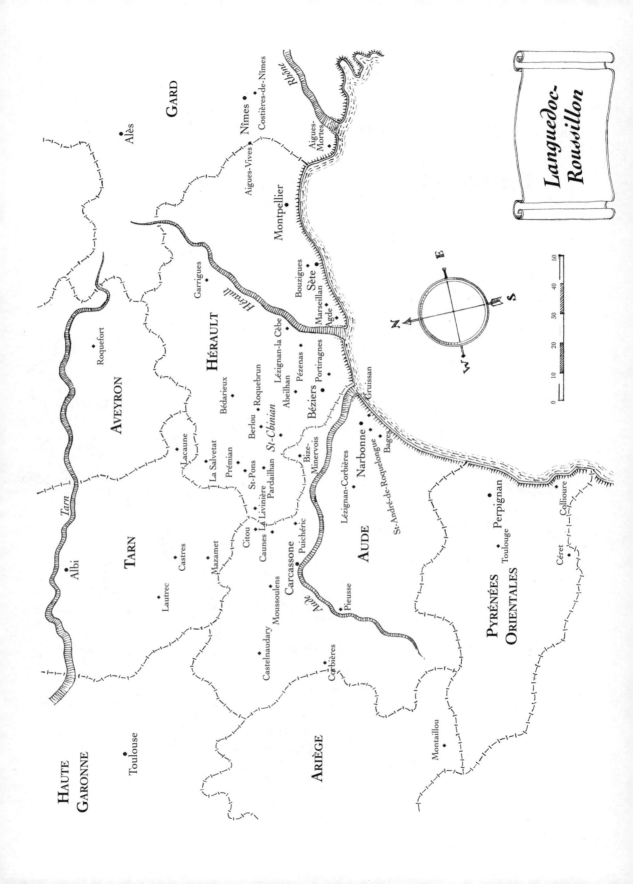

Languedoc-Roussillon

Introduction

A new country, when it is profoundly interesting, is often like a muddled manuscript that has to be decoded.

Henri Matisse

Some years ago now, leaving familiar French pathways, I stepped into the hall of an abandoned wine-maker's house in the Languedoc, and because it was near my friends and the light was so good I decided to stay – it was a step into a new country.

Near the house is a river called the Argent-Double – Double Silver or, as some people call it, Double Your Money. This runs at two levels. On the surface there is a clear stream, full of little grey fish, gliding over smooth rock. In a drought, it appears to dry up, it stops and then magically restarts a kilometre or so further on. But it has not stopped. A second, secret underground stream runs beneath, through the rock, in a hidden channel.

The village is equally disconcerting: one minute all noise – the *vigneron*'s tractor bouncing over ruts, people shouting, swifts screaming, dogs barking, people shouting at dogs barking; next, just as one decides to step out to buy a few things, it turns its face away and closes up, presenting sun-faded shutters and empty streets. Only a few lines of washing, a smell of food and a couple of empty chairs sitting in the street show that there are people living nearby. Is this the root of the occasional feeling of melancholy, in an otherwise loud and cheerful countryside?

France seems, in some aspects, to be very much a country of progress, pink and yellow villas among the old stone buildings, flying wind turbines, out-of-town shopping, municipal roundabouts, Norman Foster buildings. But something steady and ancient flows on, just beneath all this, that has held it together over time.

Everyone has a mental picture of the south of France, bathed in a golden aura, a sort of paradise of lavender fields and apricots, old stone farms and pink-washed villages, but I find that many people know nothing about the Languedoc, which covers half of the entire south of France, they are not even sure where it is, or they regard it as a remote part of the country, *la France profonde,* with not much going for it except wine.

Those who find it – lots of holiday makers do, especially from Britain and the Netherlands – find a magnificent land, and a people with a different, more democratic spirit to the rest of France and, until the nineteenth century, a different language.

Before the thirteenth century and the crusades against the Cathars, it was governed by its own feudal nobility, had close ties with the nations south of the Pyrenees and was effectively independent from the king in Paris: it was not part of France at all. The bloody and vicious way in which it was incorporated with France, in order to bring it into line and prevent its religious independence, has led to a fundamental dislike of outside interference and a very real lack of of respect for authority. In a country where the people in the next village or across the stream were strangers who spoke a different dialect, the north of France was a faraway place and of little or no interest.

However, indifferent monarchs based in Paris, and a corrupt Catholic Church, imposed their unwelcome laws and taxes on the people of Languedoc and such impositions led, over the years, to boiling rage and defiance. I can detect no reverence for the government or the Church today and have observed a complete failure to be impressed by officials, particularly high-up, religious ones. The Pope and his cardinals are considered, where I live, to be freeloaders. So the people are often inclined to turn their backs on 'fashionable France' and get on with their own way of living.

Central to most lives here is wine and, after wine, food. And one of the things that has struck me about the food is how it divides into two – mountain food and the food of the coast, where Greeks, Romans, Moors and the residue of old alliances with Spain and above all Catalonia have left gifts in so many ways.

Mountain regions have a topographcial approach to their cooking – robust, sturdy and often pork-based, all dishes rely on the fabulous local produce. The food is hearty, particularly in winter; it centres on game, beans, cheese mixed with potatoes and bacon, pumpkin, chestnuts, and air-dried meats, hams and *saucissons* aged in smoke-filled rooms, alternating with stews of giblets, a sheep's head, or some spiced-up tripe.

In its original form this is not designer-food – in fact the last thing on anybody's mind is spending time on the way it looks. It's the taste that matters, no necessity to make it look fancy, unless, of course, you are buying a dessert from the local pâtisserie and inviting people for a meal.

Here is the place to find the comfort of long-cooked dishes involving game, poultry, meat or offal with wild mushrooms, olives, garlic and onions. Garages are full of preserved tomatoes, dried mushrooms, hams, salted capers, olive oil, freezers full of wild boar, and of course barrels or *bidons* (large plastic containers) of olive oil and wine. The better wines of the region can now hold their own with pricier Rhônes and Bordeaux and as a result Californian wine-makers are trying to move in here.

A visit to the coast and the food becomes fresh and colourful – fish and shellfish based, tinted yellow with saffron (or with Spigol, a popular saffron substitute) and red with *pimentón*, steeped in olive oil and garlic, sometimes hotly spiced, with powerful flavours. For much of the year, it is life in the shade, under trees or beneath awnings. The barbecue rules here, and in every yard stands a brick-built hearth with a chimney. The air is perfumed with the smoke from grilling sardines or merguez sausages.

As you move closer to Spain, you feel the Spanish influence. Around Perpignan, capital of the *Pays catalan* and once the seat of the kings of Majorca, Moorish and Spanish foodways have taken root – here you find dishes that are sweet and salt, sweet and sharp, salty and hot, spicy food with rich juices, garlic sauces and a long-cooked onion, garlic and tomato mixture called *sofregit*. Olives, peppers, anchovies, aïoli and nuts feature often, and so do paella, stuffed squid and fish stew – all three served generously from enormous flat pans at every weekend market.

Alongside the take-away stalls are those selling cheese. Languedoc cheeses include Roquefort, strong and smelly mountain *tomes*, and sheep and goats' cheeses in all forms and sizes. Seductive *fromagiers* from the Cantal region bring their huge, bursting Salers, Laguioles, Cantals and Gruyères. Seductive? Because, for them, a small piece weighs over a kilo. Elsewhere, stalls are piled with pumpkins, *blettes*, tomatoes, vine peaches, figs, melons and, of course, onions and garlic. This is not polite France nor, according to Christopher Hope (author of *Signs of the Heart: Love and Death in Languedoc*, an affectionate book about his village), 'fancy France', this is France the way the locals like it, 'in your face

France'; Languedoc, democratic, independent, mad about hunting and foraging and all forms of self-sufficiency, has a flavour all its own, more southern, simpler, more earthy and pretty well indifferent to Michelin-style cooking from northern French provinces.

I have cooked and eaten here for some years now, and I haven't always eaten well in local restaurants and have heard some harsh things said about the food. One also hears over and over again that the restaurants are struggling, because they cannot afford to employ enough staff. Some are trying too hard and others not hard enough. It would be wonderful if there were more places that served well-cooked traditional local dishes. Because a little research uncovers how good the traditional local dishes are, and this book sets out to give a wider audience to their inspiriting, home-style cooking.

In the Languedoc, being Mediterranean through and through, everyone enjoys life, food is important, town benches, supermarket and market queues and cafés are loud with both men and women discussing this cheese or that way of cooking monkfish. Even tomatoes are a seasonal vegetable. This is how we all used to cook. Gardening here means growing vegetables and fruit; *potagers* are found at the edge of every village and town, continuously cultivated since Roman times. Men love hunting and fishing, women love foraging, two pastimes that go back to our hunter-gatherer ancestors, and the children are fed with the resulting rabbits, wild boar, snails, wild leeks and asparagus and, of course, wild mushrooms; thyme and fennel are gathered from the *garrigue* and the verges, and everywhere grow the vines that make the wine – nearly everyone has relatives working in winemaking, one way or another.

Tenaciously, in Languedoc, succeeding generations have continued to make use of local produce, and have always, sometimes out of poverty, enjoyed wild foods and dishes that contain just a little meat. And, over time, Languedociens have evolved their cuisine, making use of any small fish or sea creatures and what they call the 'lower cuts' (cheap cuts and offal) of beef, lamb, pork and poultry, ending up with their matchless fish soups and comforting fricassées and ragoûts. Everything is cooked in olive oil, goose fat or pork dripping, with considerably more than a *soupçon* of garlic.

Languedoc stretches in crescent shape from the Pyrenees to the Cévennes, from Spain to the Rhône. This arc of country is criss-crossed by Roman roads and pilgrim routes, bordered by mountains to the south and the vast limestone *causses* to the north and washed by the Mediterranean to the east and south-east. The plains, chequered with vineyards and olive groves, are threaded by that most remarkable canal, the Canal du Midi, which connects Languedoc to Bordeaux and the Atlantic coast, and by some major rivers: the Aude, muddy, treacherous and prone to flooding; the Hérault, clear and also given to the occasional spate; the Orb, travelling through beautiful gorges; and, of course, the Rhône, the region's border with the Vaucluse and Provence.

To embark on a three-page history of Languedoc would be to risk infinite accusation of inaccuracy and blind prejudice. Enough to say that it enters the mainstream of western European culture with the first coastal settlements by intrepid Greek traders in the fifth century BC, succeeded by more extensive colonization by the Romans three centuries later. They called their first province beyond the Alps *Provincia Romana*, hence Provence, and the western part of the region, beyond the Rhône, was called *Septimania*, perhaps because it was settled by veterans of the Seventh Legion in and around Béziers. The cultures that the Greeks and Romans encountered and displaced can be studied today at the museum of the Oppidum of Ensérune between Béziers and Narbonne, while the later remains of the colonists themselves are still to be seen at Arles or Nîmes, or laid out for our instruction in the museum housed in the Archbishop's Palace at Narbonne.

In the centuries which followed the Roman Empire, the characteristics of the region evolved through the ebb and flow of conquest and occupation, of settlement, cultivation and commerce. We know that the name Languedoc means 'the language that says *oc*' ('yes' in Occitan) as opposed to the northern 'language that says *oyi* or *oui*' or Languedoïl. Usually translated as 'language' or 'mother-tongue', the word *langue* can also be read as 'people' or 'land'. Occitan has more in common with Catalan than with the ancestor of modern French that was spoken in the north. There was a true difference between the two halves.

To the outsider, the history of Languedoc seems to revolve around a strong sense of independence and self-reliance allied to periods of outside interference and repression.

The centre of gravity of the region is southwards: towards the Mediterranean, Italy or Spain. Yet the political control, at least for the last eight hundred years, has been from the north, from Paris and France. Small wonder there were moments of collision and rupture. These have usually been expressed culturally, through differences of religion or opinion, even though the settling of the arguments came through the use of force.

In no episode is this seen more brutally than the Albigensian Crusades of the early thirteenth century when the French monarchy (based in Paris) and the established Church (based in Rome) combined to root out the Cathar heretics (or maybe they were merely critics) and their local supporters and to snuff out any latent political, cultural or commercial independence. The violence of the campaign is legendary, the suffering was great.

It was probably no coincidence that the process was repeated in the sixteenth and seventeenth centuries when France was riven by the Wars of Religion. Many in Languedoc were Protestant, it was only to be expected. The decades of repression that followed have seared the memory. Yet a sense of independence survived. In World War II, the Protestants of the Cévennes protected many thousands of Jews from Nazi persecution, and the region continues to be a home to dissenters, while rumours of Catharism are still alive in Toulouse.

This history of invasions, pogroms, wars, famines and plagues provides a picture of a corner of the world swept by constant turbulence and trouble. The people have lived through hard times and many masters but somehow have never let go of the thread of their own identity; one part of this is bound up with their food, and although people say the French have lost their way as far as cooking is concerned, a deep food culture is still to be found by anyone who looks. I have taken a look and I have found that the scope of the food and cooking of the Languedoc, like its beautiful landscape, is vast and timeless; I hope this book will reveal a small part of it.

Chapter One

The Tastes of
Languedoc

This chapter introduces some of the special foods of Languedoc – favourite ingredients and local produce, both familiar and unfamiliar. Some have a Spanish connection, or are special to the French *Pays catalan*; others have Moorish roots; many are products of the Mediterranean, like the oysters and mussels of the coastal lagoons.

Foraging is important in Languedoc; there are local methods of foraging and hunting in the mountains and forests, and practical ways of eating these free wild foods.

It would be impossible to find room for everything of interest, so I have simply described some of the things to look out for, and attempted to introduce a few of the unusual ingredients of the *pays*, all part of the siren song of the Sud de France that makes us long to be there.

Catalan Influences in Languedoc-Roussillon

I spent several summers in Spanish Catalonia. We ate well there, living on *pan amb tomàt* (Occitan, *pa amb tomàquet* in Catalan), tomato bread (see page 80), and grilled fish, prawns or chicken. More recently, I encountered Colman Andrews' book, *Catalan Cuisine*, and *A Catalan Cookery Book* by Irving Davis, and I began to realize what a fantastic and special way of cooking the Catalan people have developed over the centuries, part Spanish, part Roman, part Moorish. The cooking of Catalonia has ancient roots, and the Roussillon has the same heritage; it is still the *Pays catalan* today.

Catalan food includes salt cod, beans and emphatic deep-flavoured sauces. It has anchovies, pigs' feet and snails, grilled onion shoots (*calçots*) dipped in a spicy nut sauce, aubergine and peppers baked in hot wood ash, duck stewed with peaches, paella, potato omelettes, crème caramel, fresh figs, and toasted hazelnuts still warm from the oven. It revels in saffron, nuts and paprika. Every kind of chilli pepper, fresh and dried, mild and hot, green or red or black, makes a contribution and blood sausage and *chorizo* are key ingredients.

The Moors were the eighth-century conquerors of Spain and part of what is now southern France. They brought Arab influences and spices into the kitchens and streets of the western Languedoc. Even in the mountains the smell of cumin perfumed the air; we know this as it is mentioned as a spice brought to the village of Montaillou in the early fourteenth century by pedlars. The book about this village, made vivid by Emmanuel Le Roy Ladurie's painstaking dissection of the trial documents of the Inquisition as it pursued Cathar heretics, offers a bird's-eye view of home and farm life, right down to what they ate (cabbage soup with bacon, snails, wild mushrooms, ewe's milk cheeses), the way the women carried their bread (on their heads) and the kind of game they preferred for their pies (ptarmigan, pheasant and squirrel).

Catalan cuisine is essentially natural; it is not expensive but it can be quite complex and even quite fiddly – lots of pounding, which is made much easier by using a food processor.

Colman Andrews laments the fact that there is not much of a record of French Catalan food, but food historian, writer and cook Éliane Thibaut-Comelade has documented it thoroughly over the last few decades and she paints a colourful and detailed picture. She describes the legacy left by the Moors as crucial – it has given a taste for meat with fruit, for hot and sweet, sweet and salty and sweet and sharp flavours.

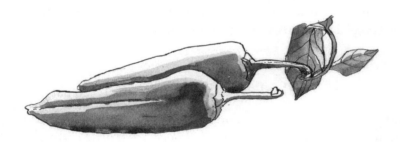

Nuts are often ground and used to thicken sauces; cinnamon and chocolate appear in savoury dishes as well as sweet ones; poultry might be cooked with prawns as in paella; and both meat and vegetables can function as dessert. In several Pézenas bakeries, little pies containing candied lemon peel and lamb, the *Petits Pâtés de Pézenas*, are still available today. Meat with preserved fruit is a popular flavour combination, for example spiced pickled figs or fig or peach chutney are eaten with roasted or boiled meat. These preserves are made with white wine vinegar, preferably home-made (*vinagre d'hostal*), cinnamon, cloves and sugar.

From Spain comes a love of mixing sea and mountain (*mar i muntanya*), shellfish and game birds or chicken, sausage and rabbit with snails, pork and chicken with squid. Rice dishes cooked in a *cassola* (a large, deep earthenware casserole) or a *cazuela* (an earthenware paella dish made north of Barcelona), such as *costellous au riz,* are ubiquitous; paprika abounds; and omelettes are thick, creamy tortillas (or *truita* in Catalan).

Although Languedoc is a major olive oil producer, Catalans like to cook in a mixture of lard and olive oil. Catalan sausages and black puddings are famously good, as are their ham and bacon – once enjoyed when slightly rancid, though less so today.

Many Spanish and also Italian immigrants ended up in the coastal towns of Perpignan, Narbonne, Agde and Sète. Pasta is indigenous and supermarket shelves are crammed with all shapes including *fideu* (Catalan, *fideo* in Spanish) – a local vermicelli – often cooked in fish stock with paprika, monkfish, calamars and prawns.

Le Ranxo – carnival feasts, *repas de carnaval* – are organized all over the *Pays catalan*, celebrating omelettes, snails, artichokes, the pig or anything else. They have been going on since the Middle Ages. Special celebration dishes such as *riz 'a la cassola'* – rice with vegetables, meat and seafood – *escudella* (page 139) and *paella* are their staples.

Black Truffles (*La truffe*)

Around Christmas and all through January there is truffle mania in Languedoc, particularly in the Gard. There are truffle festivals and fairs scattered across the region and chefs dream all night of new recipes involving truffles. Recent delights have included a hot toasted truffle sandwich fried in olive oil and served with a glass of iced champagne, black truffle macaroons, and truffled soup of *boudin blanc*.

In Moussoulens, north of Carcassonne, the January truffle fair, the Ampélofolies, is a fête day. It is often freezing cold and all around the centre of the village are stalls selling local winter produce (confit of duck, duck breasts and giblets, turkeys and other poultry from the Cabardes, nuts from Narbonne, spicy gingerbread, rosemary or lavender honey, huge mountain cheeses, charcuterie, bread, nougat, chocolate with nuts, rose petal jam, live snails, onions and the rose garlic of Lautrec), as well as hot food to keep out the cold (little meat pies, chips, grilled duck-breasts or Toulouse sausages, tripe, hot chestnuts, *millas* or polenta, beignets, oysters and omelettes). Stalls overflow with plastic cups of local wine, people picnic and snack everywhere, spilling onto the grass roundabout and verges, even into the bus shelter.

At the very centre, under the bare trees, trestle tables are set out, with a rope barrier round to keep jostling customers at bay. At a given time, country men and women (and children) drift in, carrying bags, baskets, holdalls, tins and boxes, from all of which exudes a powerful smell. Small hunting spaniels run amongst the excited crowd. The brushed truffles are laid out in baskets and on boards. 'Tonton a faim', a small marching band, plays loudly, while the buyers decide, from a distance, whose truffles they like best. The Mayor announces that there are altogether 22kg of tubers to be sold. Everyone cheers.

Finally, a figure appears holding a gun which he fires into the air; this is the signal for all the buyers (including me) to duck under the rope and rush forward to their chosen dealer, shoving their way to the front to grab the best truffles. It is hugely chaotic, competitive and exciting.

The knowing buyers choose round, large, smooth truffles which they weigh in their hands and sniff before buying, to make sure they are not worm-eaten and smell sufficiently strong. Some people pick out one, others five or six. Then they are weighed, wrapped in a twist of paper and put into little plastic pouches.

The idea is to take them home and use them immediately in omelettes and so forth, or to make pâtés, or to preserve them for an important occasion, for a truffled sauce for beef or chicken. Many buy truffles to eat at the Christmas or New Year's dinner, but they are at their best at the end of January and the first week in February.

There are quite a few of these small country fairs going on through January but, like the truffle itself, they can be hard to find, partly because of the general air of secrecy that envelopes the trade, partly due to the unreliability of the truffle – some years plenty, some years none – so these markets are not widely publicized. In order to track them down, contact the local Syndicat des Trufficulteurs.

In more sophisticated Uzès, they celebrate 'La journée de la truffe' which starts with 'Une nuit de la truffe', when all the best chefs get together to cook a magnificent truffle dinner, followed the next day by a truffle market. Demonstrations by truffling pigs and dogs show animals who seem to be very happy in their work. There are truffle-cooking lessons by chefs and at lunch time, usually midday in Languedoc, a giant truffle omelette is shared out.

Cultivating truffles

Growing truffles is far from an exact science, but they are cultivated in quite large quantities. They grow in symbiosis with plant roots. They are called mycorrhizal fungi, and they mainly grow on the roots of oak trees. These can be injected with the spores of the truffle and planted out in scruffy plantations where the soil is poor, dry, meagre and calcareous. Because of climate change, these plantations may now need automatic watering systems.

It is usually possible to buy bunches of inoculated oak, evergreen oak or hazel saplings at the truffle markets to establish your own plantation. You may have to enclose it with electric deer fencing, as much to protect the ground against human, as faunal, incursion. There have been a number of cases of truffle-rustling in recent years – in one an intruder was shot dead: and serve him right, say the truffle growers.

Out of 32 types of edible truffle, these are the five main varieties in France.

Tuber melanospermum Vittadini. Known as *truffe noire* or *truffe de Périgord* or *du Tricastin*. This is a fine black truffle with violet-black flesh, veined with white. The aromas include black radish, hazelnuts, woody humus and damp woods.

Tuber brumale Vittadini. This is dark blackish brown outside, greyish black inside. Its aromas are strong, musky, a little bitter and earthy.

Tuber uncinatum Chatin. Known as the *truffe de Bourgogne*. This is blackish outside, deep brown with white veins inside. It tastes of mushrooms and of hazelnuts when ripe, and is faintly bitter.

Tuber aestivum Vittadini. Known as *truffe blanche d'été* or the *truffe de Saint Jean*. This summer truffle is the most prolific but the least sought-after; it has beige flesh with white veins and a faint mushroom aroma, it tastes bitter and earthy.

Tuber mesentericum. This is a small truffle, black outside, brown inside. It has a strong and not particularly pleasant aroma, but tastes good if a little bitter.

Truffle know-how

Truffles can be kept for up to a week, wrapped in a loose piece of kitchen paper, in an airtight box, in the refrigerator. They may also be kept in a paper bag with eggs, which absorb the truffle flavour, ready to make a delicious omelette, or in a jar of rice. Truffles transpire, breathing in oxygen and breathing out a mixture of gases, including carbonic gas, which carry their aromas; keeping them at 0°C reduces this transpiration to a minimum. However it is best to eat them as soon as possible.

Preserving truffles

Truffes à l'huile is a way of preserving them in oil for up to a fortnight – any longer and off-flavours may develop. Slice the truffle and put it into olive or grape seed oil in a sealed jar. The oil can be used in a salad dressing, trickled over eggs or onto a steak.

Truffes à l'alcool is another way of keeping truffles. The cleaned tuber can be steeped, whole or sliced, in pure white alcohol or brandy or even Armagnac. If using a commercial preserved truffle, use it within a day or two of opening the tin or jar. The alcohol and the truffle can be used in omelettes or pâtés or for flambéing shellfish.

Cooking truffles

The first rule is they should be cooked as briefly as possible. Cook them with such things as eggs, chicken, fillet of beef, pasta, rice or potatoes, to provide a rather gentle background for their perfume, rather than with ingredients with strong flavours, which will smother them.

Leaving whatever ingredient you are going to use in your truffle recipe inside an airtight box with the truffle allows the aromas to start working their magic. This works extremely well with eggs (particularly if you wash the shells first to make them more porous) and with rice, but you can also, for example, put slices of the washed truffle inside or under the skin of an uncooked chicken for a few hours or overnight in the refrigerator.

Clean the truffle by washing and brushing it, if necessary, paring the skin off as thinly as possible. The peelings can go in a jar of brandy to flavour it.

Slice the truffle thinly and use it in a simple recipe – scrambled eggs or omelette are two favourites in the south of France, while my personal choice is for tiny baked potatoes topped with sliced truffles heated in cream.

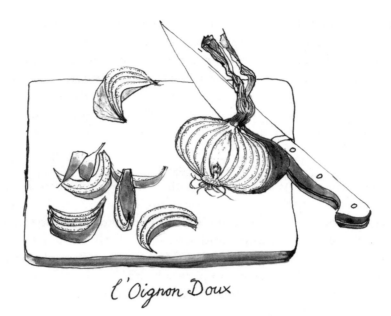

l'Oignon Doux

Sweet Onions and *Calçots*

Onions have a special meaning in Languedoc. They are grown and eaten in huge quantities, and villages such as Citou and Lézignan in the Hérault have their own varieties. One of the two settlements bearing the name of Lézignan is actually called Lézignan-la-Cèbe (Cèbe being a Frenchification of the Occitan *ceba*, onion). In the Gard, a wedding was not complete unless the brothers and sisters of the bride and groom ate raw onions, to ensure that they would meet their sweethearts in turn. The symbolic onion also meant that the marriage would be a happy and long one.

Raw onions provide a prized flavour in the region – large quantities are strewn on every salad, which may be why they have developed the most delicate and delicious sweet onions, cultivated from special local seeds, saved each year and guarded jealously. These are the most important varieties.

Cèbes de Lézignan, in season from June to August, are the largest sweet onions you are likely to come across – prize ones weigh up to 2kg, and they are said to taste as mild as bread. Grown competitively in the *potagers* and commercially in the alluvial soil of the plains, they are flattish globes of pale, tender, translucent flesh that can be eaten just as happily raw as cooked. Because of their high water content they do not keep over the winter. People like them raw with tomatoes, peppers or potato salad, baked whole in the fire, the oven or, traditionally, in a *diable* – an unglazed terracotta pot similar to a chicken brick.

The delicate pink onions of Citou, which grow amongst the cherry, apple, apricot, peach and pear orchards above Caunes-Minervois, are sold from open barns up and down the main street in August and September. Their shape is flat, with a sweet, mild flavour. They are eaten raw in green salads, *anchoïade* or with tomato salad. They are excellent for cooking too.

Rayolettes, also known as *oignons doux des Cévennes*, are the large, rounded, sweet onions of the Cévennes and from the northern Gard. They are grown on high and dry terraces once used for growing mulberry trees for silk worms. Their chief characteristic is their long keeping quality; they stay fresh from September to April. They are delicious baked in the embers of a wood fire or in the oven, and then served warm or cold with a vinaigrette.

The sweet onions of Toulouges (in the Pyrénées-Orientales) are ruby red and can grow to an enormous size. Local people make a wonderful onion tart with them, but they are also very good raw. They are cultivated east of Perpignan, where water from the mountains is plentiful; because of their high water content, they do not keep well.

Calçots (see the recipe on page 113), pronounced *calso*, are a passion in the *Pays catalan*, appearing at almond blossom time, starting in February. They are eaten with friends or in a crowd, an occasion called a *calçotada*, a hugely jolly, noisy feast, where people wrapped in anoraks and fleeces put on bibs and gorge on these fat juicy onion shoots, grilled over flames and dipped in a special red sauce, until the juice runs down their chins. And, as Irving Davis says, 'If it snows, so much the better'. They are available in London during the season from Tayshaw Ltd., Seasonal Produce, 60 Druid Street, SE1 2EZ – (0207 378 8666).

Beans

Was cassoulet originally made with dried broad beans? Possibly. I once saw a jar labelled *Févoulet* in Narbonne's poshest grocer, which was just that, and haricot beans, when they first came to France, were often called *fèves* or *fèves de haricot*, so the picture is linguistically confusing. In any case, broad beans, which came from Egypt, and black-eyed beans *(Vigna)* from Africa were staple foods in France long before the beans we now know as white haricots were introduced.

Haricot beans, along with maize and pumpkins, were first brought to Spain from the New World in the sixteenth century and given to monasteries in Seville who gave them, in turn, to the Pope, who no doubt had wonderful, extensive vegetable gardens at his palaces. Pope Clement VII was Catherine de Medici's cousin and he, among others, received, in Rome, some of the new beans.

Reputedly he offered Catherine some seed-beans to take to France; he was certainly present when she married the future King Henri II in 1533. Catherine then inherited the Comté du Lauragais (between Toulouse and Carcassonne); her daughter Marguerite de Valois married the future Henri IV, and it was in their lands in south-west France that the bean was first developed. It soon became a staple and the great bean dish of the region was, and still is, cassoulet.

What counts in a cassoulet is the choice of white bean. In Castelnaudary, the small, round *cocos de Pamier* are considered the best. Highly rated in Carcassonne are *les haricots de Mazères* and in Toulouse *le haricot de Lavelanet*; these small white haricot beans are also known as *le lingot* in Bas-Languedoc. The larger *lingots de Soissons* were considered the best around Béziers, according to Albin Marty, whose grandparents ran a bakery in the area. He can remember the time when everybody brought their dishes of cassoulet, already made-up in pottery bowls or *cassoles*, on Fridays, Sundays and fête days, to be cooked in the cooling bakery oven after the bread was baked.

In the nineteenth and early twentieth centuries, particularly in Toulouse, climbing beans were highly favoured; the best were the *haricots de maïs*. One in particular stands out, called *Tarbais* (for Tarbes, whose bishop first introduced the variety in the eighteenth century), a large, flat, very white bean, liked for its creamy texture and thin skin and for the fact that it does not break up in long cooking. Buy them whenever you see them, as they are the best.

In the spring, it was always the women who did the job of planting this crop. The beans had to be sown alongside maize kernels, and in order to make this easier, the planters wore special aprons with two pockets, one for beans, one for maize. The haricots would then clamber up the standing maize plants and, in return for their support, would provide them with nitrogen. The widespread use of weedkiller on maize crops more or less put an end to these excellent beans.

The name *mongette* or *mogette* is likely today to be applied to either *coco* or *lingot* but was originally the local name for black-eyed beans. (*Cocos* have round beans, *lingots* longer beans, while *flageolets* have smaller beans and *sabre* have kidney-shaped beans.)

Flageolets verts, green dried beans, are varieties that can be picked early on in their development and which retain their green colour when they are dried. They are at their best with roast lamb.

In the mid-twentieth century, food snobbery started to set in, even in rural areas. Fresh green beans were considered, together with asparagus, to be an altogether finer, classier food to serve than dried haricots, which were regarded as a shade too rustic and associated with harder times, along with potatoes and the good, healthy cabbage. Young green beans – bush (*haricots nains)* and climbing (*haricots à rames*) – known as *haricots verts* or as *barraquets* in the south-west, and delicate *haricots beurres,* yellow podded beans, were finer, took less cooking, and could be preserved by salting, bottling and canning. The fact that, once preserved, they bore no resemblance to the freshly picked bean did not seem to matter.

When deep-freezing came along, many took to the freezer to preserve their green bean crops, but there are still whole shopfuls of preserving jars. Even supermarkets carry them and older people still grow and bottle their own beans, peas and tomatoes as well as home-made *confit* and pâtés. A wonderful nineteenth-century photograph shows a young girl in a kitchen stuffing peas and beans into empty wine bottles ready for sterilizing.

At one time, the indigestibility of haricot beans was much discussed: 'refined' people could no longer tolerate the vulgar farting that usually follows the eating of beans. So from having been a staple food, served in soups, cassoulets and in other ways at least twice a week, dried beans are now barely eaten once a month and most growers have succumbed to concentrating on the modern, easily cultivated hybrids.

However there are still a few of the older sorts to be had. In autumn and early winter one can still find *cocos de Pamiers, cocos roses* (similar to borlotti or pinto beans) or *Tarbais* beans at good grocers and in the markets. From August they can be bought fresh – as *haricots à écosser* or *haricots en grains,* and they make the most wonderful soups.

If you buy these semi-fresh early in the season, say in November or December, they will take less time to soak and cook – they get more recalcitrant with age. More than a year old and they may never get really tender. It is sometimes suggested that the beans must be cooked in rainwater as hard water toughens them up; another tip introduces bicarbonate of soda to the cooking water.

Foie Gras

Foie gras, fattened goose or duck liver, is one of the main treats on every menu in Languedoc. Produced in traditional poultry farms, mainly from *mulard* ducks (a Muscovy/Pekin hybrid), it is a food that has become controversial in some parts of the world. Animal-rights activists object to the production methods involved and in America, after a now-repealed ban in Chicago, its sale is forbidden in California from 2012. Other places, for example Turkey and Argentina, do not permit the production of *foie gras*, although there is no restriction on its sale.

These criticisms have done some harm to a traditional practice, but *foie gras* producers and others, in order to set the record straight, have now done a great deal of research into *gavage* (the feeding of large quantities of food directly into the bird's stomach) to see if it really is harming the birds. Below are some of the facts set out by Ariane Daguin, the daughter of three-star Gascon chef André Daguin and an expert on the subject. (Incidentally, I personally have seen a cormorant swallowing a whole, enormous live eel, with difficulty but obvious enjoyment, and I am convinced that the *gavage* does not cause pain or discomfort.)

> *Fact no. 1*: Ducks have no gag reflex and their oesophagi have a tough lining so they can swallow huge fish or other prey without pain. As the National Audubon Society states: 'birds have a remarkable ability to expand the mouth and stretch the esophagus to swallow large prey.' *Gavage* takes advantage of a natural trait of the bird – its ability to swallow large volumes of food without feeling pain. Veterinarians use this same feeding technique to save the lives of waterfowl, and parent birds use it to feed their young by plunging their long sharp beaks into their baby bird's oesophagus. Nature

does not operate according to the animal rights agenda, and numerous videos attest to the capacity of ducks to swallow whole prey.

Fact no. 2: In nature, web-footed birds gorge themselves and store calories as fat in their livers before migration. The effect is reversible, proving that a fattened liver (*foie gras*) is a natural propensity in ducks and geese. When waterfowl arrive at their migration destination, the fattened liver has returned to normal size, after being reabsorbed by the body for energy. Likewise, the liver of ducks fed for *foie gras* will return to normal if the feeding is halted.

Anyone who has been to a winter Foire au Gras will have seen the enormous pride that the people take in producing the best *foie gras* for the Christmas and New Year celebrations. It is sold raw or cooked, and is easy to cook at home.

The best buy is raw, vacuum-packed goose or duck *foie gras*, ready to cook. To cook it yourself, see the recipe of page 96. A slice or two of the classic, silky, just-cooked *foie gras*, lightly flavoured with pepper and Armagnac, together with toasted *pain de campagne* and a glass of sweet muscat wine, sets the perfect mood at any feast. Muscat de St-Jean-de-Minervois and Beaumes-de-Venise are popular, as is Sauternes. I prefer a glass of chilled Blanquette de Limoux, light and clean and sparkling.

Garlic

The rose-coloured garlic of Lautrec

The romantically named *ail rose de Lautrec*, plaited into silvery pink tresses, is endowed with two qualities that make it sought-after – it is delicately flavoured, sweet, concentrated and juicy, and the bulbs keep better and longer than any other garlic; in the right conditions (cool, dry and dark – think barn or wine cellar), they will last for up to a year.

The Tarn village of Lautrec, a steep, ancient *village perché* close to Castres, is the hub of the garlic growing industry, whose abundant, pink striped bunches – 4,000 tons of them each year – shedding the thinnest of papery integuments, find their way into every market and most barns, outhouses, kitchens and, eventually, on to tables throughout the region.

Lautrec has a market on Fridays where the garlic is on sale, and once a year, at the beginning of August, they hold a garlic fête, complete with sculptures of snails, castles and swans (all in garlic) competing for a prize. There is street dancing, and a typical, creamy garlic soup served *al fresco* at midday.

Buyers are keen but choosy. They know what to look for – clean, firm, plump, rosy garlic with no signs of bolting (green shoots) or of mould. They buy several kilos at a time, piling it into the boots of their cars, and they will use it all over the winter and early spring. Then the immature, new season's garlic comes and they will enjoy that for a month or two, until, in August, the main crop is perfectly ripe and ready to store again.

Purple garlic

L'ail violet is plump, juicy and attractive to look at. If pungency is what you are after, it can also be extremely strong. It is grown near Toulouse, Cadours being the centre of the growers' syndicate. At their garlic festival they build all sorts of decorated little houses, follies and even lighthouses out of garlic to show it off.

Chocolate

Cocoa beans came to Spain with Cortés in 1528 and were at first available, crushed and pounded, as a stimulating, seductive chocolate drink, a drink too good for common people and kept only for the nobility of the Spanish court. It was not until 1585 that it escaped into the wider world. The first record of Jewish chocolate makers in France was in the early 1600s. Their relatives who, like them, fled from the Portuguese and Spanish Inquisitions, had landed in South America, Curaçao and Jamaica and there they learned how to cultivate and process cocoa beans. They were soon ready to market them in Europe, and a number of these enterprising plantation founders decided to form trading companies to export the beans that would make a drink so irresistible it would seduce all the Catholic ladies of Spain and south-west France .

These refugee Jewish families in South America shared their knowledge with French relations, who learned how to roll and crush the beans to a paste, to make a drink, and to flavour their frothy chocolate with sugar and cinnamon and sometimes vanilla, not a bad combination. They kept all the details of the process secret. According to the food historian, the late Sophie Coe, what then happened to the Jewish chocolatiers is 'the dark secret'. This is a précis of her research.

> The Musée Basque, located in Bayonne, France, has an interesting exhibition which shows how, as early as 1609, Jewish immigrants roasted cocoa beans in a small oven and then ground them with a roller on a heated concave table … to make a thick paste. This table was dragged by its owners from house to house in order to prepare the hot chocolate drink.
>
> Eventually, the secret of preparation was let out and in 1681 Catholic chocolatiers, who had learned the lengthy process of making the chocolate drink, united and had the local leaders issue ordinances against the Jewish chocolatiers in order to make it difficult for them to trade. … Before long the Jews could not own or rent any properties and had to pay special taxes. By 1761 eleven French and Spanish chocolatiers had formed a Guild of Chocolatiers. This gave them the exclusive right, according to the statutes of the guild, to be the sole chocolatiers licensed to sell chocolate or own stores. This was annulled in 1767 by a court in Bordeaux. However by 1802 only two Jewish chocolate makers remained.

It is not an edifying story. What did remain was great expertise in the making and eating of chocolate. Yves Thuriès at Cordes in the Tarn, winner of the Meilleur Ouvrier de France Award, is an example of the legacy of fine chocolate-making left by the Jewish chocolatiers.

Rosé des Prés

Ceps and Other Fungi

Wild mushrooms in all shapes and colours are an ancestral food in Languedoc. Any recipe called *à la languedocienne* is more or less guaranteed to have dried or fresh mushrooms in it somewhere. There is a huge variety, and the following are some of the most popular.

Rovellos

One of the most sought-after mushrooms is the milk cap, *Lactarius sanguifluus* (*lactaire vineux*), a Catalan favourite growing mainly in limestone areas. Known locally as *rovellos* or *sang de Christ* (blood of Christ), these are fragrant milk caps of a reddish-bronze colour, which weep a tiny tear of strange, blood-red milk when they are cut. You will find them piled up on the market stalls in autumn, looking a little alarming, as they bruise so easily.

Roussillous

Another local milk cap, good but not quite as good, is found in spruce or pine woods and appears in autumn, vividly piled on market stalls at Carcassonne and elsewhere. Look for conical, amber-coloured mushrooms, stained blue on the cap. It's the *Lactarius deliciosus*, also known as *barigoule* or *catalan*. Spicy and crisp, these are much appreciated straight from the grill, although they may also be pickled before they are eaten, to remove the bitterness. See the recipe on page 257 for marinated mushrooms with raisins.

Roussillous and *rovellos* are often grilled over vine prunings, with drips of lard or bacon fat poured onto them to crisp them up. Another method of barbecuing them is the *Roussillonade* – the fire composed of pine-cones. You have brought with you a small metal grill, some olive oil, salt, bread and a fresh sausage, about 250g for each picnicker. Place the grill over the embers and grill the sausage and the mushrooms, lightly sprinkled with olive oil and salt. A scattering of chopped garlic and parsley is also good with any wood-grilled fungi.

Another fine Catalan dish combines *roussillous* or *rovellos* with black pudding; the mushrooms are fried with garlic and a few lardons in olive oil, then black pudding, cut in pieces, is added to the pan (see page 234).

Girolles

Often called *chanterelles* in other parts of France, the apricot-scented orange-yellow *Cantharellus cibarius* is a strong contender in the mushroom popularity contest, and occasionally even has its own weather forecast on a sideshoot of the French *météo* map. It comes relatively early in the season, in August; is frequently found in great masses; and is probably one of the most delicate, delicious and appetizing of all mushrooms. You may find them in troops, large and small together, under beech trees. They emerge in fortnightly cycles, so if you walk to your chosen spot and pick them all, when you come back a fortnight later, more will have grown. They tend to be gritty. To prepare them see page 259.

Cèpes

My first mushroom hunt, or *cueillette de champignons*, took place in the Montagne Noire with Lionel and Françoise Raviat, friends and fine cooks from the neighbouring village of Caunes-Minervois. This Montagne is in fact a range across the south-western corner of the Massif Central, rising at its highest to over 1200 metres, and straddling the boundaries of the Tarn, the Aude, the Hérault and Haute-Garonne. After a lifetime of hunting and identifying edible fungi, it was extremely humbling to find out how much I did not know.

We set out early on a chill but fine September morning to meet at their house, a wooden cabin with many mod. cons., high up in the Montagne Noire, where they spend the whole summer to escape the heat. We had espresso coffee from their machine and set out in a van, driving up higher and deeper into the interior of the chestnut, beech and pine forests that cover the mountains, called black because there was once a charcoal industry there, although they do also look very black from a distance, if the rain is coming and the light is clear.

We were looking for ceps. There are many different varieties in the *boletus* species, each one with its own particular habitat, growing close to, and symbiotic with particular trees. Birch, beech, pine, fir, oak and hornbeam are all host trees.

When mushroom hunting, it is important to have the right kit; a sleeveless jacket is good, leaving your arms free to grab a branch as you slide down a bank, although all too often the branch snaps off in your hand and you fall down anyway.

You need a basket, and a folding knife to cut the mushroom and to slice the stalk in order to inspect suspect fungi for worms and to cut off the dirty bits of each specimen as you pick it, so it does not soil the others. Some of these knives have a little brush at one end to brush off leaf-mould and grit, and it is correct to fasten the knife to the basket with a leather thong so it does not get lost.

The basket has two purposes, one is that it lets the mushrooms breathe; in a plastic bag they squash and go soggy. The second is more interesting – as you walk through the forest, spores, drifting from the undersides of your mushrooms, fall through the basket onto the ground, where hopefully they may start to grow. This is cited as one reason why you often find more mushrooms along the sides of rides (wide tracks used by foresters and hunters) – another is that the ride is usually a bit sunnier and warmer than the dark spaces under the trees.

Seasoned mushroom hunters often take a long stick; this is to steady you as you jump across ditches, climb up banks and generally scramble about, and it is useful for pushing plants aside in order to look underneath. It may have a forked end, which can be used for lifting brambles out of the way and, of course, for dealing with adders. In Mazamet, a town on the north side of the Montagne Noire, they traditionally have walking sticks with baskets attached, but this is cumbersome.

Mushroom hunting in this part of the world is very serious. Children are taught to identify the edible ones at school. Every chemist has charts on show and you can take your pick to the pharmacist, who will identify them and take out any that are poisonous or suspect.

We were given to understand that if a car with number-plates from another department were to park near someone else's mushroom patch or *nid*, the tyres might be slashed.

The fascinating thing about mushrooms is that when they come, they sometimes come in big quantities – Françoise once picked 40 kilos in one morning.

But what can you do with so many mushrooms? You can sell them, which means either standing on the side of a busy road with your basket, or having an outlet, usually a stall at one of the markets – Carcassonne Saturday market is a particularly rich hunting ground for buying wild mushrooms of all sorts. Or you can dry them – slice them and perhaps thread them on a string to hang near a fire (the dying Louis XIII passed his last hours stringing fresh mushrooms for drying), or place them on racks or *clayettes* in a dryer or the plate-oven of a stove.

Wood-fired drying racks were traditionally used to dry prunes and chestnuts as well as mushrooms and imparted an extra dimension, smoke, to the flavour. Wormy mushrooms can be used for this purpose as all the worms fall out as they dry.

The better specimens can be frozen. This is an art in itself. The cleaned and sliced mushrooms are spread out on waxed paper and frozen. They are then taken out, the ice-crystals brushed off and they are packed in bags in the freezer. When you want to use them, they can be eaten fried in lard, olive oil, butter or goose fat until they are a light golden colour, then sprinkled with parsley or a mixture of parsley and garlic.

There are numerous different ceps, each one with its own particular habitat, texture, flavour, colour and smell. The best of all is the *Boletus edulis*. They are firm, plump and crisp when young, with hazelnut brown caps wrapped tightly over bulbous, white-fleshed stalks. The caps soon open to reveal a pale spongy underside. With ceps, firmness and freshness are everything; they lose some of their allure as they soften and the sponge-like gills become rather slimy and not so good to eat.

When choosing them make sure they are firm and solid, with no traces of worm holes. Young ceps can be eaten raw in salads or with thinly flaked Gruyère cheese and olive oil, older ones are sliced and fried with *persillade* – goose fat is a good medium – they also make a good soup, tarts and potato dishes.

Confits, Poultry and Meat Preserved in Duck or Goose Fat

As you drive through the countryside of Haut-Languedoc, you will often see green meadows, sheltered by trees, scattered with flocks of white and grey geese and ducks. They are enjoying their freedom but they are shortly destined to be fattened up by force-feeding, in order to provide marvellous things to eat – *foie gras*, duck breasts (fresh, cured and smoked), goose and duck fat for cooking and legs and wings for *confit*. Every butcher in Languedoc sells *confit de canard* or *confit d'oie*, often displayed in large trays, with plenty of creamy fat adhering to it.

Crusty and golden preserved duck or goose legs, fried slowly in their own fat until crisp on the outside and meltingly tender inside and served with ceps scattered with *persillade*, potatoes sautéed in duck fat or Puy green lentils, is one of the great dishes of the region. The other splendid use for *confit* of goose or duck is in cassoulet, the famous and popular trademark bean dish of Carcassonne and Castelnaudary.

In the past, although big landowners could eat *confit* regularly, among the poor tenant farmers who had to make much out of little (and there have been plenty of hard times in Languedoc), poultry and their products were kept for market or for special occasions – to share with neighbours at a celebration. Sometimes, during the summer, when harvesting took everyone out to the fields, *confit* would be served at lunch, as there was no time to cook.

The fat was used in soups or spread on bread, and was often eaten rancid – in fact many preferred it that way. The giblets were preserved in fat in the same way as the legs, for a salad of *confit de gésiers*, and the neck was stuffed and turned into sausage.

The process of making *confit* is simple. The legs (*cuisses*) or sometimes the wings (*manchons*, a rather bony alternative and a bit cheaper) are salted to get rid of some of their moisture and then simmered very slowly in enough of their own delicious, transparent, melted fat to cover them. Sometimes pork fat is added to the poultry fat.

When they are tender they are placed in jars – originally round-bellied earthenware pots with lids and two little handles made locally, now sterilized glass jars or cans – and the liquid fat is strained over them until they are completely covered. The jars are shaken to remove any air pockets, allowed to cool, then sealed and placed in a cool place. Commercial *confit* is pasteurized, to make doubly certain that no bacteria can survive.

Confit, like ham, salami and all cured, fermented, salted and smoked foods, was devised as a way of keeping meat for the winter store cupboard. I have sometimes, when duck legs were available, made *confit* myself (see page 207 for the recipe). It was good, but it would be even better with the right kind of duck. The *mulard*, a Muscovy cross, has more robust flesh than our roasting ducks, which tend to give a softer result. Bought *confit* has the advantage that it can be kept in the cupboard for a long time, ready for eating on a crisp autumn day.

Coca or Coques

These are Catalan flatbreads, usually made with yeast, and can have all sorts of different ingredients, savoury or sweet. They can also be savoury *and* sweet, like the chard *coca* with pine nuts and raisins (page 297). Different *coques* are eaten for different saints' days. The *coques de Saint Jean* are eaten at Perpignan's favourite religious festival, a week-long jamboree starting on 23 June and featuring life-size painted saints lined up outside the Casa Parail at the Castillet in the centre of town. There are processions, bagpipes, singing, dancing in the streets, fireworks, *bonnets rouges*, costumes, and eating. St Jean's favourite pastry is a sweet *coca* with glaçé fruits and pine nuts on top. At the beginning of Lent, on Mardi Gras, there are *coques* stuffed with bits of deep-fried pork crackling called *grattons* or *fritons*. And on Sundays families, with children dressed in their best, share a grand *coca de recapte* (see page 295), which translates as '*coca* with everything'.

Chestnuts, Almonds and Pine Nuts

Chestnuts

The Spanish chestnut trees stood each four-square to heaven under its tented foliage. Some were planted each on its own terrace no larger than a bed; some, trusting in their roots, found strength to grow and prosper and be straight and large upon the rapid slopes of the valley; others, where there was a margin to the river, stood marshalled in a line and mighty like cedars of Lebanon. Yet even where they grew most thickly they were not to be thought of as a wood, but as a herd of stalwart individuals; and the dome of each tree stood forth separate and large, and as it were a little hill, from among the domes of its companions. They gave forth a faint, sweet perfume which pervaded the air of the afternoon; autumn had put tints of gold and tarnish in the green; and the sun so shone through and kindled the broad foliage, that each chestnut was relieved against another, not in shadow but in light.

This evocative description of chestnut gardens in the Tarn is from *Travels with a Donkey* by Robert Louis Stevenson.

Drive through the woods of the Cévennes, or above Olargues, in October, and you will be driving under the same trees, beneath a cascade of falling yellow leaves and plummeting nuts. Baskets of large and smaller chestnuts appear in the markets. In Prémian the baker sells chestnut bread, while in Olargues the butcher makes a juicy chestnut *pâté*.

After the *vendanges* in the ancient village of Berlou, surrounded by vineyards turning red, gold and bronze under the autumn sun, the winegrowers put out barrels to serve as tables and pour hundreds of litres of their wine to celebrate *le vin nouveau*, and in the streets of the village they serve, free, the 'bread from the woods', roasted chestnuts.

Saint-Pons has an enormous celebration lasting a whole weekend, during which two tons of chestnuts are cooked in the streets, roasted in great rotating cages over flaming branches of wood and eaten scorching hot in the cold mountain air. The town was a major depot for the dried chestnuts of the Cévennes. The crop used once to be brought in sacks on the backs of the peasants themselves, or in mule-trains, from the *châtaigneries* or chestnut gardens, and from here it was distributed all over Languedoc. Even now the growers come down from the hills with their chestnut harvest – in lorries – and set themselves up on the side of the road, in such unromantic places as the Zone Industrielle of Narbonne, to sell their crop. Another fair, Saint Firmin's in Uzès, takes place on 11 October.

The chestnuts at the autumn markets of Saint-Chinian come in two sizes, *châtaignes*, which are big and grow in pairs in their prickly shells, and *marrons*, which grow singly, are darker brown and absolutely enormous. They are a fiddle to peel but they are definitely superior, plump, firm and juicy, quite different from the somewhat floury, vacuum-packed variety that we tend to rely on at Christmas.

Chestnuts – *les arbres à pain* – have a big history in the Haut-Languedoc and the Cévennes; in the mid-nineteenth century cultivated chestnut woods – together with mulberry trees – covered the steep hillsides. *Châtaignes* were a most important source of food and income and whole families would be involved in their picking and shelling. Walking in the woods, it is still possible to see traces of the terracing, where slopes were planted with the handsome trees, to provide food for people, a cash crop, fodder and bedding for animals, firewood and timber for building and for furniture .

Varieties of chestnuts – there are over 100 – were developed to provide different qualities and to suit different growing conditions, much like the different varieties of olives, aubergines or figs developed in Languedoc, or, indeed, the different varieties of vines. In the Cévennes, round Mazamet in the Montagne Noire and through Olargues and on to Saint-Pons, chestnut trees supported lives.

The 'bread of the poor' bulked up winter soups, replaced flour in cakes, pastries and bread, even turned into a jam or a spread, sometimes flavoured with chocolate or orange peel.

Chestnuts also provided food for the pigs, it gave them good fat (lard was an important cooking medium) and good meat. Particular varieties of nut were grown to be turned into *châtaignons*, which were dried for a couple of weeks in racks over slow fires which imparted a smoky flavour and allowed them to be kept all winter. And over centuries country people sent their children to the fields or to walk to school on a winter's morning comforted with a bowl of chestnuts boiled in milk.

Almonds (*l'amande, Prunus amygdalus var. dulcis*)

Almonds have flourished in Languedoc and Provence since the fifth century. Once there were plenty of orchards, but this is a hard crop to grow successfully and the blossoms come so early they often succumb to frost; sadly, today, they are mainly grown in Spain and, increasingly, in America.

But the naturalized almond trees remain, growing wild in the hedgerows everywhere, unfolding the first beautiful, pink and white buds, creating wild bursts of joy along the edges of the lifeless vineyards in February, usually with some blue mountains and blue sky to set them off.

By July their pale green, velvet unripe nuts appear on the markets, ready to be eaten with drinks, either whole or peeled. The thick, soft, shells contain a mildly almond-tasting jelly at this point.

The nuts themselves ripen in September – there are bitter almonds and sweet almonds – two separate varieties; you can find both in the vineyards of the Minervois. In the Midi people often like to add a couple of bitter almonds to the sweet ones when making pâtisserie, in order to increase the almond flavour, but there is a limit to how much you can add, as they contain *cyanhydrique* acid (hydrogen cyanide) which is highly poisonous.

A delicate drink, *l'orgeat*, made by macerating almonds and making a syrup with the filtered liquid, contains quite high quantities of bitter almonds, but is then diluted to make something pleasingly refreshing. It is sometimes flavoured with rosewater or orange-flower water.

Sweet almonds are used fresh or dried, grilled or salted, with drinks, ground in soups and sauces, blanched, with fish and chicken, and of course in all kinds of pâtisseries, in particular *frangipane* for the *galette des Rois* to celebrate Twelfth Night and sweets such as *nougat, pralines, dragées* (sugared almonds) and marzipan.

Pine Nuts and the Umbrella Pine
(pin pignon, pin pignier, pin parasol)

The sculptural umbrella pine is a native of the Mediterranean basin. Its cones take three years to ripen, while other species fall at the end of two years. Inside and enclosed in the large handsome cones are *'pignons doux'*, pine nuts, encased in hard sooty little shells.

The resinous flavour of the *pignons* is an essential local taste. We find them in the *Pays catalan* accompanying fish, rabbit or chicken, in sauces and cold aubergine dishes and in pâtisseries. *La Languedocienne*, a flat, biscuity gâteau with a cross on it, is sprinkled with them, as is the apple-filled pastry called *la Narbonnaise*. Pine nut biscuits and meringues are in every pastry shop.

If you can get it, pine nut oil can be used to combat arthritis. There are other pine trees with edible nuts, such as *Pinus cembra* (*pin cembra* or *arolle*), but the umbrella pine nuts give the characteristic, authentic taste of the Midi.

Cheeses of Languedoc

Sheep and Goat's Milk Cheese

There are so many sheep and goats' cheeses to choose from, fresh or aged, dozens and dozens of shapes and different sizes, from a soft fresh lemon-shaped one to a large curdy cone, a linen-white basket shape, a disc with ferns, one with pink peppercorns, ash, wrinkled skin, smooth skin, a covering of vine leaves, black pepper, chives, to a tiny, hard little disc called *bouton de pantalon*.

They are eaten at every occasion; if not as part of a cheeseboard, then served with honey and walnuts, or melted under the grill and put on top of a salad. They are nearly all delicious – although you may not yet have developed a taste for the cheese rubbed with *marc* and preserved in oil. But here are a few that are due a special mention.

Pélardon. Every market has a stall selling small round flat goat's cheeses, little white discs whose pristine freshness makes it impossible to resist buying them. But the ones to look out for are *Pélardon* – these are the real thing. Cheeses can be adulterated in all sorts of ways, using frozen or unpasteurized milk, milk powder, and many kinds of industrial cheats. But these flower-fresh, creamy little cheeses, whose history goes back 2,000 years, have to be made in the authentic, traditional way and have been granted an AOC, which means they must only be made in their region of origin (the Aveyron and Lozère). The milk must be fresh, unpasteurized, from small, family-owned herds of goats who graze on the high pastures of the *causses* (limestone plateaux) and *garrigue* (rocky areas of low evergreen oaks and aromatic shrubs). Their fodder must be 80 per cent from grazing this natural, flower- and herb-rich flora. And the result is a cheese scented with broom, heather and acorns – not to be missed.

Picodon. Another small goat's cheese, from the Rhône area, made in summer with the milk of mountain goats. It has a spicy, sweet and sour taste and a firm texture.

Pérail. A delicate, creamy, round flat sheep's cheese made in the same limestone *causses* as Roquefort and from the same rich, Lacaune sheep's milk. A cheese of this type has been made here for centuries and was popular with the pilgrims on their jouney to Spain, but the earliest mention of the name Pérail occurs in the nineteenth century.

Roquefort. Salty and tingling, creamy and sweet, Roquefort, one of the world's great cheeses, goes back a long, long way – it was first mentioned in AD 79 by Pliny, and was the favourite cheese of Charlemagne. Since 1411 all Roquefort must be aged in the caves of Roquefort-sur-Soulzon for at least four months.

    The fresh and airy vaulted caves were carved out in prehistoric times by underground streams that undermined the rock and then formed a large reservoir beneath the mountain of Combalou. This then drained,

leaving the caves. The site is approached through beetling gorges of white rock and surrounded by dry, tawny grasslands.

The caves used by the Roquefort Societé can be visited. A walk through descending stone corridors ends in a cavern that takes up three immense floors, each housing 23,000 cheeses.

Originally the ivory-coloured cylinders, speckled with greenish mould, would have been pierced and left in rows in the cool, dark caves with some mouldy rye bread, to acquire *Penicillium roquefortii* moulds, the source of the blue veins and special taste. Today Roquefort is very big business, the principal sheep farmers keep a thousand or more milking sheep and most of the cheesemakers introduce their bacillium in a liquid culture grown in laboratory conditions.

The milk comes from long-legged sheep of the Red Lacaune breed, whose milk is buttery and sweet. They have to graze on the local *causses*, within 90 kilometres of the caves, an immense area which takes in parts of the Aveyron, the Gard, the Hérault, the Aude, the Lozère and the Tarn.

The Roquefort cheese bought in small local shops is sweeter and less salty than the one we are used to; the added salt presumably helps it withstand being sent abroad.

Roquefort prefers cave-like conditions, so keep it wrapped in foil in the vegetable drawer of the refrigerator; it does not like temperatures below 10°C, nor does it like to be warm for long periods. Paula Wolfert, the author of *The Cooking of South West France*, recommends eating it with black figs accompanied by a glass of muscat – I recommend the wine of St-Jean-de-Minervois for this, or a sweet red Banyuls, chilled.

Cow's milk cheese

Bleu des Causses. Produced in the north of the Aveyron and Lozère, this is a creamy blue cow's milk cheese, made from the milk of the old races of Montbéliarde or Aubrac cows, fed in the traditional way on the untreated, flowering pastures of the *causses*.

All the cheeses are aged for several months in north-facing, limestone caves in the beautiful Gorges du Tarn, rudely termed *caves bâtards*, simply because they are not Roquefort caves. They have natural chimneys called *fleurines*, which provide a flow of air lightly peppered with the microflora that play a crucial role in developing the cheeses. The summer-made cheeses are a little more creamy than those made in winter.

Wrongly regarded as a poor relation of Roquefort, Bleu des Causses is a splendid cheese in its own right, and has its AOC status; the flavour is unctuous and peppery with a long finish. A glass of Muscat from Banyuls is excellent with this. Like Roquefort, it likes to sit in a cave-like atmosphere, so keep it as I mentioned before and remove it an hour before serving.

Laguiole, Tome de Laguiole. Weighing 50 kilos, the mighty Laguiole appears on the markets, the rind coated with brownish dust, looking like part of a column from an ancient civilization whose hieroglyphics declare this is a noble cheese. It is indeed ancient, made from the unpasteurized milk of an ancient breed of cow, the Aubrac, in the mountains of the Lozère, Aveyron and Auvergne. The cheese is pressed, semi-hard, smooth and a bit creamy; it tastes sweet but has a distinctive bite. It is made in the highlands where the Aubrac cattle are pastured, night and day, for four months during the late summer.

It is certain that cheese was made here in the fifth century, and by the twelfth century it was produced in quantity by monks, who sold it to the bands of pilgrims on the Via Podiensis from Lyons and le Puy, jostling their way towards the relics of Saint James of Compostella and salvation.

This trade was highly successful; by the fourteenth century the whole area was a vast cheesemaking factory. However, the Church lost its sway after the Revolution, and the monastic properties were sold to farmers, called *buronniers*, who spent the summer in the high pastures in *burons* – the small stone dwellings where the cheese was made.

Today the cheese is made under strict conditions (no silage allowed) by a co-operative called Jeune Montagne. There are about 80 Laguiole cheesemakers; they also make a fresh white *tome* or *tomme*, that is used to make *aligot*, a glorious, gloopy mixture of cheese and potatoes (another favourite food of the pilgrims) still sold at Lézignan market.

For the best Laguiole, look for the name 'Laguiole Grand Aubrac', made between 23 September and 13 October. Accompany it with a good red wine from Costières-de-Nîmes.

Polenta – *Millas*

A light and fluffy polenta made with a little goose fat to enrich it, called *millas*, has been made locally since maize arrived in Europe from South America in the sixteenth century and became a staple crop in Languedoc for humans and livestock alike. Maize is still grown in vast quantities and *millas*, although no longer a crucial food, is still served at festivals and events such as the Foire des Truffes at Moussoulens.

It was made above all in the villages of the *garrigue*, when families killed their household pig in winter. Once the mixture of ground maize, water, salt and a spoonful of goose fat has boiled for the required time, it is poured onto a marble slab or into a container to a depth of one or two centimetres. When it has cooled and firmed up it is cut in small squares and fried, then served with sausages and a good tomato sauce. Or it may be baked in the oven under a rich béchamel or eaten with a sprinkling of sugar and a little fig or rosehip jam or crab apple jelly. For a full recipe, see page 132.

Charcuterie

Now we come to the cold times
When ice and snow come and mud
And the little birds are mute,
For not one is inclined to sing.

Azalais de Porcairagues, a twelfth-century woman
troubadour from Portiragnes, near Béziers

In Languedoc, with cold weather comes the pig-killing, or at least this is how it always was. The friendly and much-prized family pig, often called 'the minister', was cosseted all through the year, to make sure he was in good health. The owner would rub him with wads of straw and feed him up to guarantee he was enormously fat and happy. Pig-killing day, *la fête du cochon*, was carefully chosen. It had to be cold, dry and crisp, and coincide with the correct phase of the moon. It usually took place in late autumn or early winter, after the pigs had guzzled on chestnuts or acorns, gathered in the woods by the young children, and on the windfall apples in the orchard. It was once the biggest family fête of the year – everyone loved the excitement and took the shrieks of the pig, burning hair, spilling blood and oozing guts in their stride. Called *tue-cochon, pele-porc, pela porc* or, more poetically, *les noces du cochon* – 'the pig's wedding – this was the day to make charcuterie for the winter – hams, *boudins*, fresh *saucisses* and *saucissons secs* – and also to thank close neighbours and family for their help in this huge task, and for any other help, by providing them with a feast – almost always the same food, a dish called *frésinat* or *fréginat* (see page 231 for recipe). The neighbours who helped were called *les voisins du porc*.

Charcuterie is essential to everyday life in the Midi, particularly in the Pyrenees and in the mountains of Haut-Languedoc, where the forests of oaks and chestnuts historically provided foraging for the pigs, and where the cold, dry mountain air is the perfect atmosphere for curing sausages and hams.

No meal would be complete without some charcuterie, whether it is ham, pâté or one of the multifarious sausages and pork-based foods such as *fricandeau, farçous* and *bougnettes*. The Catalan word for charcuterie is *embotits* and these are some of the favourites, with both a French and Spanish flavour.

Saucissons secs: artisan-made *saucissons secs* – salamis made with cured prime pork meat – come in daring variety; you can buy them on any market, flavoured with blueberries, chestnuts, hazel- or walnuts, red pepper, black pepper, fennel, dried herbs, juniper, and enriched with any variety of meat or game, especially wild boar, horse, donkey, pig's tongues, skin and ears and even with duck. They are made large and small, according to which end of the pig's intestine is used as a casing. Each part of the intestine gives a different flavour; the larger *saucissons* tend to be more pungent!

Recently a new variety has been introduced – very tiny ones, to pick up in your fingers and eat whole with drinks at the hour of the apéritif, late on a sun-drenched afternoon. These are sold in bundles and aptly named *apéro.*

The long thin variety, called *fuets* (Catalan; *fouets* in French) or whips, are eaten, sliced on the bias, with a glass of wine.

Jambon cru and jambon cuit: the hams of La Salvetat-sur-Agout in the Hérault and Lacaune, in the mountains of the Tarn, are well known to be delicious. There are still several firms making a small number of fine hams, which are salted, air dried and sometimes smoked in large sheds in the towns. They also make and sell *jambonettes* – small pear-shaped hams made up of bits of cured pork – fat, smoked bacon (*poitrine fumée*) and cured pork shoulder fillets called *échines* (cf. the English word, chine).

Feche or fetge: one taste I have very nearly acquired is the taste for *feche* – pig's liver salted for 3–7 days, rolled into a sausage shape, tied with string into a roll like a joint of roast pork or put into a net, sometimes salted again with coarse salt and then left to cure.

It is quite hard, dark purplish brown and desperately strong and salty, and the butcher sells it by the slice, like pâté. It can be added to vegetables in order to make them taste more satisfyingly like meat: just one slice, cut into strips and fried, will flavour a whole dish of artichokes. It is also eaten cold with radishes *en apéritif*, with green salad, or with snails.

Pa de fetge: fresh liver sausage made with eggs, pork and pork fat. It is eaten fried and is strong and savoury.

Botifarró, botifarra negra: also known as *boudin noir* and *bisbe negre* are cooked black puddings. These may contain, in addition to pig's blood, diced pork fat, onions, pine nuts, bread, rice and spices. Particularly in the south, they may be fragrantly spiced with paprika, or more exotically with cinnamon, cloves, cumin or coriander, the Moorish

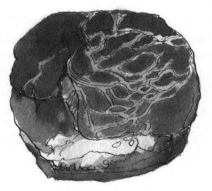

La Bougnette

touch, while in the Pyrenees they may be flavoured with garlic and parsley or fennel. *Bisbe negro de lengua* is black pudding with tongue in gem-like pink cubes spread through the sausage.

Botifarra blanca: a gelatinous, pale, boiled pork sausage containing a lot of fat, which sometimes plays an important part in *escudella* – Catalan stew (see page 139).

Botifarra d'ou: yellow in colour, this cooked sausage contains eggs. It can be eaten cold, sliced and served with other charcuterie. Or it can be lightly fried or grilled, though it does not require further cooking. Serve it with beans, with mushrooms or in omelettes. Small amounts can be added to soups or broad bean dishes. It should be kept in the refrigerator, but taken out well in advance of serving.

Bull: a unique boiled Catalan sausage made of pig's trotters, head and ears. Heftily spiced, it is served thinly sliced on *tostado*, toasted bread. *Bull negre*, black bull, is a black pudding version, also eaten sliced, delicious on top of *pan amb tomàt*, toasted bread rubbed with garlic and ripe tomato, and sprinkled with olive oil.

Le fricandeau: a sort of faggot, a mixture of pig's liver and throat seasoned with pepper, thyme and bay, rolled in a sheet of caul fat and baked (see page 233).

La bougnette: a lovely mixture of fresh pork, bread and eggs rolled into balls and fried in lard. It is good sliced and cooked like fried bread, for breakfast, or with a green salad, and it can be eaten cold like pâté. At Saint-Pons-de-Thomières they take it seriously enough to have a Confrérie de la Bougnette, with special meals in its honour. *Bougnette* may also be a simple beignet.

Le sac d'os : a sort of salted haggis from the Lozère, made from a pig's stomach filled with all the trimmings of the hams, gristle and odd bits of meat, including bits of tail, that were too humble to go into anything else. In order to cook it, it had to be soaked for three days and cooked for three hours. I have never seen it or tried it, and probably that is a good decision.

La saucisse d'herbe: a delicious sausage made with a mixture of half chopped cabbage or chard and half chopped pork and pork fat. It is eaten boiled in a soup or grilled as an accompaniment to *aligot*.

Les manouls: sheep stomach stuffed with tripe, sheep's feet, garlic and herbs all cooked in a court-bouillon with thyme, bay, carrots, onions and white wine.

Les tripous: small parcels of sheep's tripe stuffed with ham, garlic and parsley, a speciality of the north Aveyron. They are cooked for eight hours in a sauce made with white wine, garlic, carrots, onions and tomatoes and traditionally eaten before mass on a Sunday morning, having simmered in their own juices all night.

Home-made Sausages

Making sausages was an important part of the pig-killing day in most country households. All the neighbours came to help and the women scrubbed out the intestines thoroughly – in the nearby stream, if there was one – ready for the *saucissons secs* and fresh *saucisses*.

To make sausages at home you can buy sausage casings and use a Porkert or other mincer to process the meat as well as funnel it into the casings once it has been seasoned (there are several brands available, hand-powered as well as electrically driven). It only remains to twist the sausage into links.

Catalan sausage

The most exquisite fresh pork sausage is a Catalonian speciality. It comes as individual sausages or, often, as one long spiral, in a casing made of the small intestine. When it is made fatter, the large intestine is used (see page 94).

Toulouse sausage

This juicy, pure pork *saucisse* is pretty plain, made from good cuts of pork, plenty of fat, pepper and salt and not much else. A little garlic and white wine can be added.

Chorizo

Sold everywhere, the hot or mild paprika flavour of this pure pork sausage is well liked and eaten everyday, just as it is on plates of charcuterie, or fried or boiled, or in such dishes as roast chicken, stuffed squid or paella. If you make your own sausages you can make this too (see page 95).

Merguez

Merguez is a lamb sausage spiced up with chilli or harissa, and perhaps mellowed with sumac or cumin. This very different sausage is normally at home in North Africa, but has also made itself perfectly comfortable here and is a great staple for the barbecue.

Aubrac Beef

'Let your beef come from prehistory, your geese from the sky, kill your own pig; those are the fundamentals.' So thought Joseph Delteil, witty author of *La Cuisine Paléolithique* (Prehistoric Cooking), whose belief in a return to simple peasant values went as far as living in a woodland cottage without electricity or telephone. Pity his poor wife!

A suitably ancient breed of cattle, and one he would have approved of, is the Aubrac race from the Aveyron – glossy-coated animals, chestnut in colour, with black-tipped crescent horns. They provide fantastic beef and rich milk, but they are also resilient, have ancient survival instincts, and do well on difficult terrain or marginal grasslands.

As with lamb, it is only possible to rear grass-fed beef in the Midi by transferring the animals to mountain pastures through the summer – this is transhumance. In spring the Aveyron, the northern tip of Languedoc and part of the Massif Central, transforms itself from a bleak, cold wilderness to pasture, rippling with grass and wild flowers. In May, the cattle are brought up from the lower farms to feed on the rich grass, and their milk, unpasteurized, is made into the superb Laguiole cheese.

The transhumance takes place as the hay on which they are fed during the winter runs out, and the grass in the low pastures becomes sparse and desiccated under a hot sun. The cowhands, known as *buronniers*, would once have made the long journey with their herds on foot, staying up in the mountain pastures with them all summer, making their cheeses.

The herds, today, are brought up by lorry to spend their summer on the Aubrac plateau. Every May, on St Urbain's day, the cattle breeders put on a fête to celebrate the arrival of the cattle at their summer pastures. The cattle are polished until they shine and decorated with bells, dyed topknots, flags and huge collars mounted with flowers. In the midst of the most tremendous racket of bells, moos, shouts and cheering crowds, they descend from their lorries, mill excitedly along the packed street of the little village of Aubrac and finally launch themselves onto the succulent grass of the uplands, and here they stay until October. The grass-fed beef is prized and *steak frites* is about the most popular dish of the region.

Game

Hunting boar is one of the chief delights and most passionate winter pastimes of Languedoc. My neighbour André Galy was often out twice a week throughout the season and would, with his syndicate and his dogs, track down and shoot up to 200 boar in a few weeks, which were shared out amongst the families and turned into stews, pâtés and *saucissons secs*. It has been estimated that there are hundreds of thousands of wild boar roaming France, while in Germany up to 200,000 are shot every year. In addition, all over Europe there are farms where they are reared for meat in strongly fenced pens, often covering large areas of *maquis* and woodland.

The boar was always invested with god-like qualities. It is understood that ancient man experienced a feeling described by André Bonnard as 'otherness'. I have certainly felt it myself, walking through the quiet forests of the Montagne Noire, knowing that there were boars about and that 'the divine may exist everywhere, in a stone, in water, in a tree or an animal'. To our ancestors, hunting the wild boar was a magical quest.

The mythological boar depicted on Greek pottery (some of which is to be found in the delightful Ensérune museum near Béziers) is terrifyingly large, with stiff-bristled crest, huge shoulders and curved tusks like the crescent moon; these animals were recognized as the agent of the wrath of deities in many parts of the world.

Today we have guns, which make them less frightening than when they had to be grappled at close quarters, but they can still gore their opponents and inflict wounds that do not heal well, which makes them an interesting prey. In Languedoc they live in great abundance in the wild forests and *maquis* and shooting them is a major passion for many residents.

I inadvertently crashed a boar hunt when out foraging for mushrooms in the Montagne Noire. We had set off in our van. After about half an hour we encountered a 4 x 4 thundering along our narrow track. As we lurched into the bushes in time to avoid it, the driver shouted, 'There are lots more coming.' And there were. About a dozen assorted vehicles packed with men and hairy, muscular beige dogs with long floppy ears careered at speed up the hill. They were the boar hunters. They have always symbolized virility and pride, and these were no exception. I was not surprised to see the mayor of our village among them. We continued winding up the hill for a further twenty minutes, on a fairly perilous, cliff-hanging track – the views were *imprenable*, a word much used by estate agents, which I always took to mean impregnable, but really means uninterrupted.

By now we were high up, 2,000 metres, and in the middle of breathtaking mountain country. We finally stopped in a ride, and immediately saw six neat-looking wild boar running along, crossing the ride and turning up hill into thick pines. The boar hunters, luckily for that family group, had by now thundered off down the hill in the opposite direction. Their method is to look for recent traces, then track the boar with dogs. The beaters then go round behind the prey and drive them towards the waiting guns. These hunters wear camouflage, but its utility is more often futility as they need to sport bright orange fluorescent waistcoats to prevent them killing each other (not always successfully). They stand in a row on the ride or track waiting for the boar to emerge, then pick them off as they appear. This is a very different method to Tuscan boar-hunting when you, and many others, run flat out through woods and thickets in pursuit of your boar until you catch up with him, which may take all day. Once killed, the boar is gutted there and then and taken proudly home on the top of the van or 4 x 4.

The French type of wild boar, *Sus scrofa scrofa*, has evolved over the centuries into a lighter and faster animal than the equivalent hefty Balkan variety, *Sus scrofa ussuricus*. The Mediterranean boar eats a sparser diet and lives in a hotter climate. Over hundreds and perhaps thousands of years, they have often interbred with their relatives, domestic pigs. Wild boar have also been cross-bred deliberately so as to improve the quality or quantity of their meat, to enable them to be fattened faster, or to produce more piglets than is natural in the wild.

Wild boar are at once desired and detested by the Languedoc peasant. A foraging herd can wreak a huge amount of destruction in a single night by trampling and rooting up a vital crop. Today, one can often see signs of wild boar activity – large patches where the ground is all ploughed up. Small wonder that these animals have always been hunted ruthlessly.

Gaston Fébus, the Count of Foix and Viscount of Béarn, known as Lord of the Pyrenees, was the celebrated author of *Livre de la Chasse* (The Book of the Hunt) written in 1387. In it he describes how the nobles hunted with packs of dogs and spears, while the commonality made pits covered with leaves into which a foraging boar might plunge. Rather than condemning the practice, he continues, 'When one thinks that many a peasant spent much of the year fattening a domestic pig in preparation for the winter, an autumn windfall such as this in one's orchard was probably as welcome as the apples themselves.'

Wild boar was always considered a noble animal with 'strong meat'. Boar meat is actually more easily digested than pork, but it is vital that the testicles and guts are removed immediately after it has been killed. If not, the meat, probably because of the animal's thick fur which keeps the carcase warm over a long period, will taint very quickly.

The fresh meat, traditionally, needed to be purged with something acid – wine vinegar, white wine in a marinade or in cooking, or a sauce such as *agrodolce* with oranges or lemon and sugar. Cooking for a long time in white wine is still the usual treatment for a piece of boar meat.

Often wild boar meat was preserved like ham in the winter – that is, salted for 8–10 days, then smoked in the chimney. Alternatively, in the summer, it could be put in brine in a vat, then hung to dry in the open air. Nowadays it all goes rapidly into the various huge freezers that sit in every barn.

Wildfowl

In Languedoc, the definition of wildfowl is quite wide. Among the birds that would have been shot to eat until quite recently, and are perhaps still poached and eaten, are numbered herons, moorhens (now scarce and protected, but once described as queens of the rivers and lakes), plovers, larks, thrushes, doves, blackbirds, starlings, robins and storm petrels.

Wildfowl shooting has always been popular among landowners along the wild lagoons of the Petit Camargue, where vast flocks of ducks and geese make their home in the salt marshes and near the *étangs* or salt lagoons. The shooters gather at dawn with their hairy dogs and their guns, share breakfast, perhaps a fat, juicy fillet of beef and plenty of alcohol to kickstart their day and keep them going, and then go off and get very wet, splashing around in the marshes. They may return at dusk with hares, waterfowl, wild boar, venison, rabbits, pheasants and partridges for the pot.

Olive Oil

An old saying goes, 'A man who eats olives every day of every year, will be as old as the rafters in an ancient house.' In Languedoc everyone eats olives or olive oil every day, and the region is well known for longevity. Between the distant blue mountains of Haut-Languedoc and the Mediterranean lie the plains, covered by seemingly endless vines but made more beautiful by an abundance of olive groves.

Growing and looking after olive trees is an art, one passed down from one generation to the next. The trees are pruned to be open in the centre, so that a bird can fly through. This allows the air to keep them free of mildew and lets the winds of late May flow through and pollinate the flowers for a good crop.

The oil produced here is of the highest quality. In the seventeenth century, the great playwright Jean Racine stated that Languedoc had the best olive oil in the world. Many excellent varieties of olive have been bred here. There have been setbacks – terrible frosts and attacks from disease – but optimism returns as the trees recover or put out new shoots from ancient roots. Even today, new groves are being planted. I have also noticed new olive oil mills appearing, notably in the Minervois, which has the most perfect conditions for these beautiful trees.

Different varieties are cherished and are planted where they will best thrive. They are selected for table olives or for oil. In Bize-Minervois, 'L'Oulibo', a large olive mill, presses the varieties separately and produces varietal olive oils. This is where I used to bring my own olives to be pressed, when the grove I planted started to produce a good crop. I was paid in kind, and after trying all their different oils, I have decided that one of my favourites is that made from Arbequina olives; it is fresh-tasting, aromatic and a lovely greenish gold colour, with a lighter texture than some of the others. The main varieties are outlined below, but there are many, many more.

Picholine. This is widely grown throughout the French Mediterranean. The olives are picked from the end of December to the middle of January and are harvested while they are still green, which gives a hint of bitter pepperiness to the flavour. Strong and full of aromas, this oil has a lot of character and is mainly used on salads.

Aglandau. This variety looks a bit like an acorn, hence the name (the French for acorn is *gland*). Picked while still green, at the end of

November, the Aglandau makes a green-tinted olive oil with a flavour of apples or newly mown hay. It is elegant, excellent for salads, endives, asparagus and artichokes.

La Bouteillan. This is a very productive olive tree, which starts fruiting in its third year after planting. It produces 1 litre of oil for 5kg of olives. The oil is very perfumed, tasting of dried fruit, hazelnuts and almonds and is the perfect salad oil.

L'Olivière. This variety is well suited to Languedoc as it is resistant to cold. In 1956 it stood up to the great frost and survived where other varieties suffered badly. It is less productive than some, taking 8kg of olives to produce 1 litre of oil. It has a rustic character, tasting of dried fruit, almonds, hazelnuts and a hint of apple. It has a deep long-lasting flavour, a slight pepperiness and a slightly thicker, unctuous texture. It can be used for cooking and on salads.

Lucques. These are usually used for the production of table olives and it is fairly rare to find oil made with them. The oil is quite sought-after as it has a subtle perfume combined with a strong pepperiness. It is used for salads but is also excellent for cooking.

Arbequina. As I said, this is one of my favourites. It is grown extensively in the *Pays catalan* and Spanish Catalonia. The small tree is wonderfully adapted to growing on hilly, stony and difficult ground and produces abundant, small, oval olives, which generally have to be picked by hand. This variety produces a clear, well-balanced golden oil with a flavour variously described as reminiscent of melon, almonds, apples or 'orchard fruits'; I would say that it is mellow, with a fine grassy aftertaste but little pepperiness. Arbequina is eaten uncooked in salad dressings or on fish, seafood, cooked vegetables, and in mayonnaise and aïoli. It can be used in cooking, but bear in mind that it burns at a lower temperature than some oils, so keep the heat moderate.

All olive oil should be stored in a dark, cool place, kept in a tin or in dark bottles to avoid oxidization, and used within 18 months of pressing.

A pan of small clams, called tellines.

Oysters and Mussels from the Bassin de Thau

Bouzigues, on the Bassin de Thau, has an open sky, water as far as you
can see, changing in colour like mother of pearl, and a whole row of
little restaurants all packed to the seams with people laughing merrily
and eating tons of shellfish. The tables are piled high with enormous
plateaux de fruits de mer, everyone is wrestling with crabs and *langoustes*,
opening mussel shells and tipping oysters into their mouths.

People seem to get into a special mood when they eat oysters, happy,
excited, amorous. And if you like oysters this is the place to come. The
Bassin de Thau, a vast salt lagoon on which Bouzigues depends for its
living, shelters an enormous oyster fishery, with many farms – these
cannot be called beds, since the oysters are raised in a different way
here. Sticking out of the water, which is freshened twice daily by the
Mediterranean, are frames from which hang a variety of ropes, and
stuck to these with cement, or twined into them, are the oysters.

They hang in a twilight underwater world, pumping seawater for their
food, until they reach a good size, when they are removed, dripping
with algae, to be scrubbed, sorted and cleansed ready for eating; you
can see how it is done at the charming shellfish museum at the end of
the village.

The Bassin, 1200 hectares of water, makes an ideal nursery for *Les Huitres Bouzigues*, deep shelled oysters – *les creuses* – of the *Crassostrea gigas* strain. The lagoon climate and water give them a rich salty tang with a light flavour of hazelnuts. The original native oysters of the lagoon were flat shelled – *les plates* – also known as *pied de cheval,* as they look like the underside of a horse's hoof when opened. Now these are almost gone, only the locals know where to get them today.

Small towns and large villages such as Saint-Chinian, and the covered markets in Sète and Narbonne, cater for the local passion for oysters by having their own shellfish stands. Run by brothers, sisters and sisters-in-law of the oyster tribes, these are cheerful booths where residents can buy mussels, whelks, crabs and *crevettes roses*, and of course fine oysters on ice, opened skilfully by the most charming of mermaids, to be eaten at once, at café tables with a glass of dry white wine, or taken home to the table in the garden.

Oysters have been eaten since Neolithic times and the oyster and fishing tribes have long been living here. There must have been a lot of children about: the largest Bouzigues tribe were always the Benezechs, with no fewer than 32 separate families bearing that name by the end of the nineteenth century (most of the other clans consist of two or three families).

According to records many Benezech oystermen and fishermen (there were no women mentioned in the literature, although you can be certain they worked at the oyster farms too) were reported to be hardy and spirited, some troublesome and one or two downright menacing. Today's Benezechs seem to be charming and civilized, and they run one of the waterside restaurants in Bouzigues known as Le Grand Bleu, Benezech Coquillages, specializing in oysters, mussels, shellfish, octopus salad and plain grilled fish.

When serving oysters at home the oyster-growers offer this advice: unopened oysters can be kept in the fridge at 5°C to 10°C for a week after collection; don't eat an oyster if the shell is half open before you go to open it; if it smells bad; or if it has a sort of secondary pocket filled with water, which may be cloudy, underneath the oyster. A no. 3 oyster is small, no. 2 is medium, and no. 1 is large. For myself, I prefer small oysters. Serve them on a bed of ice or seaweed (or both) and eat them with fresh bread and butter, fresh lemon, Tabasco sauce and red wine vinegar with a few chopped shallots stirred into it. A chilled Picpoul de Pinet is good with oysters.

Snails

A little rush basket, hanging by the door of a stone farmhouse, catches the eye of a Victorian Englishman as he explores, on foot, some of the remote villages of southern France. He peers into the basket, and finds himself looking at a mass of snails. The owner of the basket, standing nearby, sees him recoil and says quietly, 'These snails disgust you, but us poor peasants eat no other meat all the year, except at Easter.'

There were indeed, many very bad years when there was no meat at all for the peasants, and when snails were vital to their diet, but they always were and still are eaten for pleasure too, in vast quantities. Languedociens adore them. I was excited, travelling through the *Pays catalan*, at being given in a small restaurant a great plate of tiny, stripy snails, all bathed in a delicious herb and tomato sauce. It was messy, but eating them with chunks of bread was a joy.

As far as health is concerned, snails have long been reputed as helpful for chest problems. The Victorian mentioned in the previous paragraph, M.S. Lovell, author of *The Edible Mullusca of Great Britain and Ireland. With Recipes for Cooking them* (1867), also recounted how:

> M. Figuier remembered, when studying botany in Montpellier, seeing the celebrated tenor, M. Laborde, every morning partake of live snails, as he was suffering from a weak chest. M. Figuier assisted in finding snails in the holes in the garden wall and under leaves, and M. Laborde crushed them with a stone, picking off the pieces of broken shell, then, rolling the fish in powdered sugar, swallowed them. [Calling them fish meant that snails could be eaten on religious fast days.] The remedy was evidently effective, as twenty years later M. Laborde still held his position as tenor, and sung at the theatre at Brussels and also at the Opera in Paris.

In the *Pays catalan*, people eat several different types of snails, enjoying some more than others, and cooking them in different ways according to their variety. In Caunes-Minervois, M. Huppé the school teacher recommends eating those flavourful, small pale or stripey snails known as *cargolettes* or *cagaraoulettes* (*Theba pisana*) that feed on the roadside fennel plants. Also known as *escargots blancs* and *escargots des dunes*, and once a speciality of Figuerolles near Montpellier, they are eaten cold, *en apéritif*, boiled, with aïoli, or cooked in a strong tomato sauce. To prepare them, put them in a bucket with a handful of flour overnight. Wash well and cook in boiling water for 5 minutes.

Then there are the very ordinary *Helix nemoralis* snails. They are known as *caracolo* in the Pyrenees, *limaia* in Montpellier and they are stewed in a richly spiced sauce, such as the one given on page 92, and eaten by sucking at the shell.

Helix aspersa the common, medium-sized brown snail, is the same as our garden snail; known as *petit gris*, they are the most popular and readily available variety, sold at markets in little string bags and eaten either in sauce, or stuffed with thyme, pounded garlic and butter then grilled over a glowing, aromatic fire of vine stumps or prunings, at a *cargolade* or snail feast, and served with aïoli. One person may eat several dozen snails at a sitting.

Vineyard snails, *Helix pomatia*, also known as Burgundy snails, are the best; enormous and handsome, with creamy coloured shells. These are rare here, and are eaten with garlic and parsley butter.

Snails come out of their hiding places in walls and fences after rain, and early in the morning, in spring and autumn, and are gathered as they feed on the wet, fresh greenery. Leave them to purge in an airy cage (some people use a barrel with a fine mesh over the top, I use the top part of a couscoussière, with the lid on) for 2–3 days, cleaning them out regularly and feeding them with bran or flour and bunches of thyme or dill, to perfume their flesh. M. Olmo of Saint-Chinian, a keen snail hunter, feeds his with fennel and bay leaves for two weeks, he then gives them a shallow plate of moistened, raw vermicelli.

Now let them fast in a cool dry place for 2 to 3 weeks.

When the fasting is completed, clean them under a jet of water, brushing the shells to clean them. Bring a large pan of water to the boil and cook the snails for 2–5 minutes. Cool in cold water. Remove from their shells with a large pin. Soak in a very strong brine for 15 minutes then drain and rinse. Remove the gut (the curly bit furthest from the head), if the snails are large.

They are now ready to cook. For those that don't fancy doing all the preparation (and you will need plenty of snails, about 20–30 per person) there is a shop in the Place de la République in Perpignan, 'Escargots de Roussillon', dedicated to selling prepared snails. Unprepared, they are sold on some markets including Carcassonne, Montolieu and Port d'Argelès.

A simple *cagouillade* may be executed thus: sauter the prepared snails in olive oil with thyme and garlic, add tomato sauce, chilli, salt and pepper and simmer for 30 minutes.

Catalan cargolade or snail feast

This takes place in the open air on a fine day and in a beautiful spot, usually at Easter, and it consists of hundreds of *petit gris* snails rubbed with salt and hot chilli pepper placed on a grill with a fine mesh and cooked over a fire of vine prunings and stumps. The fire must not flame. While they cook they are drizzled with melted pork fat until they sizzle; they take 10–12 minutes to cook. There is a special instrument, a metal funnel attached to a long handle, which is used for basting spit-roasted meat. Called an *entonnoir*, it has a small hole in the bottom, and as it heats, the piece of pork fat placed in the funnel melts and can be dripped carefully into each snail, drop by drop. Once cooked they are eaten with aïoli spread on large slices of toasted *pain de campagne.* The snails are followed by grilled black puddings, *butifarre* sausages and lamb cutlets, and it is all washed down with a red Collioure or a Corbières, served lightly chilled.

The Turnips of Pardailhan
Les Navets de Pardailhan

The crisp, silver-black turnips of Pardailhan are treasured for their dense, frost white flesh and sweet flavour. When I went to the mountain village in the Haut-Languedoc, it was spring. Wild thyme was in flower and I could hear donkeys braying. In a vegetable garden below the road a handsome gardener in a straw hat was planting the famous vegetable and he told me that if I came back on 15 October I would find him digging them up. These, he said, were the old ones grown by his father and grandfather, with the special taste – other people were growing new varieties that were not quite the same.

I did come back on 15 October – through autumn landscape spread with red, yellow and golden vineyards glowing in the sunlight, then up into the mountains. When I got into the village there were the donkeys and a charming farmer, M. Robert, who came briskly out of the vegetable garden at the foot of his fortified farm. Within a minute he had given me three different ways to eat the turnips and promised they would be ready in three days, but first they had to imbibe the rain that had fallen, to plump themselves up.

When I finally got my turnips, which are only grown here, as the soil has to be super fine and worked to a fudge, they were silvery with a hint of rose – still fresh and young. When peeled they were ivory white inside and juicy. 'Do you like sweet and salty?' he asked. Of course I do, and his recipe for sweet and salty turnips is on page 276.

Foraging for Wild Foods – *La cueillette*

The two old girls knew about walking. Best of all they liked taking a shortcut by a fallow, wooded rise, where according to the season, they gathered a very good harvest, whether it was wild asparagus and the shoots of wild hops – *lous pares et lous aoberus* – or *petit gris* snails or small snails called *cagarolettes*, or blackberries or rose-hips, *les gratte-culs*, for jelly – we had no raspberries or wild strawberries where we lived of course – or simply mixed, wild salad-leaves including *rouquette*.

The resourceful ladies described by Albin Marty were enjoying what is called in French *la cueillette* – a term which describes the gathering of quite a wide range of wild foods, including mushrooms, nuts, berries, wild fruits, roots, snails, *herbettes* and *saladettes* and other wild plants; the equivalent English word would be foraging.

From earliest times *la chasse, la pêche* and *la cueillette* were important supplements to resources. The Stone Age hunter-gatherers, of whom there are wonderful and exciting traces in this part of the world, roamed freely over the country and included as the main elements of their subsistence diet the fruits of their hunting, fishing and gathering expeditions. As they took up growing grain and keeping animals, they continued to supplement their harvests with wild foods.

In the Middle Ages, much grazing and forest in Languedoc was still common land. In addition to the commons, traditional practices of *vaine pâture* (sending cattle or flocks onto private fallow land or *friches*) and *droit de parcours* (allowing livestock access to forests across private land) were followed and wild plants could be gathered from these spaces. The people regarded this as a right.

As late as the sixteenth century, they were practising *assolement*, a biennial harvest system in which fields were cropped every other year and allowed to lie fallow for a year in between to recover their fertility. It was on fallow land, untainted by artificial fertilizers and herbicides, and also in the *garrigues,* that an enormous number of species of edible wild plants grew in spring, emerging between January and the end of April. The season was over when they started to flower and became tough and stringy, or when the grasses grew up to smother them. These plants formed an important and cost-free element of the late winter and spring diet, particularly when other foods were scarce.

Understandably, then, the peasants' view was that wastelands, woodlands and water were in some way at their disposal, and that they could take what they liked at the times they deemed best and in reasonable quantities. These rights were disputed in the sixteenth century by the landowners, but the peasants protested and eventually put their case in the list of grievances, the *Cahiers de Doléances*, compiled before the French Revolution and they won their rights back.

Since then *la cueillette* has been free to anyone who likes finding their own food. To the inhabitants of Languedoc there is decidedly more to *la cueillette* than a culinary interest or a fascinating walk; a full basket, is a right and also answers a very basic urge. This free food is part of their local identity, along with fêtes, local legends, folk tales, sayings and songs, and the reason they still have these rights is because over the centuries they have protested and fought against any attempt by landowners and politicians to take them away.

The older generation, the *troisième age*, knows all about wild herbs, the young not so much. But a knowledge of edible and toxic plants and the ability to forage has frequently meant the difference between health and sickness, even, at times, the difference between life and death.

In hard times, you will at least know where to get your greens, but if you pick the wrong plant and feed it to your family, you could poison them. There have been, thanks to wars, plagues, bad management and bad weather, recurrent famines in Languedoc, and as recently as 1943, during the deprivations of the Second World War, mothers have kept their children alive on bread made from acorns or fern roots, or, as one doctor reported, poisoned their families on hemlock, trying to fill their empty stomachs. To be totally safe, choose your wild foodstuffs from the considerable quantity of such easily identifiable vegetables as wild leeks, dandelions and wild asparagus sold on the markets, together with snails, lime-blossoms for tisanes, chestnuts and chestnut flour, wild mushrooms and wild strawberries.

In better times many of the *herbettes* and *saladettes,* which are often wincingly peppery and bitter, were favoured because they were health-giving, often for very specific ailments or for cleaning the blood in spring time. Most adults have a vestige of this love for peppery and bitter herbs – think of rocket and watercress – while in Languedoc many have developed a real taste for their acerbic bite.

Edible wild plants do have specific medicinal properties: dandelions, for example, stimulate the circulation, liver, digestive organs, kidneys and bladder. They also provide copper, iron and vitamins A and C. The wild thyme which grows in the *garrigue*, a grey variety used in the *herbes de Provence* mixture, used once to be fed to the babies of Corbières (renowned for their fat good health) in a garlic soup made against the time they were weaned.

The Languedoc, until not so long ago, has had two kinds of medicine, the medicine of the doctors, trained in the excellent medical schools of Montpellier and Toulouse, and the medicine of the local healers, whose knowledge was handed down, and who used used *simples*, plants gathered in the countryside, to cure all ills. In the 1880s the official medical establishment still had not won a social victory over their rural rivals, the herbalists, religious healers and witches who proliferated in the countryside. Moreover, until the new epidemiological understanding of the 1880s, their herbal and spiritual remedies were at least as effective as the cures of professional doctors.

As recently as the mid-1990s there was a herbalist practising in the Montagne Noire, and she was frequently observed by a friend of mine who lived near Mazamet picking wild plants to cure her patients. These healers were often considered miracle-workers. The writer René Nelli said of them, 'They know how to talk to animals, to dogs and sheep, they

can foretell the weather by the sky and heal by means of plants.' When
I spoke to Frédéric, the proprietor of the excellent Hôtel d'Alibert in
Caunes-Minervois, he stated that people only eat wild herbs in spring
because they regard them as necessary for their health; others disagree.
Benoit Huppé, schoolteacher in the same village, forages regularly in
spring and enjoys the flavours of these wild plants. He and his wife make
salads and soup from the harvest of their *cueillettes* from mid-winter until
the end of April.

As well as saladings, wild herbs grow everywhere and are often used
as flavourings – foragers pick thyme, fennel, rosemary and marjoram.
The yellow fennel pollen can be shaken onto fish before cooking, and
the seeds were used in little pastries called *rousquilles,* in the bread called
fougasse and at one time, when the *vignerons* were allowed to make their
own, fennel was sometimes used as a flavouring for *pastis* .

Guide des Plantes Sauvages Comestibles et Toxiques by François Couplan
and Eva Styner describes eighty poisonous plants and two hundred
edible wild plants. Here are a few of the key varieties which are still
sold at local markets and remain part of the food culture.

Wild leeks, dandelions, *raiponce* or rampion, wild garlic, *arroucat* or false
dandelion and wild asparagus appear on the markets of Carcassonne,
Narbonne, Lézignan and Perpignan. The season lasts from December
or January to April, although one authority cites dandelions as being
edible between September and April.

Wild leek, *poireau sauvage, poireau de vigne, poireau maragane, baragane,
pouragane, ail faux-poireau, taradels (Allium polyanthum or Allium ampelo-
prasum)*: these small leek-shaped vegetables are really a member of
the garlic family but in taste and appearance they are miniature leeks,
with a delicate texture and flavour. They grow in the woods and
along the borders of vineyards and are making a reappearance in the
vineyards themselves, with the introduction by so many wine-growers
today of bio-dynamic methods of viticulture. They can be bought in
local markets, tied in bundles. In Languedoc, they say the water the
leeks have cooked in can be made into a delicious healthy soup by
combining it with puréed potatoes and butter.

The leeks themselves are very often served as a salad with a mustard
vinaigrette and a chopped hard-boiled egg. Another local dish is *les
poireaux au four,* said to be much finer in taste and texture than the
same dish made with cultivated leeks.

Once they are trimmed and cooked the leeks must be boiled in salted water until tender, never 'underdone like green beans in modern cooking' says Albin Marty. Then layer them with grated Gruyère cheese in a gratin dish, pour over a good béchamel sauce and bake in the oven, without breadcrumbs, until nicely browned. The same composition, in a pastry shell instead of a gratin dish, is a *tarte à poireau*.

They were once eaten in quantities with lampreys. They were also wrapped in damp greaseproof paper and cooked in the embers of a fire.

Wild asparagus, *asperge sauvage, repunchus, espargue salvatge* (*Asparagus acutifolius*) is a climbing woodland creeper, whose young, edible shoots can be found in March and April, at the start of spring. Not only is it sold, tied in bunches, on the market stalls of Carcassonne, Lézignan and Perpignan, but it can be bought daily during the short season, in the superb covered Narbonne Halles Mirabeau, with its zinc bars and vaulted iron framework. In March at least two stalls in these Halles sell wild asparagus in good-sized bunches. I asked one stall-holder if she picked it herself and she told me that a gentleman gathers the asparagus and wild leeks for her and he picks them on La Clape, a small limestone mountain between Narbonne and the Mediterranean, criss-crossed by tracks, once a well-used pilgrim route, and covered in *garrigue* (aromatic evergreen plants and evergreen oaks). Walking here is a joy, with the blue sea in the distance. At the end of March the freshly soaked rocky terrain is, here and there, brightened by pools of tiny blue or white irises about two inches high, abundant spider orchids and other rarer wild flowers, some of which only grow here. It is a common sight at weekends to see walkers with knives and baskets scouring the hedgerows for enough wild asparagus shoots to eat *en famille*.

Wild asparagus grows in shady places, for example on verges, beneath pines, rosemary bushes, cistus and evergreen kermes oaks and in *les friches*, meaning land that was once cultivated but is now abandoned or set aside. The green spring shoots are eaten while still very young. The top 20 centimetres should be crisp, tender and edible, about as thick as a straw. As they mature, they become long, tough, prickly and tangled, rather like brambles, as they attempt to climb up any host tree or bush towards the light.

The Occitan people consider asparagus to be a diuretic and in this respect the wild is as good as or better than the cultivated variety. Wild asparagus can be eaten raw, *croque à sel*, or cooked and served on its own with a vinaigrette, in a *salade composée* or, most traditionally of all, cut into small pieces or left whole and fried gently in goose fat, lard or olive oil before being incorporated in an omelette. On Easter Monday young and old like to eat wild asparagus omelette in the open air. Probably the origins of this picnic lay with the finding of wild birds' eggs at the same time as the asparagus, and with the early belief that eggs represented renewal and rebirth

Saladettes and *herbettes:* if you want to collect a salad of mixed greens, you can find an enormous variety of edible leaves in the vineyards, banks, verges and uncultivated ground of Languedoc. Bitter greens can be made more appetizing when eaten fresh and raw by introducing a sweetener such as tomatoes, cheese or eggs. Often olive oil or walnut oil, vinegar, garlic or onion are introduced to tame the heat. Some are also eaten cooked, with the bitterness blanched out.

In Gruissan, on the coast near Narbonne, before being made into soup, they are soaked overnight, rinsed twice, then blanched in salted water for 10 minutes. After that they are boiled for 2 hours with a piece of salt pork or a ham bone and potatoes to make a healthy soup. These soups may also be flavoured with garlic and tomatoes.

The greens can be cooked as a dish of greens, with olive oil, pork fat or goose fat or used to flavour omelettes and other egg dishes.

In her book *Petit Traité Romanesque de Cuisine*, Marie Rouanet suggests the following dizzying list of plants for a winter salad: the very young leaves of daisies, poppies, valerian, sow thistle, milk thistle, wild watercress, all kinds of dandelions (which she says taste of nuts), strong wild rocket or *fausse roquette* (which in spring grows in such profusion in the vineyards that when it flowers it looks like snow), wild lettuce or blue lettuce – *Lactuca perennis* – with its blue flowers, common reichardia, called in Languedoc *couscounille,* wild purslane, field scabious, known picturesquely as *broute lapin* (rabbit food) or *oreille d'âne* (donkey's ear), and all kinds of land cress, including lady's smock (*Cardamine pratensis)*, which is bitingly hot like mustard. Dress this with a traditional vinaigrette, adding fried lardons and croûtons rubbed with garlic and fried in olive oil and perhaps a chopped hard-boiled egg. You can crush Roquefort into the dressing or add hot goat's cheese.

I have also found much mention of the eating of burdock and of bistort. Black briony shoots are boiled and eaten, and waterdocks and other docks, *patiences,* are cooked like rhubarb.

Dandelion, *pissenlit* (*Taraxacum officinale*): large quantities of a small variety, forming tight rosettes, are readily available on the markets of Languedoc, as well as a long, pale yellow, forced variety. They are eaten as a salad on their own, perhaps with bacon or torn or cut fine in a salad of mixed leaves (*mesclun*). An interesting recipe for cooked dandelion, described as a *recette diététique*, comes from Prosper Montagné and turns out to be a simple form of dandelion soufflé.

Creeping bellflower, *raiponce* (*Campanula rapunculus*) is sold on Carcassonne market. This plant is eaten before it flowers, when it turns out to be a very tall, blue campanula, lovely enough to pick and put in a vase. The white, crisp root is prized and eaten raw like a sweet crunchy radish, or can be cooked, while the leaves are eaten in a mixed salad.

Wild garlic or ramsons, *ail des ours* (*Allium ursinum*) should be eaten for its leaves before the plant flowers, when the hot, garlic-mustard flavour becomes too strong. Bunches of bright green wild garlic are sold on Olonzac market in March. The stall-holder picks them in the Montagne Noire and recommends them, first wilted in butter, in an omelette or tortilla; she also puts them in soup and in meat and vegetable stews.

Beaked hawksbeard, *arroucat, arrucat* (*Crespis vesicaria*) comes as rosettes of incredibly bitter, dark green, deeply cut, toothed leaves that fold back on themselves when picked and washed, like a parasol. They are sold on Carcassonne, Olonzac and Narbonne markets. One stall-holder gathers them on La Clape. They are eaten in salads both for pleasure and for health reasons. If you cut them up very finely they can give a robust flavour to a bland salad, but you might like to soak them in salt water for a while first.

Wild salsify, *barbabouc, galinette* (*Scorzonera laciniata*) is eaten during the winter. It is the white flesh of the root that is prized, and is by all accounts excellent, as is the wild scorzonera or black salsify. The roots can be eaten boiled, and the young leaves are good in salads, while the 1930s chef and writer X. Marcel Boulestin recommends enjoying the young buds in an omelette.

Wild chicory, *lacheta, barbe de capucine, cheveux de paysanne*: the root of this herb is famous for its use as ersatz coffee. The whole plant is excessively bitter.

Milk thistle and sow thistle are two species eaten with gusto (and sometimes cultivated). The sow thistle (*Sonchus oleraceus*) is *laitisson* in Occitan and *laiteron* in French. It is found from September to April. The young shoots are tender and taste delicious, you might almost think you were eating spinach. Some people also eat the handsome milk thistle (*Silybum marianum*) or *chardon marie*, whose tender stems are supposed to taste deliciously of artichoke, and whose roots can also be eaten like salsify. Another prized edible thistle is the *Carlina acanthifolia* with a flower which looks like the sun, which appears as a motif on hand-blocked Provençal fabrics.

Prickly lettuce, *penche, laitue des vignes, laitue sauvage* (*Lactuca serriola*) is a bit of a challenge; an ancestor of endive, the leaves (not the root) are eaten from October to March, but are extremely bitter.

Common reichardia, *couscounille* (*Reichardia picroides*) has tender leaves which are supposed to taste perfumed. Expert forager Benoit Huppé recommends *soupe de couscounille*, which he and his wife like to eat every week in spring.

Poppy, *rosela, langagne, coquelicot, pavot, ponceau* (*Papaver rhoeas*) has leaves which can be eaten from September to March and are said to taste of nuts. They can be eaten cooked, like spinach. However the flower has a reputation of bringing on eye problems and in Arles is called *mal d'iue* – eye sickness.

Nettles, *orties* (*Urtica dioica*): I have not seen nettles sold on market stalls, which means they are not considered very highly in the region and are picked only by those who want to eat them. However, they do appear in cookbooks. One southern French version of nettle soup, called *soupe verte*, contains garlic and watercress which give a deep green colour and a much better flavour than nettles on their own. They are also eaten as a purée.

Unfortunately, or fortunately, there are too many edible plants in Languedoc to describe all their culinary and medicinal uses. I will just give a few general hints on eating them and I have made a list of all the kinds I know of with their Latin, French and English names.

On the general cooking of wild plants remember that: you can pick several species and cook them together; that you should wash wild greens very well in several waters, shake dry and store rolled in kitchen paper inside storage boxes, in the fridge; if the *herbettes* are to be cooked, they can first be blanched two or three times or, if very bitter, soaked in salted water for an hour or overnight; if making soups, cook them for a long time – up to 2 hours – to improve the flavours; you can also cut up the youngest and most tender of the washed greens and fry them in olive oil with crumbled sausage or lardons of streaky bacon and thyme; or you can boil them until tender and serve with olive oil, or use for a *farçous* (a patty containing breadcrumbs, egg, garlic and sausage meat or ham), an omelette or a tortilla.

The sometimes savage, hot and bitter flavours of wild salads are genuinely quite addictive in spring; I am not surprised to find they are popular, when I remember our own taste for radishes, mustard, horseradish and rocket.

Here is that table:

Latin	French	English
Aegopodium podagraria	*Herbe St Gérard; pied de bouc; herbe-au-goutteux*	Ground elder
Allium ampeloprasum	*Ail faux-poireau; poireau d'été; pouragane; poireau sauvage*	Wild leek
Allium ursinum	*Ail des ours*	Ramsons; wild garlic
Amaranthus acutifolius	*Amaranthe réfléchie*	Pigweed
Anchusa italica	*Buglosse bleue; azurea; langue de boeuf*	Italian bugloss
Arctium lappa	*Bardane; la patience*	Burdock
Asparagus acutifolius	*Asperge sauvage; repunchus*	Wild asparagus
Bellis perennis	*Pâquerette*	Daisy
Beta vulgaris	*Bette; bette sauvage*	Wild spinach beet
Borago	*La bourrache*	Borage
Brionyia dioica; tamus communis	*Tamier commun; herbe aux femmes battues; herbe du diable; vigne blanche*	Black briony (cooked shoots only, the berries are toxic)
Campanula rapunculoides	*Raiponce; le repounchu*	Creeping bellflower
Capsella bursa-pastoris	*Bourse à Judas*	Shepherd's purse

Cardamine pratensis	*Cardamine des prés; cresson des prés*	Lady's smock
Centranthus ruber	*Lilas d'Espagne; barbe de Jupiter*	Red valerian
Cichorium intybus	*Chicorée sauvage; lacheta cicori*	Chicory
Crepis versicaria	*Arroucat; faux pissenlit*	Beaked hawksbeard
Diplotaxis ericoides	*Fausse-roquette*	White wall rocket
Eruca versicaria	*Roquette*	Salad mustard; rocket
Foeniculum vulgare	*Fenouil*	Wild fennel
Humulus lupulus	*Houblon*	Hop
Knautia arvensis	*Oreille d'âne; broute lapin*	Field scabious
Lactuca perennis	*Laitue vivace; escarola*	Blue lettuce
Lathyrus tuberosus	*Gesse tubéreuse; gland de terre; châtaigne de terre*	Earthnut peas
Lavatera arborea	*Mauve royale*	Tree mallow
Leontodon autumnale	*Liondent d'automne*	Hawkbit
Lepidium latifolium; Cardaria draba	*Passerage*	Hoary pepperwort
Malva sylvestris	*Mauve*	Common mallow
Mentha aquatica	*Menthe aquatique*	Watermint
Mentha arvensis	*Menthe des champs*	Corn mint
Mentha piperata	*Menthe poivrée*	Peppermint
Mentha pulegium	*Menthe puliot*	Pennyroyal
Nasturtium officinale; Rorippa nasturtium-aquaticum	*Cresson de fontaine*	Wild watercress
Origanum vulgare	*Origan; marjolaine sauvage*	Wild marjoram
Ornithogalum umbellatum	*Bela de jour; pénitent blanc; ornithogale en ombelle*	Star of Bethlehem; Bath asparagus
Papaver rhœas	*Coquelicot; pavot; ponceau*	Field poppy

Phyteuma, see campanula rapunculoides		
Picridium vulgaris	*Couscounille; la terra grapia; picridie*	Common reichardia
Plantago lanceolata	*Plantain lancéolé*	Ribwort plantain
Polygonum bistorta	*Bistorte*	Bistort
Portulaca oleracea	*Pourpier sauvage*	Common purslane
Rosmarinus officinalis	*Romarin*	Rosemary
Rumex acetosa	*Oseille des prés; surette*	Sorrel
Rumex acetosella	*Oseille des brebis; petite oseille*	Sheep's sorrel
Rumex hydrolapathum	*Patience des eaux*	Great waterdock
Salicornia europaea	*Passe-pierre; salicorne*	Marsh samphire
Sanguisorba minor	*Petite pimprenelle; petite sanguisorbe*	Salad burnet
Satureja montana	*Sarriette*	Winter savory
Scorzonera hispanica	*Scorsonère*	Scorzonera
Silene vulgaris	*Silène enflée*	Bladder campion
Silybum marianum	*Chardon marie*	Milk thistle; holy thistle
Sonchus arvensis	*Laiteron*	Sow thistle
Sonchus oleraceus	*Laiteron potager*	Smooth sow thistle
Symphytum officinale	*Consoude*	Comfrey
Tamus communis	*Herbe aux femmes battues; herbe du diable; vigne blanche; tamier commun*	Black briony (shoots only; the berries are poisonous)
Taraxacum officinale	*Pissenlit*	Dandelion
Thymus serpilloides	*Thym serpolet*	Wild thyme
Thymus vulgaris	*Farigoule; Frigoula; Thyum*	Thyme
Tragopogon porrifolius	*Salsifis à feuilles de poireau*	Salsify

Tragopogon pratensis	*Salsifis*	Salsify
Urtica pilulifera	*Ortie à pillules*	Roman nettle
Urtica dioica; U. pubescens	*Grande ortie*	Stinging nettle

Berries, *fruits sauvages*

M. Benoit Huppé mentions delicious liqueurs made with juniper berries, thyme flowers or mulberries. With hawthorn berries he makes a strong-flavoured jelly to eat with meat, and I have come across a local jelly made with *azerole*, a large-berried hawthorn variant, with pretty, rosy fruits which grows luxuriantly in the wild near Berlou, north of Saint-Chinian.

There are many wild fig trees and, of course, blackberries, although they tend to be less juicy than northern blackberries.

L'apéritif

Everyone takes part in *l'heure de l'apéritif*, the winding-down period when, sitting outside, in the garden, under a tree, by the barbecue, in the yard, or even in the street if necessary, one mulls over the day with family and friends in the clear evening air – away from the cities, even on a warm evening, Languedoc air is as clear and delicious as spring water.

Apéro is short for apéritif, and to invite someone for *l'apéro* or *l'apéritif* may mean different things, from Spanish-style tapas to accompany the sunset glass of wine, snacks with drinks in a café and so on – or, if it is an invitation from people like Françoise and Lionel Raviat, a huge and never-ending procession of home-made and toothsome things to eat, starting with *foie gras* on toasted *pain de campagne*, a big plate of *jambon cru*, wild mushrooms in a quiche straight from the oven, some spicy merguez and other sausages on the outside grill and, the final coup, *le Vieux Garçon* – a jar filled with different fruits preserved in alcohol and sugar. You keep putting more fruit in as the season goes forward and eventually take the liqueur off and drink it.

The apéritif part of a meal is not always so substantial or lavish, and often precedes a barbecue of meat, sausages or fish. Outdoor fireplaces for grilling are popular and can be tended while you talk and drink. But first there may be such things as:

Saucisson sec and other kinds of charcuterie cut into manageable pieces and placed on a board.

Pan amb tomàt: grilled or toasted *pain de campagne* rubbed vigorously with a cut clove of garlic and then with half a large, juicy, raw tomato. Trickle olive oil over the tomato-soaked bread and season with salt and pepper.

Olives: shiny black and matt green, large and tiny, fresh and pickled or done in a variety of strongly flavoured marinades of hot paprika, spices, chilli and herbs, garlic and even aïoli – perfume the air of the local markets. As a rule, the *vendeuses* are are stunningly beautiful girls, dressed as if going to perform in a Texan night club alongside Dolly Parton, and dressed in laced corsets and impossibly high heels.

Radishes are the easiest and most popular appetizers. The French Breakfast variety are long with a white tip and should be served chilled with crystals of salt and cold, unsalted butter.

Nuts: toasted almonds and green, unripe almonds.

Raw vegetables: baby purple artichokes, baby broad beans, tiny little red and yellow tomatoes, served with sea salt to dip into.

Toasts (slices of baguette, toasted) spread with any number of different types of *tapenade* (see page 104), black or green, or with *anchoïade*, anchovies mashed with garlic and olive oil, or with *tomatade*, a paste of sun-dried tomatoes with olive oil and garlic or, finally, with *brandade de morue* (see page 173). All these can be bought ready-made on the market from the olive stalls.

Jambon cru, jambon sec: the raw ham or *prosciutto* of the Midi, cut into shavings, which may be accompanied by slices of juicy local melon.

Two ideas for tapas from chef Alain Liorca, whose restaurant at La-Colle-sur-Loup is actually in Provence, but whose food often has Catalan flavours, are a salad of baby squid on top of anchovy on top of a fried potato slice, on top of rocket and tomato with a dressing perhaps containing chives; and one made of micro-sized pieces of baguette with a white bean purée (not too much) topped with lobster.

This not-so-much-an-apéritif-more-of-a-banquet will be served with chilled bottles of the wine of the *pays*. It is important that any red wine is served lightly chilled – at 16°C – which helps keep its structure.

Camargue Rice

The Camargue, that wind-tormented delta of vines, salt marshes and lagoons at the mouth of the Rhône, grows a quarter of all the rice eaten in France – and they eat a lot, particularly in the south, where rice is served as a vegetable with grilled or roasted meat, or even with fish and is a hugely popular salad ingredient. I have never liked rice salad particularly, but in the Camargue itself they know how to do it, and it can be seriously good (see page 131).

Round grain and long grain are both grown in quantity, but the most interesting is the red, *riz rouge,* which is a cross between a wild and cultivated grain. It is a rosy-russet colour, tastes nutty and savoury, and makes a beautiful change to white.

Rice has been grown in the Camargue since the 1600s and at one time provided three-quarters of France's requirement. The crop is sown in May and irrigated by a series of canals and pumps which flood the fields. Ten thousand hectares are planted and, sorry to say, they are often sprayed, Hitchcock-style, from the air. Harvest is between September and November, when the wide blue skies fill with towering columns of smoke as they burn the stubble.

Sel de Mer, Fleur de Sel and Other Salts

The wild seashore of the Camargue, parched by the sun and stripped to a salty desert by the Mistral and the Tramontane, has its own harvest; *sel de mer* is one of the great products of Provence and Languedoc.

Once there were dozens of salt works, now there are three, producing 500,000 tons a year, continuing a trade that has probably been going since settlers arrived from Rhodes in the fifth century BC. When the Romans colonized Septimania (Settimanie in modern French), as the Romans called Languedoc, an engineer called Peccaius was sent to build an official salt works, pumping seawater into ponds for evaporation, on a site near Aigues-Mortes in the Petit Camargue; this site was named Peccais. At the time salt was precious, so much so that Roman soldiers were at one time paid in salt; each man 'worth his salt'.

These ancient salt works in the Petit Camargue and the lesser ones of Gruissan on the coast at Narbonne, were vital to Gaul. Salt was the great preservative, and those unfortunates who lived far away from the sea relied upon fish and shellfish – mussels, oysters and sea urchins – preserved in brine, transported into the interior by pack-trains of mules and donkeys, in pottery jars and, later, furry goatskin containers, just like the camel caravans of the Middle East.

The Romans used salt in the making of their favourite sauces garum and liquamen (fermented fish intestines and small fish in brine). Salt was and still is used to preserve salt cod, herrings, sardines, tuna, olives, cucumbers, capers, cheeses, confit of goose and duck, hams, bacon and sausages (the Romans were very partial to all forms of sausage) and, at Collioure, the finest cured anchovies. It was occasionally used in spice mixtures – (spiced salt is still available from Saint-André-de-Roquelongue in the Aude). To supply the Burgundians, who were famous for their ham, the salt was shipped up the Rhône in enormous barges hauled by mules, and later horses, in teams of up to 60 animals. (Not surprisingly, a taste for donkey and horse *saucisson* developed, and these are still popular.)

It is salutory to remember how important salt was in the region throughout the Middle Ages. It was important for trade – there were large salt markets in Valence – and essential to survival through the winter months. It remained so until the introduction of refrigerators and freezers. And it was not just in the kitchen that salt was valued, as Mark Kurlansky lays out in his wonderful book on the subject. Newborn babies, before they were baptized, were sprinkled with salt to ward off the Devil. And it was also used to keep infection at bay, particularly after Collioure, where salting anchovies was the main trade, remained immune to the Black Death, while the plague infected every other village in the area.

At Aigues-Mortes in the Petit Camargue, at Saint-Lucie and at Gruissan, the last remaining salt works are still in operation. Aigues-Mortes alone supplies one third of France's salt, under the name of La Baleine (part of the Salins du Midi operation), and les salins de l'îles St-Martin in Gruissan make a very special pink *fleur de sel*. Their large, rectangular salt pools are a beautiful pink colour at certain times of year due to tiny algae that live in brine, *Dunaliella salina*, which are green but turn red when seawater reaches a certain level of saltiness. The salt pools also harbour minuscule reddish shrimps, native to the lagoons of the Camargue, which flamingoes love to eat, and which give them their pink colour.

Salt-making is a seasonal occupation. After the winter is over, in February and March, the *sauniers*, salt-makers, let seawater into long, snaking canals, where the sun and wind start to evaporate and concentrate the brine as it moves around. It is then retained, by a series of locks, in vast pools, some more than 900 acres. More water is let in as it reduces and concentrates and, by the end of the summer, 90 per cent has evaporated. The *saumure* or saline solution is then directed into shallow, rectangular salt pools called *cristallisoirs,* where it stays until September. It is now that it fully evaporates to make a layer of salt 12 centimetres thick. This is moved to *camelles*, huge mountains of salt 20 metres high and almost a kilometre long, which are washed by the autumn rains. The salt is then graded into salt for industry and roads, the standard bay salt, *gros sel,* used for charcuterie and hams, *sel de mer*, used for the table, and *sel fin*, fine salt.

Fleur de sel

Anyone who has paid an astronomical price for *fleur de sel* will know that it is worth it. The floating crystals that are *fleur de sel* form on the surface of the salt pools and have to be taken off by hand, hence their great cost. During the time of the *gabelle*, the notorious salt tax of the *ancien régime*, the resentful salt-makers kept the *fleur de sel* for themselves. It consists of light, slightly humid crystals with a perfect crumbling texture and a saltiness and delicate structure that melts gently on the tongue.

Sel épicé, spiced salt

In St-André-de-Roquelongue in the Aude an artisan manufacturer makes a spiced salt from raw materials supplied from Gruissan. The Sel Épicé Garrigue is mixed with herbs – rosemary, savory, thyme and bay – and is excellent on any kind of grilled fish or meat, particularly lamb. The spicier version is mixed with dried lemon peel, star anise or liquorice, coriander and Sechuan pepper; use it on barbecued lamb or to season any kind of long-braised meat.

Salt cod, morue

Row upon row of pungent racks of kite-shaped, yellowish flaps of salt cod, hard as planks, once hung in every fish market of Languedoc. Beneath stood the fishmongers, busy with their miniature guillotines for cutting up the cod, which were kept constantly slicing down, as the housewives queued for their *morue*. There are reputed to be three hundred salt cod recipes; it is eaten with béchamel sauce, potatoes, haricot beans, with peppers, chillies, tomatoes, olives, whole heads of garlic, with capers, anchovies and with cabbage, with rice, with honey, with chick peas – with everything. In Mediterranean France, this was the one dish you were certain to see on the tables of peasants as well as the bourgeoisie and aristocracy throughout the year. Traditionally it is eaten during Lent, when the sky is a tender blue, the pink peach blossom is in flower and there is still snow on the mountain tops.

It remains a favourite food, a taste acquired when *morue* was the Church's answer to feeding the faithful during all the dreaded fasts it imposed. The duty of every good Catholic was to eat fish on Fridays and during Lent, on Christmas Eve and on many saints' days. These fasts proliferated and, if you lived far from the coast, your options were few. But pack mules could bring the heavily salted fish, which had already travelled from Newfoundland, to the most remote mountain villages.

Mainly fished and cured by Basques, it was brought in through the port of Sète, where, along with Nîmes, the manufacture of *brandade de morue*, that satisfying purée of salt cod, olive oil, garlic and milk, is still a tradition (recipe on page 173).

Left-over Bread

My favourite experience of baking was actually in the Lot, although the process was typical of much bread-making in the south of France. Our neighbour Madame Malbec would make bread once a month or once a fortnight. The wood-fired oven, outside a crumbling house that her family had long since abandoned, had to be heated up a day ahead by her husband and son. Then she would arrive, black sprigged pinny in place and covered in flour, with her trusty barrowload of large, flat, cloth-lined baskets brimming with risen dough. The dough was transferred onto a large wooden paddle and shoved to the back of the heated oven. When it was cooked, she would stand in the road and, if you wanted her splendid bread, she sawed off a piece from one of the giant round, discus loaves and hung it on a hook to weigh it; this bread was delicious, substantial and chewy. The loaf lasted for at least a week, getting progressively harder to masticate. But it was never thrown away; what we might call 'stale' bread became an ingredient in cooking.

Bread soups were the most convenient, since the poorer and more rural families, including the Malbecs, would eat soup every day, and 'Have you made your soup?' was a form of morning greeting. Often appearing today as a floating slice of toasted baguette, *dans le temps* (in the old days) there was more likely a whole tureen full of bread in cheese soup, almost a kilo per soup tureen (everyone had a soup tureen), with stock poured over it to allow it to swell up and become soft again. Cheese soup (see page 144) makes use of *chou fourrager* (forage kale); if you see tall stalks with a few green cabbagey leaves sprouting from the top, this is the handy 'walking stick' cabbage that you can pick a few leaves at a time.

To make a delicious *bougnette*, you mix bread with pork, roll it into balls, bake them in the oven, then slice and fry them; there are also a variety of dumplings and stuffings for birds based on stale bread.

Salads and soups may be garnished with large croûtons fried in oil (see *Salade fermière*, page 108), and slices of toast are frequently floated on soup and dolloped with aïoli and grated Gruyère (see *Bisquebouille*, page 154).

Toasted or baked rounds of bread can be served as a starter, spread with chicken liver pâté or Roquefort cheese and walnuts.

A strange loaf called *pounti* is a mixture of bread, eggs, chard and prunes, sometimes with pieces of ham included, while the appetizing-sounding *farçun* is a mixture of breadcrumbs, bacon, spinach or chard, onions, garlic and herbs, spiced with cumin and combined with béchamel and eggs. This is put into a gratin dish, covered with tomato sauce and cheese and baked.

Bread is often made into breadcrumbs, of course, for gratins and croquettes, or used for stuffing tomatoes, courgettes, onions, cabbages – anything.

Then there are a variety of puddings: some, like *coupetado*, not unlike bread and butter pudding, layered with raisins or prunes or with pieces of fresh fruit. One I like the sound of is an apple bread and butter pudding with rum in it, while another from the Aveyron called *soupe de cerises* contains slices of fried bread sprinkled with sugar and mixed with cooked cherries and cinnamon. I think all these sorts of dishes are a great solution; it is thrifty to avoid wasting the half-eaten loaf of good bread hidden in the bottom of the bread bin by something fresher.

The *Cazuela*

Round, shallow terracotta pots made from a warm russet clay are piled up at the Saint-Chinian Sunday market. This is the *cazuela* – the

centuries old pot used in all Catalan cooking. It appears in the beautiful
seventeenth-century still-lifes of the Spanish painter Zurbarán, and is
still made today. You can buy the *cazuela* online; it costs next to nothing
and is the perfect pot for every kind of gratin and for little stews, tomato
sauces, paella, crème caramel – more or less anything.

To prepare a new purchase and to prevent it becoming porous: soak
it in cold water for 24 hours; dry it; fill it with water to two centimetres
from the brim, then add half a cup of vinegar; put it on a heat-diffusing
disc over a low flame or medium heat and bring the water to a simmer;
let it boil away until you are left with about half a cupful; turn off the
heat and allow the *cazuela* to cool down. It is then ready for use. Always
use a heat-diffuser when cooking on an open flame.

Wine in Languedoc

'In Languedoc all roads lead to wine, or start from it,' wrote the historian Emmanuel Le Roy Ladurie. My first drive through the Languedoc plains and their tight little villages was before this broad wine country had its change of heart; we saw hundreds upon hundreds of miles of vines, and we knew it as the place that made *vin ordinaire* or, in translation, plonk.

Today those who still make large quantities of everyday wine to be sold for almost nothing are the conservative souls who cling to tradition. The enterprising, and the younger wine-makers, have built on the marvellous discovery that this terrain is not only perfect for making quality wine, it is as good as the very best. Today there are top-quality wines to be found here at a fraction of the price of their counterparts in Burgundy and Bordeaux.

Old methods die hard, but die they must. In the sixteenth century, as now, the *vendange* came in September, when wasps and thrushes descended upon the vines, which were allowed to trail along the ground, unlike Austrian vines which were held up on trellises. The grapes, once picked, were carried by donkeys or mules in tubs to the *caves* where, according to Le Roy Ladurie, 'a naked man hanging by his arms from a beam in the wine cellar trampled the grapes in their tubs; care had to be taken lest the trampler succumb to the fumes of carbon dioxide given off.'

There were rats everywhere and ropes were left hanging over the sides of the vats so that if a rodent fell off a beam, it could hopefully climb out, and not spoil the wine. One need not be surprised that this wine did not keep or travel well. It was not expected to last more than a year.

After fermentation the wine was put in barrels, and was then available in three qualities – a light *clairette,* a dark red of medium quality and lastly a *piquette* which was of the very poorest and was given to the wine-maker's servants. The red wine was usually served from flagons and mixed with water, and people drank plenty.

The making of vast oceans of wine for the masses took place in small barns and cellars in villages and towns throughout Languedoc; we are told that the earth beneath Montpellier was as riddled with holes as a Swiss cheese owing to the many vaulted wine cellars.

Wine continued to be the major industry for three centuries. By the nineteenth the business was dominated by successful southern wine barons, making good money out of the northern industrial workers' need for three litres of red wine a day to keep them going.

These successful *vignerons* were making *le gros rouge* and building the most outlandish and grand châteaux for themselves with the profits. The countryside round Béziers is a joy for lovers of elaborate architecture – there are dozens of exuberant, oversized castles with more turrets, towers and castellations, terraces, battlements and arrow-slits than any medieval stronghold ever had. This boom lasted until phylloxera hit the vines. The disease came from the US, and it was a catastrophe.

The twentieth-century history of wine from the Hérault and the other departments of Languedoc was not one of undiluted triumph. The region as a whole continued to be the source of *vins ordinaires*, in such quantity and of such poor quality that much was converted to industrial alcohol. It lost its place in the market in the face of competition from wines from eastern Europe and the New World, and it ceased to be an ever-ready source of a good living to its makers. Hence their conversion to more modern ways of making wine, their decision to rip up the old varieties and plant vineyards for better grapes, and their lifting of standards right across the board. Today, a wine-lover can make as invigorating and satisfying a tour of the South-West as he or she can of Burgundy, the Loire, or Bordeaux. The wines are good, the wines are interesting.

Chapter Two

*Basic Recipes, Sauces, Dressings
and Aïoli*

Think of this chapter as supplying the formulas for essential preparations that you turn to without thinking when cooking (the dressings, base sauces and so forth), as well as offering suggestions for dishes that depend on your shopping basket and the time of year, such as grilled vegetables, simple snail dishes or grilled mussels. These recipes are less about precise quantities, more about method.

A Catalan Herb *farçellet*

This Catalan version of the *bouquet garni* is a deliciously scented little parcel of dried thyme, winter savory and oregano, wrapped in bay-leaves and tied up with string. Use it to flavour long-cooked dishes, as you would a *bouquet garni*. Keep it in an airtight container.

Blender Mayonnaise

Mayonnaise is such a blessing in the hot summertime, it makes cold food so much more delicious, even cold fish becomes delectable when served with a herb mayonnaise, and cold chicken is definitely at its best with mayo.

This recipe can be varied by adding more or less mustard, and by altering the proportions of olive oil and sunflower oil. Adding more olive oil gives a richer, heavier result. Some people find mayonnaise made entirely with olive oil tends to be too strong and even rather bitter.

Add *crème fraîche*, as much as you like, to lighten the mayonnaise, and, of course, add chopped herbs. Parsley, chives and chervil, plus a few chopped capers, is a fresh combination for fish.

> 2 tsp **lemon juice**; 2 **egg yolks**; 1 tsp **Dijon mustard**; 250ml **olive and sunflower oil**, half and half; ½–1 tbsp **water; sea salt.**

Put the lemon juice and mustard into the bowl of a food processor and add the egg yolks and a little salt. Blend them together and with the blender still running, gradually trickle in the oil, drop by drop for a minute, and then in a thin trickle. Continue until all the oil is used up, adding a little warm water if the mixture gets too stiff, but it should end up stiff enough to stand up a spoon.

Aïoli (by hand)

*2–4 fat cloves of **garlic**, finely chopped; 2 **egg yolks**; 300ml **olive oil** or **sunflower oil**, or a mixture of the two; (optional, but not authentic – juice ¼ **lemon**, 1 tbsp **hot water**, 1 tsp **Dijon mustard**); **sea salt, pepper**.*

Wet a tea towel and wring out the surplus moisture. Fold it and put it on the work surface to anchor the bowl in which you make the mayonnaise.

Mash the garlic with coarse salt, using the flat side of a knife blade, working it hard against the chopping board until it has emulsified.

Add it to the egg yolks in a bowl, or a mortar, and combine with a small hand-held whisk or, if you prefer, a pestle. Gradually add the oil, drop by drop to begin with, as if you were making mayonnaise, stirring all the time.

Gradually incorporate all the oil, adding a little water and perhaps a few drops of lemon juice (not authentic!) when it gets very stiff. Taste and add more salt and pepper if necesssary.

Blender Aïoli

*4 cloves **garlic**, finely chopped; 2 tsp **lemon juice**; 2 **egg yolks**; 250ml **olive** and **sunflower oil**, half and half; ½ tbsp **water**; **sea salt**.*

Mash the garlic with a little salt, using the flat of a knife blade or a fork and working it to a fine paste on the chopping board.

Put it with the lemon juice into the bowl of a food processor and add the egg yolks. Blend them together and gradually trickle in the oil, drop by drop for a minute, and then in a thin stream. Continue until all the oil is used up, adding a little warm water if the mixture gets too stiff, but it should end up stiff enough to stand up a spoon.

To Cook Snails

Once the snails have been purged (see page 65 for more details), give them a good clean in several changes of water, scrubbing if necessary to clean the shells.

Make a *court bouillon* of thyme, bay leaves, fennel, basil, onion, shallot, salt, white wine and about a litre of water. Boil for 20 minutes to extract the flavours and allow to cool.

Simmer the snails in their shells in this *court bouillon* for 60–90 minutes. Now they are ready for all sorts of ways of cooking.

Snails with *sauce cargolade*

*20–30 **snails** per person.*

*100g **poitrine fumée** or **pancetta** cut into lardons, or **streaky bacon** if in England; 3–4 tbsp **olive oil**; 1 medium **onion**, finely chopped; 1 **shallot**, finely chopped; 3 cloves **garlic**, chopped; 2 **bay leaves**; bunch of **thyme**; 5 sprigs **parsley**, chopped; 5 sprigs **basil**, chopped; 5 sprigs of **fennel**, chopped; 1kg ripe red **tomatoes**, skinned, deseeded and chopped; 1–2 tsp **tomato purée**; 150ml **white wine**; 200ml **water**; **salt, pepper, cayenne pepper**.*

Heat the olive oil in a sauté pan with the lardons. Add the onion, shallot and garlic and let them soften for 15 minutes until tender. Add the herbs, tomatoes and tomato purée, season with salt, pepper and cayenne and cook for 30 minutes, until the sauce is thick. Add the snails in their shells, stir in the white wine and water and simmer, covered, for 20 minutes, so that the snails are bathed in delicious sauce. (Serves 3–6.)

The recipe above is based on one from *Recettes Paysannes de l'Hérault* by Mark Béziat; there are plenty of snail suggestions in this good little book, including with ginger, with walnuts, on skewers, in a bouillabaisse, and with saffron.

I have also come across snails with nettles, and the following idea for snails with ceps, based on one by the Internet chef Patrick Asfaux (see the site www.aftouch-cuisine).

Snails with Ceps
Escargots aux cèpes

*36 cooked **snails**; 1 tbsp chopped **garlic**; 2 tbsp chopped **parsley**; 100g softened **butter**; 300g fresh **ceps** (you could try substituting other mushrooms, **button chestnut mushrooms**, thickly sliced, are particularly good); 1 tbsp **goose fat**.*

Make snail butter by pounding the garlic and parsley together and working them into the butter.

Sauter the ceps in the goose fat for 5–6 minutes, until golden, then add the snail butter and the snails and heat through, shaking the pan. Season with salt and pepper. (Serves 3–6)

Une cagouillade – a simple version

Sauter the snails in olive oil with thyme and garlic, add tomato sauce, chilli, salt and pepper and simmer for 30 minutes.

Catalan Sausage
Embutido de cerdo, botifarra crua

There is something thrilling about making your own sausages, even if it means ordering the casings from the butcher and wrestling with a funnel and a wooden spoon. Many have attempted this successfully. The following recipe is based on one by the Catalan food-writer, supporter of Ferran Adrià (of El Bulli fame) and gastronomer Jaume Fàbrega, who says, 'It's delicious!'

Use chopped fresh pork: either neck, shoulder, fat back or belly. Add some lard, if you wish – for a juicier sausage, increase the amount of fat. This will be enough for 6 small sausages, or one continuous spiral if you prefer to make it in that form.

Suggested proportions are:

> 375 *chopped fresh neck or shoulder of* **pork**; 175g *chopped* **pork belly fat**; 1.5 *metres* **pig's intestine**, *cleaned and washed and dried or* **sausage casing** *from your butcher, soaked in cold water;* ¾ *tsp* **salt**; 1 *tsp ground* **black pepper**.

Tie a knot at one end of your sausage casing, which will probably have a piece of stiff plastic inside that helps to guide it onto the nozzle. Push the casing onto the nozzle of your Porkalt mincing machine/sausage maker or the plastic or metal nozzle of a very large piping bag. Continue doing this until all of the sausage skin is gathered up onto the nozzle.

Mix the sausage ingredients well with your hands and funnel the sausage meat into the ready-cleaned intestine or sausage skin, coaxing it gently off the nozzle as it fills with the minced meat. Twist at regular intervals to make sausages of the size you like or make a continuous sausage; remember that they will shrink during cooking. Let everything mature for 2–3 hours in a cool place, wrapped in a cotton cloth. After that, the sausage is ready. You can keep it in the fridge for some days.

To the plain sausage mixture, you can add aïoli, mushrooms, truffles, herbs, *foie gras,* and so forth. Then you can grill them over charcoal or on a griddle pan, roast them or serve them fried with beans (when they become *Botifarra amb mongetes*). This sausage can also be added to casseroles or to cassoulet.

Chorizo

Curiously enough, in northern Catalonia they do not put garlic or *pimentón* (paprika) in their sausages. However in Languedoc-Roussillon, they like spicy *chorizo* and it is available in many butchers'.

Use the same ingredients as Catalan sausage above but add *choricero* pimentos (about 5) soaked and scraped off their skins, or 1 teaspoon hot or smoked paprika (*pimentón*), or a mixture of both, to the minced pork and work it in thoroughly with your hands before stuffing the casings.

Sausage with White Wine
Saucisses au vin blanc

This recipe makes 12 sausages. Increase the proportion of fat to lean for a juicier result.

> *750g **lean pork** such as loin, neck or shoulder, minced or finely chopped; 250g **pork belly fat**, minced or finely chopped; 100ml **dry white wine**; 1.5 metres **sausage casing**, soaked in cold water; 1 clove **garlic** (optional), mashed with a fork; 1½ tsp **fine salt**; 1–2 tsp cracked **black pepper**.*

Mix all the ingredients together in a large bowl and let the mixture mature for a couple of hours or overnight.

Follow the instructions in the recipe for Catalan sausage.

To Cook Salt Cod

The best cod is dry-salted, thick and creamy-white in colour. Choose a middle piece, which comes apart in big flakes once the fish has been soaked and cooked. It should be soaked in a bowl of cold water for 24–36 hours, on two crossed forks, skin-side down, and the water should be changed three times. Some people change to warm water for the last 2 hours of soaking.

The flesh will have swollen and softened and be ready for very gentle poaching. Place the soaked cod in a saucepan and pour plenty of boiling water over it. Let it come back to a simmer, then remove it from the heat. Cover and let it stand for 15 minutes. It will then flake off the skin and bones.

To Cook *foie gras*

For me, the only way to eat *foie gras* is as simply as possible. I was instructed by Madame Bonomi of Martel, a village to the east of Sarlat, a centre of *foie gras* production. It took her about four minutes to prepare the liver and push it into its terrine.

Choose a fine, raw, vacuum-packed, fattened duck liver, a pink or yellow shade of beige, weighing 500–600g and showing no off-colour patches.

Carefully remove it from its wrapping and let it come to room temperature. In order to remove any inner veins, it must be opened out: to facilitate this it can be soaked in a basin of lukewarm water. Gently prize apart the two lobes, large and small, and with a tiny knife cut out the sinews and veins, handling the liver with great care so as not to crush it.

Open it flat and sprinkle the inside surface lightly with salt and pepper and a drop or two of Armagnac or port.

Close the lobes together, push the *foie gras* into a terrine into which it just fits, cover with foil and leave to absorb the flavours for an hour or two.

When you are ready to cook it, pour off any liquid from the terrine, mix about 100g of duck fat with a teaspoon of Armagnac or port and spread this over the liver.

Heat the oven to 100°C. Place an oval gratin dish of water in the oven to heat up. Put the terrine in the *bain marie* in the middle of the oven and cook for 60 minutes. Switch off the oven, leave the terrine to cool slowly for an hour and then remove it from the oven.

When it is cold, place it in the fridge to mature for at least 24 hours before eating.

When you want to serve it, you can put it in the freezer for 10–15 minutes to chill, which makes it easier to slice. Serve it in rather thick slices with toasted *pain de campagne.* Chef Michel Guérard would serve very thin slices of raw apple with it, to add a fresh note.

Picada

Picada, according to Colman Andrews, author of *Catalan Cuisine*, is one of the 'bookends' of Catalan cooking. It isn't quite a sauce, it is a gentle, creamy, exquisitely flavoured medium with which to finish cooking fish or meat, adding body to the sauce. But instead of adding the neutral taste of flour, it adds a whole harmony of warm flavours.

Picada is made with toasted bread or fried bread and nuts, aromatized with spices, garlic and herbs. It can be made, authentically, in pestle and mortar or quickly in a food processor. You can use it with monkfish, lobster, rabbit, chicken or partridge and many other things.

*40g blanched **almonds** or **hazelnuts**; 2 cloves **garlic**; 1 slice of **white bread**; 1 tbsp **olive oil**; ½ tsp **saffron**; 1 tbsp chopped **parsley**; ¼ tsp ground **cinnamon**; 100ml **sherry** or **white wine**; 100ml **water**; **sea salt**; (optional: 25g **dark chocolate**, a few **pine nuts**).*

Toast the nuts in a frying-pan over a low heat, shaking them frequently, until they are pale brown and give off a warm, nutty smell. Chop the garlic coarsely. Fry the bread on both sides in olive oil until it is a deep golden brown. Drain and cut it into cubes.

Put the toasted nuts with the saffron, garlic, fried bread, parsley, cinnamon, salt and sherry or wine and water in a mortar or the bowl of a food processor and grind to a fine paste. (If you are cooking rabbit or partridge, you may wish to add to the mixture the two optional ingredients, the grated chocolate or the pine nuts.)

This sauce can then be added to sliced monkfish previously dipped in flour and fried, or pieces of cooked lobster, browned meatballs, rabbit browned in oil, briefly browned partridge or lightly fried chicken, or cooked vegetables such as cardoons. Once the addition is made, carry on cooking for a further 10 minutes.

Catalan Red Pepper Sauce
Sauce romesco

Introduced to Europe by the Spanish *conquistadores*, red peppers are ardent contributors to Spanish-influenced sauces. Kitchens in the *Pays catalan* are redolent with the smell of cooking capsicums, in all their varieties: sweet bell peppers both round and long, dried peppers such as the plum-shaped *romesco*, sweet *ñoras* and the dusky, smoky *choricero*, *pébrines* (hot bird peppers) and ground peppers like cayenne, paprika – hot, sweet or smoked – chilli powder and chilli flakes.

This hot, red sauce, named for the pepper, comes from Tarragona in Catalonia. It can be made ahead of time, and is excellent with grilled prawns, clams, mussels and grilled fish, or mixed grilled seafood. The recipe makes 300g of sauce.

> 4–5 **dried peppers** (romescos or ñoras) or 2 dessertspoons **sweet paprika**; 1 **small dried chilli pepper**, crumbled, or ¼ tsp of **chilli flakes**; 3 **tomatoes**; 1 small head of **garlic**; 25g blanched **hazelnuts**, skins preferably removed (fiddly job, skip it); 12 **blanched almonds**; 1 slice **bread**; 1 tbsp chopped **parsley**; a few **mint leaves**, chopped; 120ml **olive oil**; 1½ tbsp **white wine** or **sherry vinegar** (or both); **salt**.

Heat the oven to 220°C. Soak the dried peppers in warm water, remove the seeds and scrape the flesh into a bowl. Roast the tomatoes and head of garlic in a roasting tin. After 15–20 minutes add the nuts and roast for 5 more minutes. Skin the tomatoes and remove the seeds. Pop the garlic cloves out of their skins. Fry the bread in olive oil until golden. Break it into pieces.

Put the peppers, tomatoes, garlic, bread, nuts and herbs into the food processor with vinegar, half the oil and salt. Whizz until smooth and then trickle in the remaining olive oil to finish the sauce. It should be the consistency of thick cream. Add more vinegar or some water if it is too thick.

Tomato Sauce
Sauce tomate maison

This invaluable Languedoc housewife's sauce is made in summer, when ripe, sweet tomatoes are weighing down the baskets of shoppers and vegetable gardeners; it can be used right away or kept in the freezer for later, it freezes well. In the past it was always pasteurized, either in preserving jars or in old wine bottles. It is vital to everyday cooking and is used to make the usual *sofregit*, a rich tomato base, and in all sorts of soups, stews and sauces.

8 large **tomatoes** *(1.5kg), chopped; 2 small* **onions**, *peeled and finely chopped;* **sea salt**, **pepper**.

Put the tomatoes and onion in a saucepan, season with salt and pepper and cook in their own juice, skins and all, for 20–25 minutes.

Now pulse the sauce in a food processor and sieve it through a conical mesh sieve to remove the skins and seeds, or sieve it through a *moulin à légumes* (food mill). Taste for seasoning and if the sauce is not quite sweet enough, add a pinch of sugar and stir it in to dissolve it.

Keep the sauce for a week in the refrigerator, with a layer of olive oil on top, or freeze it.

Sofregit

If you follow the expert on Catalan cuisine, Colman Andrews, softening sweet, finely chopped onions in plenty of olive oil very slowly until they turn beyond yellow, beyond golden, beyond hazelnut brown, and then adding tomatoes, is the usual start of making dinner. This is how to make *sofregit*, the source of that warm appetizing smell that wafts round a Catalan house and draws people into the kitchen, the essential flavour that brings all the other ingredients together.

To the mixture of onions and tomatoes you can add peppers, aubergines, mushrooms or lardons. Reduce the mixture down, to make what is elegantly described as a *confiture*, a jam. There can be no such thing as a wet *sofregit.*

However, if you watch a Catalan chef making a *sofregit*, he just chops up onions, peppers and aubergines, sticks them in a blackened pan, adds grated tomatoes, garlic, plenty of olive oil and seasoning and cooks everything together for a while, not particularly gently, until it turns into a rich sauce – adding a little water from time to time if it gets too dry.

Either method works well, but I am a slow cook myself and I think the long method gives a deeper flavour.

You are now ready to add flavourings and your main ingredient. *Sofregit* can be used to cook crabs, eels and all sorts of fish and shellfish, rabbit, rice, pasta, artichokes, snails, meat dishes – almost anything whatever that you like the look of in the market today, although obviously not all at once! It gives a good intensity to your food, once you have acquired a feel for the approach, as it eliminates wateriness; the trick is to melt your ingredients together with the juicy vegetables, made sweet and succulent by onions, olive oil and long cooking.

Think about adding wild mushrooms, dried mushrooms, peppers, carrots, potatoes, lardons, pig's feet and ears, ham bones, sausage meat, olives, pine nuts, hazelnuts and almonds, capers and gherkins, or anchovies.

Garlic is not essential, only the sweet onions are, saffron is sometimes added – and herbs – wild fennel, earthy thyme from the *garrigue*, parsley, basil – and spices – cinnamon and, surprisingly, star anise.

Liquids can include wine, sweet Muscat wine, vinegar, sherry, cognac, water and stock.

Roasted Garlic

A whole head of garlic cooked in the fire, with its smoky, creamy taste, is a fine addition to any roast or grilled meat or poultry. It can be presented by giving each person a few cloves as they are, or they can be taken out of their skins and mashed into the meat juices. This last, highly seasoned, is called a *saupiquet*(see page 250). This is often eaten with game such as rabbit or hare, preferably cooked on a spit in front of a wood fire; it is also good with some birds – for instance duck or pheasant.

A *saupiquet* can also include the mashed poultry or game liver and a dash of vinegar mixed into the juices.

Heat the oven to 200°C. Tear some aluminium foil into 4 squares, each about 30 cm square. With a sharp knife cut the tops off 4 whole heads of garlic, removing just enough to expose the flesh at the top of each clove. Sprinkle them with olive oil, salt and pepper. Wrap each one in the foil. Place them on a roasting tin and bake for 20–30 minutes, until soft; take care not to let them brown too deeply or the taste will go from sweet to bitter.

Grilled and Roasted Vegetables
Escalivada

Grilled vegetables are a vital companion to lamb, steak and roast chicken. They are used in salads, or served hot, with or without tomato sauce. Close to the Spanish border in the delightful fishing port of Collioure, once home to Seurat and Matisse, I ate *escalivada*: aubergines, peppers and tomatoes, cut up, sprinkled with oil and grilled over a wood fire and ever since I have been trying to achieve the same smoky, succulent result.

For best results, the ideal is to cook this over wood, on a barbecue or in a fireplace in the kitchen or outside, using a sturdy iron grill. Alternatively, you could use a large, heavy ridged grill pan. This works really well, but will not impart the delicious aromas that come from the smoke of a wood fire.

You can grill all the usual things – aubergines, courgettes, peppers, tomatoes and you can also grill endives (chicory), large mushrooms, radicchio and spring onions.

Prepare the vegetables by slicing them: fairly thinly in the case of courgettes, aubergines and radicchio; peppers, tomatoes and chicory can be cut in half; mushrooms and spring onions are left whole and everything is brushed with olive oil.

Grill them until they go limp, about 7–8 minutes on each side, turning them from time to time (unless you want very smart stripes, in which case turn them only once), and when they are cooked all the way through, remove them with tongs and sprinkle them with sea salt.

If you are grilling over a wood fire, light it fairly well in advance and boost it 15 minutes before you start the grilling with a bunch (a *fagot*) of vine prunings, or some kindling. Let it die down to strongly glowing embers. Heat the grill before you place the vegetables on it.

Once cooked, you can eat them as they are, or sprinkled with a little olive oil and a *persillade* of chopped garlic and parsley, or with the wonderful red sauce for *calçots* (page 113). If you want to eat them cold, put them in a dish and sprinkle them with vinegar – sherry or red wine mixed with a little honey is good – a little fresh olive oil and chopped basil or mint.

Grilled Mussels

Our friend Bruno Pérolari from Marseillan first introduced us to mussels grilled over pine needles. He started by collecting a bucketful of long pine needles from an umbrella pine, and placing some fine wire netting over the half of a metal oil-barrel we used as a barbecue. He then brought lemons, glasses, a bottle of chilled white wine, and a colander full of washed mussels from the Bassin de Thau, between Sète and Cap d'Agde.

He put a thick layer of dry pine needles on the netting and arranged the mussels on top, propped against each other in concentric circles, with their hinged sides facing down. Then he covered them with another thick layer of pine needles.

The pine needles were suddenly blazing, they frizzled and shrank and flared, the mussels opened and we ate them, with a squeeze of lemon, burning our fingers and our lips. They were specially good washed down with light local wine.

Bruno also gave us the following amazing salad dressing.

Sweet and Sour Pomegranate Dressing
Sauce grenade amère

2–3 ripe, red **pomegranates**; *120ml* **olive oil**; **salt, pepper**.

To remove the seeds from the pomegranate, cut a slice off the top end with a sharp knife then cut through the skin, down the sides of the pomegranate, as if you were preparing to peel an orange.

Now take hold of the pomegranate with both hands and twist it so that it breaks in half. Pick out the pockets of jewel-like seeds, removing all the yellow inner skin.

Put the seeds into the food processor and whizz them. Strain the juice through a fine mesh or a muslin. Cook it gently until it thickens. Cool it in its pan, in a bowl or basin of very cold water. Mix it with olive oil, season with salt and pepper. Use as a dressing for a large green salad or on grilled vegetables.

Anchovy Vinaigrette

This is the dressing for a salad containing hard-boiled eggs, or for an anchoïade (see page 109). It is also very good with tomatoes, avocado and goat's cheese. This will be ample for a large salad.

*6–8 **anchovy fillets**, chopped; 6 **spring onions**, green tops removed, cut into thin rounds; 3 tbsp chopped **flat parsley**; juice of half a **lemon** (about 2 tbsp); 2 tsp **sherry vinegar**; 150ml **olive oil**; **salt, pepper**.*

Mix all the ingredients together in a bowl. Taste for seasoning.

Walnut Oil Vinaigrette

Use this warm-flavoured dressing on strong or bitter salads such as *frisée*, dandelion, batavia or oak leaf lettuce.

*1 tbsp **walnut oil**; 3 tbsp **olive oil**; 1 to 1 ½ tbsp **sherry vinegar** or **red wine vinegar**; 1 small **shallot**, finely chopped; 1 clove **garlic**, finely crushed; **sea salt, pepper**.*

If you find the shallots too strong, wash them in a small sieve and then shake them dry. Mix all the ingredients together and season well.

Garlic Sauce
Crème d'ail

A simple and appetizing way of providing a sauce for a grilled lamb chop or steak, or for grilled fish.

*100g **butter**; 8 cloves **garlic**, peeled and halved; 250ml **white wine**; pinch **salt**.*

Put all the ingredients into a small saucepan and simmer, covered, for 40 minutes. Whizz in the food processor until creamy and frothy. Try flavouring the sauce with thyme or tarragon. This should be enough for 4–6 people.

Black Olive Tapenade

My neighbour in Saint-Chinian, M. Galy, has planted a caper bush by the fence at the bottom of his *potager*. It is placed to get full sun and he is proud of it, as they are notoriously difficult to get going. He and Mme. Galy pickle the capers in vinegar, and it is from pickled capers *(tapèno* in Provençal; *tapera* in Occitan, tapenade is *taperada* in Occitan) that one makes tapenade – pounding them together with stoned black olives and anchovies in olive oil.

Nowadays, on the spice and olive stalls at the outdoor market of Saint-Chinian, they also sell green tapenade (made with green olives), red tapenade (made with sun-dried tomatoes instead of olives), and there is a tapenade made with tinned tuna fish and mustard. This recipe is based on Mireille Johnston's advice, and was passed on to me by our actor-friend Robin Ellis who lives near Castres. It will serve 6–8 people.

> *200g **black olives**, stoned are best; 6 **anchovy fillets**, chopped; 2 tbsp **capers**; 2 cloves of **garlic**, crushed; 1 tsp **fresh thyme**; 1 tbsp **Dijon mustard**; juice of a **lemon**; 120ml **olive oil**; **pepper**.*

Put all the ingredients except the oil into a food processor and pulse briefly, as you pour in the olive oil. The texture should not be too smooth. Taste a bit, to see if it needs more lemon or more oil. Keep covered, in the fridge.

Green Olive Tapenade

> *150g **stoned green olives**; 50g **capers in vinegar**; 30g **anchovy fillets in olive oil**; a few sprigs **parsley**, chopped; 3 tsp **olive oil**; **pepper**.*

Drain the olives and the capers. Put them in to the food processor with the anchovies and the parsley. Pulse until you have a coarse purée, then trickle in the olive oil and pulse a few seconds more. Season generously with black pepper. Eat on grilled *pain de campagne* with a glass of rosé.

Chapter Three

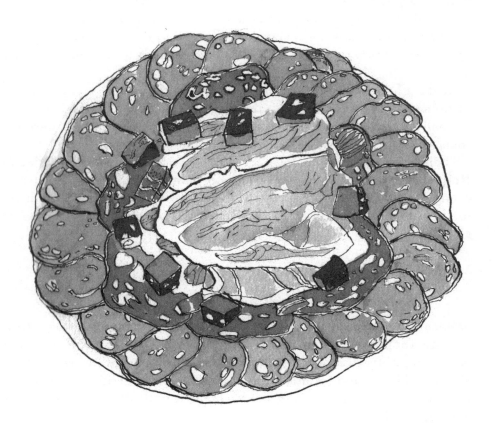

*First Courses, Salads,
Gratins and Eggs*

Les grandes salades

The *grande salade* is very big in Languedoc; on most menus you will find a list of them and if you order one, even a keen salad-lover's first impression will be 'too much'. But in hot weather the best choice will often be one of these jumbles of fresh green salad with any number of delicacies piled on top, and then a dessert or cheese.

In the Cévennes you may find a *grande salade de cuisses de cailles fumées* with smoked confit quails' legs, slices of silky cured duck breast and *gésiers* (gizzards), *mesclun* (mixed leaves), tomatoes and a strong, mustardy dressing.

At the Fleur d'Olargues in the Orb valley they serve a *grande salade* of home-smoked salmon, the salmon crumbled and scattered through a small mountain of mixed leaves with sliced *puntarella*, ripe heritage tomatoes, and thin strips of salted and drained courgette.

There are plenty of *grandes salades* to choose from at the Petit Nice in Roquebrun, a little town in the Hérault mountains where palm trees, oranges and lemon trees flourish above a huge weir alive with swimmers in the summer. One of their favourites is the salad with Roquefort cheese.

Salad with Roquefort and Walnuts
Salade aveyronnaise

Salade aveyronnaise consists of crunchy green leaves, crumbled Roquefort, walnuts (hopefully, if it is autumn, they will be fresh) and sliced white onions in a nutty dressing, all placed in an enormous pile on a large plate. This salad looks and sounds harmless, but packs a terrific punch and is not for delicate palates. You can also make it with Bleu des Causses or even goat's cheese.

*1 head **frisée** (frizzy endive); 1 small **onion**, cut into thin crescents; 100– 150g **Roquefort** or **Bleu des Causses**, crumbled, or **goat's cheese** cut into thin rounds; 50g shelled **walnuts**, broken into pieces; 18–20 **chives**, finely chopped.*

For the vinaigrette:
*1 small clove **garlic**, finely chopped or crushed; 25ml **white wine vinegar**; 75ml extra virgin **olive oil**; 1 tsp **walnut oil** or more, according to taste; **salt** (go easy as the cheese is salty), **pepper**.*

Cut the base off the frizzy endive and wash the leaves well; dry in a salad spinner and leave while you prepare the other ingredients. Make the vinaigrette in the usual way, adding a small quantity of walnut oil – too much can be a bit overwhelming. To make the salad, tear the leaves into manageable pieces and place in a salad bowl with the onion and half the walnuts. Toss well with the vinaigrette. Put the salad on serving plates and top with the cheese. Sprinkle on the remaining walnuts and a scattering of chives. Serve with country bread. (Serves 4–6.)

Peasant-style Salad
Salade paysanne

This salad is perfect for an autumn lunch or as a first course.

1 thick slice of bread torn into pieces to make croûtons; 2 tbsp olive oil; 1 clove garlic; 100g smoked ham in thick slices; 125g Beaufort, Cantal or other hard cheese; 1 frizzy endive (frisée), cos lettuce or 2 little gem lettuces, washed and torn into manageable pieces; 2–3 handfuls of baby spinach leaves; a few sprigs of tarragon; a few sprigs of fresh basil; handful of parsley, coarsely chopped; 50g fresh walnut halves.

For the dressing:
1 tsp Dijon mustard; 2 tbsp olive oil; 2 tsp lemon juice; 2 tsp sherry vinegar; salt, pepper.

Put the torn bread in a bowl and sprinkle it with olive oil. Turn it over, then put it in an oven heated to 220°C to crisp. Take the croûtons out when they are golden and rub them lightly with a cut clove of garlic.

Cut the ham and cheese into thick matchstick-sized pieces. Put the lettuce, spinach, herbs, ham, cheese and walnuts in a good, large salad bowl. Make the vinaigrette by stirring the mustard, salt and pepper together in a bowl and gradually adding the oil to make an emulsion. Add the lemon juice and vinegar to taste. Toss the salad (not too much) and serve, mounding it into the middle of four plates. Throw a few croûtons on top of each plateful. (Serves 4–6.)

Country Salad
Salade fermière

This is a large plate of green leaves of crisp lettuce or *frisée*, on top of which are piled succulent pink, sizzling hot, fried *gésiers confits* (duck gizzards), sometimes with lardons, and the fat from the pan, deglazed with a little red wine vinegar. Fresh croûtons are added and some raw onion is not unusual. You can sometimes see sliced *foie gras* or fried chicken or duck livers along with the *gésiers* or, occasionally, fried shredded duck *confit*, which is a useful substitute if you cannot find *gésiers*.

1 head **frizzy endive** or **Batavia** (escarole); 1 **duck leg** (confit) or 150g **duck gizzards**; 2 large slices **rustic bread**; 3 tbsp **olive oil**; 1 small **sweet onion** (red will do), chopped ; 1 tbsp chopped **chives**.

For the vinaigrette:
1 **shallot**, chopped; 1 tsp **sherry vinegar**; 1 tbsp **red wine vinegar**; 3 tbsp **olive oil**; 1 tbsp **walnut oil**; **salt, pepper**.

Wash the frizzy endive and spin it dry; tear the leaves into smaller pieces. Make the vinaigrette by whisking together the shallot, sherry vinegar, half the red wine vinegar, salt and pepper. Whisk in the oils. Make the croûtons – cut or tear the bread into pieces and toss with the oil, then brown slowly in a frying-pan for 10–15 minutes (or cook until golden in an oven heated to 220°C). Put the duck leg *confit* in a small heavy frying-pan with the skin side down and cook very slowly until the skin is crisp and deeply browned. Turn and brown the other side. (This can take as long as 30 minutes and should not be rushed.) When done, remove it to a plate and leave until cool enough to handle but still warm. Deglaze the pan with the remaining vinegar from the vinaigrette and keep it hot. Tear or cut the duck into small pieces. Keep them hot.

Put the salad in a large bowl, pour on the hot vinegar from the pan, then the dressing and toss thoroughly. Distribute between 4–6 plates. Scatter each plate with pieces of duck, followed by the onion, croûtons and chives. (For 4–6.)

Corsican Fig and Goat's Cheese Salad

Salade Corsica is an early-autumn salad made with green leaves, goat's cheese, chestnuts, walnuts and fresh figs.

Melted Camembert Salad

Salade camembert au four, as it suggests, is a green salad, dressed as usual, perhaps with a few fried lardons, and a whole melted Camembert on top. Each person gets a share of the cheese with their salad.

Melted Goat's Cheese Salad

Salade au chèvre chaud, is a green salad dressed as usual and decorated with a few sliced onions, chives and toasted walnuts or pine-nuts and a slice of a large goat's cheese or a whole small goat's cheese per person, melted in the oven, on top.

Christmas Salad

Salade de noël nîmoise is a beautiful bowl of finely sliced celery hearts dressed with olive oil into which you have melted a few anchovies, with black truffle grated over the top.

Anchovy and Tomato Salad
Anchoïade bouzigaude

Le Marin Restaurant in the fishing village of Bouzigues, on the edge of the shining Bassin de Thau and in full view of the oyster fisheries, serves this simple dish. It is traditional to serve this salad without vinegar, but you can add it if you think it needed.

*2 large, firm **tomatoes**; 2 **green peppers**, preferably the long type, grilled or roasted, skinned and sliced; 12 **anchovy fillets**; 3–4 **spring onions**, cut lengthways into four; 6 **hard-boiled eggs**, halved; 2 tbsp **black olives**, preferably stoned; 4 tbsp **olive oil**; **salt crystals**.*

Roughly slice the tomatoes and arrange on a nice earthenware dish. Arrange the peppers on top, season lightly and then add the anchovies. Scatter on the spring onions, and lastly place the halved eggs and black olives on top. Dribble olive oil copiously over everything and sprinkle with a few salt crystals. It looks like summer itself. (Serves 6.)

Octopus, Fennel and Potato Salad with Aïoli
Salade de poulpe

To tenderize an octopus, some people suggest throwing it hard into the sink about ten times; others, banging it with a mallet; and others use the timeless method of hanging it on a rope by the sea, to dry in the wind and sun for a day or so and then beating it against a nearby rock. One recipe recommends putting the cleaned octopus in a dry, covered pan over a medium heat for 15 minutes, before adding any liquid. Another, much the best, simply leaves it in the freezer for a few hours and then defrosts it. The worst suggestion for softening it that I came across recommends marinating the octopus in pineapple juice overnight.

Follow any, or all, of these methods but, particularly if you choose smaller octopus, freezing overnight followed by long cooking, is the best.

> *2 small **octopus**, about 350g – 400g each, frozen overnight; 3–4 tbsp **olive oil**; 3 tbsp **white wine**; ½ tsp **salt**; 400ml **water**; 6 small **yellow waxy potatoes**; plain **vinaigrette** dressing; 1 **red onion**, sliced into crescents; ½ **bulb fennel**, thinly sliced; 4 tbsp **capers with their vinegar**; 1 bunch **flat parsley**, chopped; 1 tsp **smoked paprika**; sea salt, **pepper**.*

To clean the octopus, cut the head off, turn it inside out, empty it out and remove any loose skin, and then turn it back and peel off the outside skin. Pop out the beak in the centre of the 'flower' of tentacles and then cut between the top of the tentacles to separate them. Wash them under the running tap. Pull off as much skin as possible and then cut in 2–3 cm lengths. Slice the body. Put the octopus into the pan with the oil, wine, salt and water and bring to the boil. Turn down the heat and simmer for 1½ hours or until tender. Allow to cool in the cooking liquid, then drain, and remove the pieces to a dish.

To make the salad, boil the potatoes in their skins. As soon as they are cool enough to handle, skin and slice them. Make a simple dressing of olive oil, lemon juice, a little vinegar, salt and pepper. Mix the pieces of octopus lightly with the potatoes, lay the onion, fennel and capers on top and sprinkle the dressing over everything; scatter on the parsley and jumble everything together lightly so the dressing is well distributed. Sprinkle on the paprika and a little more olive oil if necessary and serve on a flat dish. Aïoli (page 91) is the correct accompaniment. (Serves 6.)

Salt Cod Salad from Bédarieux
Morue maître d'hôtel

When I first had a fish salad, it was *turbot à la monégasque*, and the firm flakes of turbot were simply dressed with shallots, capers and parsley, oil and vinegar. It was delicious and is equally good made with salt cod, a recipe from Bédarieux in the valley of the Orb in the Hérault.

> *400g **salt cod** previously soaked for 36 hours; 1 **sweet onion**, finely chopped; 1 tbsp chopped **chives**; 1 tbsp chopped **parsley**; pinch **nutmeg**; 1½ tbsp **olive oil**; 1 tbsp **white wine vinegar** (or try a mixture of lemon juice and sherry vinegar); 1 tbsp **capers**; **pepper**.*

Cook the salt cod lightly, according to the method on page 171. Mix the onions, chives, parsley and nutmeg together in a bowl. Whisk the oil and vinegar in a separate bowl, then combine with the herbs. Season with plenty of pepper. Flake the cod and mix with the onion, capers and herb dressing. You can do this with your hands. Taste for seasoning and serve chilled or at at room temperature. (Serves 2.)

Salad of Salt Cod with Beans and Olives
Salade de la province de Bages

This is a typically Catalan dish, although there the cod is sometimes used raw. The province of Bages, near Barcelona, is a wine-producing district and its capital Manresa was refuge to St Ignatius Loyola, the founder of the Jesuits, as he prepared for his religious vocation. Much later, it was the site of a serious defeat for Napoleon, whose troops destroyed the town before they fled. The residents rebuilt it from the rubble which gives some of the old city a curious appearance.

*300g white fillet of **salt cod**, soaked for 36 hours in frequently changed cold water; ½ **onion**, sliced; 2 tbsp **black olives**, stoned; 2 tbsp **green olives**, stoned; 1 **red** and 1 **green pepper**, roasted, skinned and cut into strips; 2 **plum tomatoes**, skinned, deseeded and cut into dice; 100g cooked or tinned **haricot** or **borlotti beans**; 1 tbsp of **flat parsley**, chopped; **salt**.*

For the vinaigrette:
*2 cloves **garlic**, chopped; 1½ tbsp good **wine vinegar**; 4 tbsp **olive oil**; **pepper**.*

Make the vinaigrette by whisking the ingredients together. Do not add salt at this point. Bring the cod to simmering-point in a pan of unsalted water, remove it from the heat before it boils and let it cool for 15 minutes in the cooking water, then drain it. Skin the cod and flake the flesh, removing every bone. Mix the flakes into the vinaigrette.

Wash the onion rings in cold water to remove some of their acridness, and pat them dry. Place the olives, the sliced peppers and the tomato in a flattish dish. Add the cod, the beans and the vinaigrette and mix lightly, so that all the different ingredients are coated with the dressing. Taste for salt – the cod and olives may be enough. Scatter the onions and chopped parsley on top. Serve at room temperature. (Serves 4–6.)

Calçots

Calçots are giant onion shoots which appear with the almond blossom in February. They are consumed in gargantuan quantities at festivals, called *calçotadas* in the *Pays catalan*. The macho test is to eat as many as possible – thirty or forty? Nowhere near enough. Grilled over bonfires of vine prunings on giant grills in the fresh air, they are served wrapped in newspaper using the curved southern roof-tiles as plates. After the onions there will be *saucisson sec* – the long thin ones called whips or *fouets* are popular – *jambon cru*, almonds, hazel nuts, olives, prawns, tomato bread, roast pork and a kind of pizza called *coca de recapte* (see page 295); and quantities of red wine and beer.

The *sauce aux calçots*, a variation on romesco sauce, is made with roasted and pounded garlic, a dried long chilli called *bitxo* or a sweet, mild heartshaped one called *ñora*, parsley and almonds or hazelnuts, bound together with olive oil and vinegar. The *calçot* looks like a bunch of fat onion shoots all coming from the same root. The method of growing them consists of starting them like ordinary onions and then earthing them up, when they produce several stems in a cluster. These are separated, trimmed and washed and are now ready for grilling.

Calçots take a year to grow and are very specialized, consequently we very seldom get them in Britain (for a supplier, see page 31). But we can make the dish with young, tender leeks which, alas, are nowhere near as fat and juicy, nor as tender and melting as the real thing.

To Grill *calçots*

In the kitchen: heat a griddle pan until very hot, brush lightly with oil and place the *calçots* on it. Turn them over with tongs and keep grilling until the outer skin is blackened and the flesh is tender when pierced with a knife.

If you are cooking out of doors: grill them over a glowing bed of charcoal, wood or, better still, vine prunings, until blackened and smoked and tender and juicy in the middle.

Almond, Garlic and Tomato Sauce
Sauce aux calçots

This velvety sauce is made smooth and clinging so that it does not drip when the *calçots* are dipped into it. Much is said about how best to eat *calçots*. You must tip your head back, raise the onion, covered in black bits and red sauce, over your mouth, and steer it in. The more you eat, the more juice runs down your chin, the better fun for everyone.

This heavenly sauce, a beautiful coral red, is a brilliant companion to any grilled or roasted vegetables. You can also eat it with the aubergine gratin on page 270.

*1 whole head of **garlic**, the top sliced off; 3 **tomatoes**; 25g **flaked almonds**; 2 dried **ñora chillies**, soaked, deseeded and scraped (optional); 2 generous pinches of **cayenne pepper**; 2 tbsp **red wine vinegar**; 120ml **olive oil**; **salt**.*

Heat the oven to 200°C. Drizzle the garlic with olive oil. Roast the tomatoes for 15 minutes, then add garlic to the roasting tin and return for 25 minutes. Toast the almonds carefully in a dry frying-pan until pale brown, 10 minutes or less. Remove the skins from the tomatoes and the garlic cloves. Put all the ingredients in the food processor and pulse to a smooth, creamy texture, adding the olive oil last in a slow and steady stream. Serve it hot with *calçots*, grilled spring onions or any grilled vegetables, or with shellfish.

Long Pimentos with Goat's Cheese
Poivrons farçis

This excellent first course was cooked for us in Saint-Chinian by my singer daughter-in-law Gertrude and, like her, it is both elegant and practical. The weather was hot and heavy, as it can be in mid-August, with occasional flashes and rumbles from the clouds hanging over the mountains, and we wanted something simple and light. She made it with the long, mild, thin-fleshed peppers that are grown throughout the *Pays catalan*, called *piments doux* or *piments du pays*. They are also called Romano peppers.

*6–8 long red or green **pimentos**; 200g **feta** or other brined goat's or sheep's cheese, cut in small cubes; 3 cloves **garlic**, peeled and sliced thinly; small bunch of fresh **basil**, leaves only, torn into small pieces; 3 tbsp **olive oil**; **salt**, **pepper**.*

Heat the oven to 200°C. Wash the pimentos and slit them all the way along one side. Don't cut off the stalk end. Working carefully with your fingers, scoop out the seeds and as much of the white pith as possible. Place them, cut side up, in a roasting tin or gratin dish. Sprinkle a little olive oil into each pepper. Divide the pieces of cheese between them, pushing them into through the slit and put the shreds of garlic on top. Put the leaves of basil on top of this and sprinkle again with oil. Season well with pepper but very little or no salt, as the cheese is salty. Put the dish in the oven and roast for 25–30 minutes until the cheese has melted and the peppers are tender. Serve hot or cold. (Serves 4.)

Fried Aubergine and Tomato Salad with Mint and Harissa
Salade frite

Harissa – the fierce red Moorish paste of chillies, garlic, coriander, caraway, cumin, tomato paste and olive oil – is a favourite ingredient in Languedoc. Usually bought ready-made, it is used in couscous, to flavour green and black olives, with snails, with mussels, in sauces and, here, as a seasoning.

*2–3 **aubergines**, about 300g altogether, sliced across diagonally into 5mm slices; 225ml **olive oil**; 1 tbsp **red wine vinegar**; 5 large ripe **tomatoes**; 1 tsp **caster sugar**; a good bunch of **mint**; 1 tbsp of **harissa paste**.*

For a plain vinaigrette:
*1 tbsp **red wine vinegar**; 3–4 tbsp **olive oil**; 1–2 cloves **garlic**, chopped; 200ml **Greek yoghurt**; **salt**.*

Sprinkle the aubergine slices with salt and place them in a colander to drain for 30 minutes. Rinse, drain and pat dry with kitchen paper. If you can, grill the aubergines over a fire, after brushing the slices with olive oil on both sides. This imparts a lovely, smoky flavour. Otherwise, fry the slices in batches in half the olive oil until well browned, tender and cooked through. Add more oil if necessary; the aubergine should be translucent. Drain on kitchen paper. Remove to a dish and arrange in overlapping slices. Sprinkle with red wine vinegar and a very little salt.

Cut the tomatoes in half across the middle, turn them cut side up and sprinkle with sugar and salt. Heat the remaining oil and fry the tomatoes skin side down, over a lowish heat, for 15 minutes. Turn carefully, lower the heat a little more, and fry for a further 10 minutes, watching to see that the sugar does not burn but lightly caramelizes with the tomato juice. Spoon the tomatoes and their juices over the aubergines or tuck them in between the slices.

Whisk the harissa together with the vinaigrette ingredients and trickle it all over the salad. Scatter chopped mint leaves over everything. Serve the salad warm, with a bowl of yoghurt for added zip. (Serves 4–6.)

Baked Aubergines with Two Cheeses and Basil
Aubergines au four

*2 **aubergines**; 1 **red onion**, chopped; 1 **tomato**, skinned, deseeded and cut into dice; 1 bunch **basil**, chopped; 50g **Parmesan cheese**, finely grated; 50g **Gruyère**, grated; 6 tbsp **olive oil**; **salt**, **pepper**.*

Cut the aubergines in half and carefully scoop out the flesh with a teaspoon, keeping the shells intact. Chop the flesh and sprinkle both the flesh and the shells with salt. Allow to drain for 20–30 minutes. Rinse briefly in cold water. Heat the oven to 200°C. Pat the shells dry, sprinkle with olive oil and bake them for 10–15 minutes, until tender.

Squeeze the flesh to extract the juice. Heat 2 tbsp olive oil in a frying-pan and soften the onion over a low heat for 10 minutes, stirring occasionally. Add the aubergine and cook for a further 15–20 minutes, until it is very soft. Lastly, add the tomato and cook without stirring for a further 5–10 minutes. Cool. Mix the chopped basil with the Parmesan and Gruyère and add to the aubergine mixture. Taste for seasoning.

Place the shells in a gratin dish or roasting tin. Pile the stuffing onto the shells, distributing it evenly, drizzle with olive oil. Bake for 15 minutes, then turn down the oven to 150°C and continue cooking for another 10–15 minutes, until brown and melting. (Serves 4.)

Light Chicken Liver Pâté
Gâteau de foie de volaille

Poultry here are strong, tall birds; my neighbour Madame Galy kept a popular, if ugly, red-feathered breed with bald necks, called *cou-nu*, that pecked and scratched, along with several ducks, beneath a couple of large fig trees. They taste wonderful.

When you buy a chicken in a good butcher in France, you are often choosing an individually reared bird; each is different. They may look rather bony, but they taste far and away better than the plump, soft-fleshed, mass-reared poultry of the supermarkets. Their livers are particularly good – firm and bright – ideal for making this smooth pâté. Serve it with a green salad. Start marinating the livers several hours in advance, or leave them in the marinade overnight.

*500g **chicken livers** (about 10), trimmed of sinews and gall.*

For the marinade:
*100ml **port**; 2 sprigs **thyme**; 2 **bay leaves**.*

For cooking the livers:
*1 small clove **garlic**, finely chopped; 100ml **milk**; 2 **eggs**; 4 tbsp **double cream**; a dab of **butter** for greasing the mould; **salt, white pepper**.*

Marinate the chicken livers, preferably in a china bowl, for 6 hours or overnight. Heat the oven to 150°C. Drain the livers and place them in a food processor with the garlic. Process finely for 2–3 minutes, then add the milk, eggs and cream. Process for a few seconds, add salt, white pepper and a tablespoonful or so of the marinade. Pulse briefly to mix it in.

Butter the inside of a soufflé dish and pour in the mixture. Stand it in a roasting tin half-full of hot water, put it in the middle of the oven and cook for 35–40 minutes, until just firm when pressed lightly with the fingertips. Remove from the *bain marie* and allow to cool for 5 minutes. Then serve with hot tomato sauce (page 98) or allow to cool and serve with toast and a green salad. (Serves 6.)

Fig Salad with Bitter Endive
Salade de figues

This salad is refreshing and beautiful, with a sweet and bitter flavour. Any ripe figs will do, but the black ones look so luscious, with their purple and pink insides, that I tend to prefer them.

*4 perfect ripe **figs**, preferably black; 2 heads of **endive**, use white or red or one of each; ½ small **red onion**, sliced into crescents; juice of half a **lemon**; 3 tbsp **olive oil**; 1 tsp **red wine vinegar** from Banyuls, or use **balsamic** or other sweetish vinegar; pinch of **sugar**; **salt, pepper**.*

Carefully cut the figs into quarters and then into eighths. Shred the endive and arrange it on an oval plate. Scatter the slices of fig on top and the sliced onion on top of that. Whisk together the lemon juice, olive oil, red wine vinegar and sugar, season with salt and pepper and pour it over the salad. (Serves 4.)

Aubergine Caviar
Caviar d'aubergines

This simple recipe comes from Gruissan, the captivating circular village surround by saltwater lagoons on the coast by Narbonne. It must have originally come into the repertoire when Spain was ruled by the Moors. I have eaten many forms of this dish in Syria and in Iran and there is nothing to beat its sweet smokiness. It does not look or taste much like caviar, but the aubergines do often have little black seeds that may give a clue to the name.

*3 large **aubergines**; 200ml best **olive oil**; **lemon juice** according to taste; ¼ tsp of **dried thyme** or leaves of 3 or 4 sprigs of **fresh thyme**; 1–2 **dried bird chillis**, crumbled; **salt**.*

Heat the oven to 200°C. Pierce the aubergines a couple of times with a knife to prevent them from exploding. Bake the aubergines for 60 minutes, until collapsing and completely soft inside. Let them cool a bit, then peel off the skin. Chop the flesh very finely with a large knife, or purée it in a food processor. Gradually mix in the oil and lemon, add the thyme and chilli. Season with salt. (Serves 4–6.)

Cep Tart
Tarte aux cèpes

This is a luxurious, creamy tart – I have tried to reproduce one cooked by Françoise Raviat, my champion mushroom-hunting guide. Her style is large and generous, and the tart should be the same.

*4 large firm **ceps** (200g) (or **portobello** or **chestnut mushrooms**); 2 **eggs**; 150ml **crème fraîche** or **double cream**; grated **nutmeg**; 2 tbsp **olive oil**; 1 **shallot**, finely chopped; 25g **butter**; 60g **Gruyère cheese**, grated; **salt**, **pepper**.*

For the pastry, either use bought puff (made with butter) or a shortcrust made with 225 g plain flour; 60g lard; 60g butter; water and salt. Roll out the pastry to line a buttered tart tin and blind-bake with beans in an oven preheated to 180°C for 30 minutes, remove the beans and continue to cook for 10 minutes until crisp.

Trim the bases of the ceps to remove any earth. Wipe the caps carefully with a damp kitchen towel. Cut them into pieces 3–4 cm across. Whisk the eggs in a bowl together with the cream. Season with salt, pepper and nutmeg. Heat the olive oil in a large pan and soften the shallot without letting it brown. Add this to the eggs, leaving the oil in the pan, and add the butter. When it is hot, put in the ceps and sauter until any moisture has run out and evaporated – this is especially noticeable if it has recently been raining. When they start to turn golden, season them lightly, let them cool a little and stir them into the egg mixture together with three-quarters of the cheese.

Transfer all of this to the tart base, sprinkle with the remaining cheese and bake in the oven for 20 minutes, until just set. (Serves 4–6.)

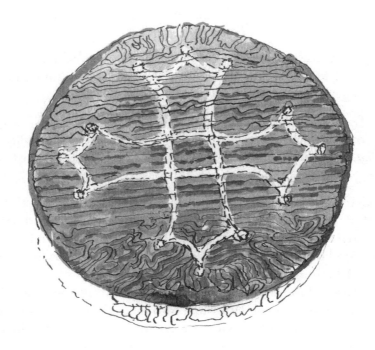

Tartiflette

This is real mountain food, rich, fragrant and melting, originating in
the Savoie rather than in Languedoc. Although the dish has traditional
origins, its current form was developed by the makers of Reblochon in
the 1980s and first served in Alpine ski resorts. It makes a wonderful
lunch. Reblochon, not too ripe and pungent, works extremely well but
there is also a special cheese called *fromage pour tartiflette*. It is easier to
handle and more authentic if you leave the rind on the cheese.

*800g **waxy potatoes**; 2–3 tbsp **olive oil** or **goose fat**; 1 **onion**, finely chopped;
150g **lardons** (use **poitrine fumée** or **pancetta**); 300ml **white wine; pepper**;
500g **Reblochon** or **fromage pour tartiflette**.*

Heat the oven to 210°C. Cook the potatoes in boiling well-salted water
until just tender. Drain, skin and slice them.

Heat the oil or goose fat in a large, sturdy frying-pan. Soften the onion
and the lardons for 10 minutes, and remove them with a slotted spoon,
leaving the fat behind. Add the potatoes to the same pan and fry until

they are just starting to brown, adding a little more fat or oil if necessary and turning them carefully so they do not break. Return the lardons and onions.

Pour in the white wine and allow to simmer for 5 minutes. Transfer everything to a large oval gratin dish and season with pepper. Cut the cheese in half horizontally across the middle and place skin side down, on top of the potatoes. Cover lightly with aluminium foil and bake for 30 minutes, then remove the foil and return for another 5 minutes. Serve with sliced baguette and a green salad. (Serves 4.)

Pasta with Mushroom Sauce
Pâtes aux champignons aux oeufs frits

This rather eccentric recipe can be a good standby for lunch on one of those days when, expecting sunshine all day, you see nothing but grey skies thanks to the Marin – the muggy wind that brings clouds up from the sea to cover the plains between Béziers and Carcassonne. It can be made with *boutons de guêtre* (false *mousserons*), with very small ceps, or with field or button mushrooms. Pasta is a common enough food in Languedoc and I love this version – mushroom pasta with fried eggs on top.

300g pasta; 225g button mushrooms; 4 cloves garlic; 1 bunch parsley, stalks removed; 50g butter; 3 tbsp olive oil; 4 eggs; salt, pepper.

Clean and slice the mushrooms. Finely chop three cloves of garlic and the parsley and mix them together to make a *persillade*. Bring a pan of salted water to the boil. Heat half the butter with 2 tbsp oil and fry the final clove of garlic (cut in half) until it turns pale golden brown. Remove it. Cook the mushrooms in the garlic-flavoured oil, seasoning them with salt and pepper. When they are golden stir in the *persillade* and take off the heat.

Cook the pasta and while it cooks fry the eggs in the remaining oil. Drain the pasta and stir in the remaining butter and the mushrooms. Toss the pasta with the sauce and serve each portion at once with a fried egg. (Serves 4.)

Tapenade and Tomato Croûte
Croûte de tapenade et tomates

You can make this with the leftovers of pastry after making a tart. It is extremely quick and easy.

> *125g **puff pastry** (made with butter); 90g **black olive tapenade** (page 104); 250g **small plum tomatoes**, cut in half across – if using large plum tomatoes cut lengthwise into 4 oval slices; 30g **anchovy fillets** (1 small tin); a sprinkling of **olive oil**.*

Heat the oven to 200°C. Roll out the pastry and cut into a rough oval. Spread it with tapenade, leaving a margin all the way round the edge. Place the tomatoes in lines, lengthwise and almost touching, on top of the tapenade, or arrange them in any pattern you may prefer. Place the anchovy fillets in lines between the tomatoes. Sprinkle or brush with olive oil. Bake for 20–25 minutes. Allow it to cool for 5 minutes before serving. You can serve this beautiful looking dish *en apéritif*, or with a salad for a light summery lunch. (Serves 4.)

Flat Tart of Brousse and Chard
Tarte de brousse aux blettes

Brousse, also known as *recuite*, is a fresh curd cheese made with sheep's or goat's milk. Hyelzas in the Lozère is famous for *brousse* made with the milk of sheep that feed high up on the rugged Causse Méjean, with its dry, herb-rich pastures. Also worth seeking out is *brousse de Rove*, made from the milk of a handsome race of hardy goats living in the windy Bouches-du-Rhône and feeding on the aromatic native plants of the *garrigue*. To make *brousse*, the milk is curdled, heated, cooled and drained in a basket. It is eaten as a dessert with jam or honey or used for cooking sweet curd tarts. It is also excellent in savoury ones, as here. A similar fresh cheese is Corsican *brocciu* or *broccio* made with whey and sheep's or goat's milk. Both *ricotta* and *fromage frais* are somewhat similar in texture and can be used as a substitute.

> *400g **brousse**, **fromage frais** or **ricotta** (or 200g cream cheese and 200g cottage cheese); 300g **shortcrust pastry**; 750g **Swiss chard**; 1 tbsp **olive oil**; 2 cloves of **garlic**, sliced; 1 tbsp **butter**; 1 tbsp **flour**; 600ml **milk**; 3 **eggs**; 100ml **single cream; salt, pepper**.*

Heat the oven to 180°C. Line a 26 cm tart tin with pastry and bake the case blind for 30 minutes. Wash the chard and remove the stalks from the green part. Heat the olive oil with 1 clove of garlic, sliced, and throw in the chard leaves with the water clinging to them, stir and cover the pan. Cook over a low heat until completely wilted, stirring from time to time. Drain and chop the leaves into manageable pieces.

Heat the butter in a medium pan, throw in the second sliced clove of garlic, stir in the flour and gradually add the milk to make a smooth sauce. Season with salt and pepper. Slice the chard stalks into small strips, throwing them into the sauce as you do so. Simmer them until they are tender, it takes about 45 minutes. Allow to cool.

Beat the *brousse* or other cheese and then whisk in the eggs one at a time. Stir in the stalks and leaves of the chard as well as the sauce. Lastly, add the cream. Check the seasoning. Pour the mixture into the tart shell and bake for 25–30 minutes, until puffed and pale golden. (Serves 6.)

Goat's Cheese, Thyme and Black Olive Tart
Tarte au chèvre frais et aux olives noires

This tart, which has a creamy, cheesecake texture, is from the Hérault, known for its olive groves; Languedociennes constantly use olives in cooking. Near Narbonne, the co-operative olive oil mill in Bize-Minervois, 'Oulibo', is open to everybody and the village holds an olive fête each July. At the mill you can taste the different varieties of local olives. You could use local green Lucques olives in this dish, instead of black olives.

> *250g **puff pastry**, made with butter; 120g soft, fresh **goat's cheese**; 200g **brousse**, **fromage frais** or other soft cheese such as **curd cheese**; 4 **eggs**, beaten; 2 tbsp **crème fraîche**; 1 tsp **thyme** leaves; 25g small stoned **black olives**; **salt**, **pepper**.*

Heat the oven to 220°C. Roll out the pastry to line a flan tin; cover the base with baking paper and beans or crumpled foil. Bake blind for 20 minutes, remove the beans or foil and allow to cool.

Whizz the goat's cheese with the *brousse* or *fromage frais* in the blender until smooth and creamy, add the eggs, cream, thyme and seasoning – it will not need much salt because of the olives. Transfer the mixture to the pastry base, arranging the olives evenly across the top. Reduce the oven temperature to 200°C and bake the flan for 20–25 minutes. Test after 20 minutes, as it is vital not to overcook it. If it is not set and the pastry is getting too brown, turn down the heat to 180°C and cook for a further 10 minutes.

Eat with a garlicky green salad with fresh herbs – basil, parsley, chives, tarragon and chervil – and possibly some slices of raw onion. (Serves 4.)

Spanish Omelette
Truita de truffas, tortilla or omelette espagnole

A hefty chunk of this classic *tortilla* (sometimes called, in the south, *la moissonneuse*, the reaper), wrapped in a printed handkerchief and taken to the fields at harvest time, provided a fine midday *casse-croûte* to refresh the weary labourer. The Spanish omelette long ago crossed the border into France and is an essential on restaurant menus throughout the *Pays catalan* and beyond. I include two versions, ancient and modern. Here we have one for everyday, eaten warm or at room temperature, cut into large rectangles, or into small squares and served with cocktail sticks *en apéro* – with drinks. It is also eaten as a snack and in sandwiches.

> *½ large* **Spanish onion**; *3 medium* **waxy yellow** *or* **red potatoes** *(about 400g) peeled;* *4* **eggs** *plus 1* **egg yolk**; *200ml* **olive oil** *or, for a lighter result,* **grapeseed oil** *or a mixture of the two;* **salt, pepper**.

Slice the onion in half from the top to the root, remove the solid bit at the root end and then slice into thin, crescent-shaped slices, again from top to root. Slice the potatoes thinly (about 4mm), either on a mandoline or with a food processor. Put these in a bowl of water for a few minutes to prevent them discolouring, then drain in a colander.

Take a heavy, well-seasoned frying-pan with deepish sides, 20–22 cm across, and heat the oil. Add the onion and let it cook for 3–4 minutes without browning, then add the potatoes. If the oil does not quite cover them, dispense a little more – they should be bathed in it. Season lightly and let them cook for 10 minutes, turning occasionally. Drain off the oil and set aside; it can be used again for frying or even for making mayonnaise.

Break the eggs into a bowl and whisk them with a little salt. Add the potatoes and onion; if you want the potatoes in layers, do this carefully without breaking them up. Set aside for 15 minutes, if there is time, so that the eggs and potatoes can get familiar with each other.

Wipe out the pan and heat it again with a teaspoon or two of oil. When it is hot (80°C) add the egg mixture and cook, shaking the pan a bit to prevent the tortilla from sticking. When it is almost set, get ready to turn it over. I do this with an oven glove and a suitable flat plate or a saucepan lid, large enough to cover the pan. Put a thinnish oven glove on your right hand, or use a cloth; grasp a plate or lid with your right hand and the frying-pan with your left. Place the cover on top of the frying-pan and quickly flip the whole thing over, keeping the cover tight on the frying-pan – the tortilla will now be on the cover, so keep it level or it will slide off. Lift off the frying-pan, now empty, and turn it the right way up. Slide the tortilla off the cover and back into the pan, cooked side up. Cook for a few more minutes until set. It should still be juicy in the middle. (Serves 2–4.)

Tortilla with Potato Crisps
Omelette de chips, sauce salmorejo

A far cry from the previous recipe, I was amused by this idea from the *Taste of Spain* magazine; it doesn't say so specifically, but I am told the recipe originally came from Ferran Adrià of el Bulli fame, and is now fairly common in the region as home cooks have followed him in bringing the Spanish omelette into the realms of 'techno-emotional' cooking.

The *salmorejo* sauce served with it is from Andalusia, but it is popular in the Roussillon, perfectly sympathizing with hot Languedoc summers – you can also serve this with fried aubergines, with rabbit or with crab.

For the salmorejo:
1 clove **garlic**; 75g day-old (or two-) **country bread**, crusts removed; 1 tbsp **sherry vinegar**; 200g ripe **red tomatoes**, skinned, deseeded and chopped; pinch **hot pimentón**; 60ml **olive oil**; **coarse salt**, **pepper**.

For the omelette:
2 **eggs** plus 1 **yolk**; ½ **onion**, sliced into crescents (see previous recipe); 100g **olive oil**; 50g **potato crisps**; **salt**, **pepper**.

To make the *salmorejo* sauce: chop the garlic and mash well with the salt to make a paste. Cut the bread into cubes, put into a bowl and sprinkle with the sherry vinegar. Liquidize the tomatoes together with the garlic using a blender or food processor, add the bread and garlic and whizz to a purée, add the paprika and then incorporate the olive oil, pouring it in gradually in a steady stream. Season with salt and pepper and set aside until needed.

To make the omelette: beat the eggs in a bowl with a little salt. Soften the onion to make a *confit* by cooking very gently for 15 minutes in 3 tbsp olive oil. Drain and remove the oil, which can be used at another time. Coat the omelette pan with a teaspoon of olive oil. Heat it while you stir the onion and crisps into the egg mixture. Tip all this into the pan when it is hot, and cook over a medium heat, shaking the while to prevent it sticking. Cook until almost set but take care not to burn the bottom. You may decide to make a French-style omelette, which works well. Otherwise, turn the tortilla in the way I described in the previous recipe. Slide it back into the pan and continue to cook for a minute or two. It should be firm but juicy. (Serves 1–2.)

Asparagus Omelette and a Little Soup
Omelette aux pointes d'asperges et sa soupe

This recipe is excellent when made with cultivated asparagus but originally took advantage of *asperges sauvages* from the hedgerow. You can find these by searching the *garrigue* in late March, and you see many parties of people setting out to do just that. But the simplest thing is to head for the market and buy them in bunches. Two stalls were selling them at Narbonne market last time I was there in the spring. Some cooks think cooking wild asparagus takes away from its character – they eat it *croque-au-sel* (raw, with sea salt) or chopped and thrown straight into an omelette. Others fry the chopped asparagus first in lard or olive oil before adding it to the eggs. This slightly more interesting recipe is adapted from one from the fishing town of Gruissan. I found it in a collection given to the editor Alain Delsol by Gruissanaise *grandmères*. These grandmothers are extremely thrifty, nothing is ever allowed to go to waste, and vegetable water is considered health-giving, so from a bunch of asparagus we make a beautiful cup of soup and a delicious omelette.

300g **asparagus** *or a large handful* **wild asparagus**; *1 dessertspoon* **crème fraîche**; *4* **eggs**; *a nut of* **butter**; *1 dessertspoon of* **olive oil**; **salt, pepper**.

Bring a pan of salted water to the boil, throw in the washed asparagus and boil 2 minutes. Drain but keep the cooking water. Cut off the first 8–10 cm of the tips, keeping the stalks separate. Cut the tips lengthwise into quarters, so they resemble the thin flexible wild asparagus tips, (they will also sit better in the omelette than left whole).

Put the stalks back in the cooking water, season with salt and pepper and boil for 12 minutes. Chop roughly and then whizz in the food processor until smooth. Put this soup back in the saucepan, heat to boiling point and stir in as much butter and *crème fraîche* as you like.

Next, make an omelette with half the asparagus tips, tossing them briefly in olive oil and then pouring on half the beaten, seasoned eggs and making the omelette as usual. Rub a nut of butter over the surface of the omelette to make it shine. Make a second omelette the same way and serve with little cups of delicate, pale green soup. (Serves 2.)

Wild Asparagus Omelette
Omelette aux asperges sauvages

There are many recent, local cookbooks containing recipes for wild asparagus omelette; this is based on one from *Petit Précis de Cuisine Occitane* by André Bonnaure.

*10 **eggs**; 1kg **wild asparagus** or use cultivated; **lard** and/or **butter**; **salt**, **pepper**.*

Beat the eggs in a bowl with the salt and pepper. Cut the base off the asparagus stalks, keeping only the tender part. Cook the asparagus tips slowly in lard (or butter) in a frying-pan until just tender. Fold them into the beaten eggs. Make an omelette in the normal way.

I have made this omelette and it is very good. Another recipe cuts the tips into little pieces and folds them, raw, into the omelette, to preserve all the flavour of the asparagus. The flavour of wild asparagus is decidedly a shade or two more bitter than that of cultivated and it has a subtlety considered superior to the domesticated vegetable by local pickers. (Serves 5–6.)

Truffle Omelette
Omelette aux truffes

*1 fresh or preserved **truffle** weighing 30–50g; 8 **eggs**; 30g **butter**; **salt**, **pepper**.*

Slice the truffle thinly. Beat the eggs in a bowl and incorporate most of the slices. If you have some brandy or the liquid from the jar if using preserved truffles, add a teaspoonful to the eggs.

Leave to stand for 30 minutes so that the eggs absorb the truffle's perfume. Heat the butter in an omelette pan. Season the eggs and pour half the mixture into the pan. Make an omelette as you are accustomed. Once you've turned this one out, make another in the same pan. Scatter your remaining truffle slices over the tops and serve forth.(Makes 2 large omelettes.)

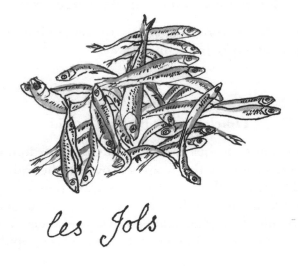

les Jols

Small Fry Omelette
Omelette de mange-tout

Mange-touts are tiny fish (when they're not peas) – they can be sea fish such as *jols* (or *joëls*, *Atherina boyeri* or sand-smelt, known sometimes as *melets*) or river fish. Start by flouring the fish by shaking them in a paper bag with some seasoned flour. Fry them briefly in oil and let them drain on kitchen paper. Mix them into beaten eggs with a *persillade* of chopped garlic and parsley and fry the omelette in olive oil in the normal way.

Wild Garlic Omelette
Omelette d'ail des bois

On Olonzac market (held every Tuesday in this pretty village in the Minervois) a stall-holder gave me a recipe for a wild garlic omelette. You make it in the same way as a sorrel omelette (you can use wild sorrel, *Rumex acetosa*, *oseille des prés*, for that too). Simply melt the washed and shredded leaves in butter, then throw in the beaten eggs and cook your omelette in the normal way. You can also add shredded wild garlic to a *tortilla* (see page 124).

Salsify Bud Omelette
Omelette aux boutons de scorzonères

Brown the buds of scorzonera or salsify flowers in butter, then pour in the beaten eggs and make in the usual way.

Acacia Flower Omelette
Omelette aux fleurs d'acacia

In *Two Vagabonds in Languedoc* by Jan and Cora Gordon, the travelling vagabonds gained culinary tips from 'a drover in the train [who] talked of acacia omelet'. Acacia flowers were once quite popular as a flavouring for desserts in Occitanie and they do have a certain honeyed taste. Just remove the blossoms from their stalks, and scatter them into a sweetened omelette as it cooks. Acacia flower fritters were also popular in country areas.

Mushroom Omelette
Omelette aux champignons

This is delicious made with ceps or *chanterelles*, and is eaten with a garlicky green salad. It is based on a recipe from Robert Ledrole's *Cuisine du Languedoc*. Try not to wash the mushrooms – rub off the dirt with damp kitchen towels or paper.

*2 **eggs** per person; 50g **mushrooms**; 2 tsp **goose fat**; generous pinch of **fresh** or **dried thyme leaves**; a little **olive oil**; salt, **pepper**.*

Beat the eggs in a bowl with a little salt and pepper. Cut the mushrooms into small pieces and sprinkle with a little salt. Heat the goose fat and fry the mushrooms for 3–4 minutes until lightly golden all over. Wipe out the pan, add the olive oil and heat. Stir the mushrooms into the eggs, add the thyme. Make the omelette in the usual way. Do not overcook it, it needs to be runny (*baveuse*) in the middle.

Roquefort Omelette from the Aveyron

This omelette is rather addictive; it has a great texture, tender, creamy, light and fluffy all at once. It can be also be made with the cheese *Bleu des Causses*. Use a medium non-stick pan rather than a small omelette pan.

100g **Roquefort cheese**; *2 tbsp* **Greek yoghurt** *and 1 tbsp* **crème fraîche** *(or use 3 tbsp* **fromage frais***); 4 fresh* **eggs**; **olive oil** *or* **butter**; *plenty of freshly ground* **pepper***.*

Crumble the Roquefort into a bowl and mash very thoroughly with a fork. Add the *fromage frais* or yoghurt and *crème fraîche*, and mix to a thick cream. Season liberally with coarsely ground pepper, but do not add salt. Beat the eggs in a bowl then gradually incorporate them into the Roquefort mixture. Heat one tablespoon of olive oil or butter in the pan, pour in half the mixture and make an omelette in the normal way, but using a spatula instead of a fork to tease up the edges. Fold it over carefully as it is quite fragile. Turn it out onto a warm plate and let it set as you make the second omelette. Let this set too for a couple of minutes. Serve with a green salad. (Serves 2.)

Red Camargue Rice Salad with Preserved Lemons and Mullet Roe
Riz rouge de Camargue à la poutargue

This is a really beautiful dish similar to one eaten at the lunches given at the *abrivados* of the Camargue; the colours are warm and glowing – russet, golden yellow and amber, with black olives to set them off. An *abrivado* is an exciting event, when the mounted cowhands herd a number of cattle, in a close group, at a fast gallop, bringing them in from the salt marshes and prairies onto the ranch. Sometimes this is done as a spectacle for the crowds – Aigues-Vives in the Gard has a good one. On these occasions a small herd of black bulls is let out into the street and chased around the village by a posse of ranch hands, with all the young boys running behind to catch hold of the tails. One of the cattle always escapes and causes lots of mayhem, and everyone feels the thrill of madness.

This salad tastes good if you add the sweetness of a dozen cherry tomatoes, cut in half.

150g red Camargue rice; 400ml water; 3 tbsp olive oil; 1 red chilli; ½ tsp salt; 20 black olives; 1 preserved lemon, flesh removed, peel cut into little strips; 1 tbsp sherry vinegar; 50g pressed mullet roe (poutargue), skin removed, thinly sliced; 12 cherry tomatoes, halved (optional).

Soak the rice in cold water for 30 minutes. Drain and rinse. Put it into a saucepan with the correct quantity of water, 1 tbsp olive oil, the chilli and salt. Bring to the boil, cover and simmer until all the water has been absorbed. Leaving the lid on, allow to cool to room temperature, then stir in the olives and the strips of preserved lemon. Add the tomatoes if you are including them. Dress the salad with the remaining olive oil and the sherry vinegar and cover the top with thin slices of amber-coloured mullet roe (you may find it offered in the shops as *botargo* or, if Italian, *bottarga*). Serve with quartered lemons. (Serves 4.)

Polenta
Millas

Millas (pronounced *millase*) is a revelation for polenta-lovers – light and delicate, pale in colour and, when fried, crisp on the outside and succulent within. Throughout south-western France, from the early seventeenth century, this maize porridge was eaten at least three times a week by most families and was described as 'the national dish of the Midi'. In the Pyrenees and around Castres it was *le mets favori* – the favourite dish. It goes under many names: called *polenta* by immigrant Italians, it was known as *millas* in the Tarn, *escautun*, *meture* or *cruchade* in the Landes. In the Béarn it was *broye*, and in the Gers it was *armotos*. Like cabbages and beans it is no longer a staple, perhaps it is too much associated with hard times. Whatever the reason, it is not often eaten today, but is still sold at country fairs, and definitely deserves a comeback. This recipe serves 6 people.

125g instant polenta; 1 tbsp goose or duck fat or lard; 75g cornflour; salt.

Slake the cornflour to a smooth consistency with 100ml water. Bring 1 litre of water to the boil in a heavy-bottomed pan, add the goose fat or lard and salt. Slowly pour the polenta into the boiling water, stirring all the time with a long-handled wooden spoon. Next pour in the cornflour mixture, stirring continuously right into the corners of the pan. Stir over a medium heat for 5 minutes; it should bubble slowly with big, bursting blops; wear an apron. Check the seasoning.

It can now be eaten in various ways:

Just as a soft porridge, hot or warm, as it is, with a spoon; you can sprinkle with sugar or dollop some jam or honey into it.

Cooled, cut in pieces and fried. To do this, pour the hot mixture into a lightly oiled rectangular roasting tin (24 x 36 cm is a good size) in an even layer. When it has cooled, spread a teaspoon of olive oil over the top with your hand, to prevent it drying out. When you want to serve the *millas*, cut it into 6 cm squares.

To fry it, heat 2 tbsp goose or duck fat in a frying-pan and put in some of the squares to fry for at least 7–8 minutes on each side, until delicately crisp and starting to brown. Fry the *millas* in batches and place each batch on kitchen paper for a minute before transferring to a dish. Serve with tomato sauce or with grilled sausages; a little stew or *ragoût;* or with a fried egg or grilled sardines.

As a dessert, fry the *millas* as I have described and then sprinkle with sugar or honey. If the intention from the outset is to make a sweet dish, then the polenta is often boiled with milk instead of water.

Hard-boiled Eggs with Aïoli
Oeufs durs à l'aïoli

Aïoli is a much-loved dish on Fridays,
     or on Fast days,
Or sometimes on Sundays, out in the country,
     With singing,
     And under a trellis.   *Maurice Brun*

The perfect dish for a hot summer's day, or a cold one. We served it after having a nostalgic conversation about the once-inevitable *hors d'oeuvres* served as the first course in every modest French restaurant. We tried to recapture the trolley but could not rustle up the tin of sardines, the salted herrings in oil or the celeriac rémoulade, instead serving these eggs, with beetroot salad, *carottes râpées*, radishes and a beautiful dish of Serrano ham, chestnuts and rocket dressed with sage-flavoured oil, invented by the chef Skye Gingell.

4 eggs plus 2 egg yolks; 2 fat cloves garlic, finely chopped or mashed with a fork; 300ml sunflower oil; 100ml olive oil; juice ¼ lemon; 1 tbsp hot water; salt, pepper.

The advantage of this version is that it is quite light but it still has plenty of character. Sometimes aïoli can almost finish you off.

Mash the garlic with some coarse salt, using a fork or the flat side of a kitchen knife, and working it hard against the chopping board until it emulsifies. Add it to two egg yolks in a bowl and combine with a small hand-held whisk. Gradually add the sunflower oil, drop by drop at first, as if you were making mayonnaise. Incorporate all the sunflower oil and then add the olive oil, with a little lemon juice and a few drops of water as it thickens and becomes stiff. Taste and add more salt and pepper, or more lemon, or olive oil, whatever you think it needs.

Boil the eggs for 8 minutes, cool them under cold water, peel carefully and cut them in half. Put them cut side down on a dish and coat with aïoli. (Serves 4.)

Fried Oysters with *chorizo* Sauce
Beignets d'huîtres

This is based on a recipe by apprentice-chef Guilhelm Challon who won first prize with it in a competition grandiloquently entitled Concours de recettes de l'Agglomération de Béziers Méditerranée in 2007. He cooks the oysters much more elaborately, by poaching them first in the oyster liquor and Noilly Prat vermouth flavoured with shallots, and then coating them in saffron-scented batter for frying. The simpler method here works very well, with much less effort. If you can get your fishmonger to open the oysters for you, that will lessen your work still further. Have them put in a plastic tub with their liquor.

24 oysters, shelled, keep the liquor; 1–2 eggs; 100g fresh breadcumbs.

For the sauce:
125g day-old rustic bread, crusts removed; 100ml chicken stock; 50ml white wine vinegar; 50ml olive oil; ½ green pepper, finely chopped; ½ red pepper, finely chopped; ½ cucumber, finely chopped; 2 cloves garlic, finely chopped; ½ onion, finely chopped; piment dEspelette or sweet pimentón de la Vera; chopped basil leaves; 100g hot chorizo cut in small dice; salt.

First, make the sauce. Soak the bread in the chicken stock and vinegar. Put all the vegetables together with the bread and its soaking liquid into a food processor and liquidize, add the olive oil and whizz to a fine purée. Taste for seasoning and add the Espelette pepper or pimentón and the shredded basil leaves. Mix in the *chorizo* and, just before serving, the chilled oyster liquor (see below).

To cook the oysters, heat sunflower oil in a frying-pan to a depth of around 8 cm. While it is heating, pour the oysters and their liquor into a fine sieve over a bowl. Reserve the liquor for flavouring the sauce. Dry the oysters, then dip into the beaten egg and roll in the breadcrumbs. Test the oil by putting in a few breadcrumbs. If they brown within 30 seconds or so, the oil is hot enough. If it seems too hot, turn down the heat. Fry the oysters in batches, taking care not to crowd the pan. Drain on paper towels. Serve the oysters either warm or hot, accompanied by the *chorizo* sauce. (Serves 4.)

Grilled Oysters
Huîtres gratinées

This recipe, given to me by Bruno Pérolari, who lives in Marseillan, near Agde, is perfectly easy and needs no measured ingredients – do not be afraid.

Simply get, 6 oysters, say, or perhaps 3, or even 12 for each person. Heat the grill. Get the oysters open, or ask the oyster-seller to open them, and throw away the juice. Loosen each one from its shell, and turn it over. Add a teaspoon of cream – *crème fraîche* or double cream – to each oyster, top with a sprinkle of grated Gruyère cheese and some coarsely ground black pepper. Cook under the grill until the cheese melts and starts to turn golden. Serve hot.

Creamed Eggs with Wild Mushrooms
Brouillade aux champignons

The first wave of Italian immigrants arrived at Sète (then known as
Cette) at the end of the seventeenth century, when it was a major
entrepot for sugar, salt, tobacco and wine. Arrivals thereafter never
ceased. The anarchist assassin of President Carnot in 1894 was an
Italian apprentice baker from Sète. More Italians settled between the
two world wars (the great singer-songwriter Georges Brassens was
born there in 1921, his mother was from the southern Italian province
of Basilicata) and consequently the region is familiar with Parmesan
cheese, which is much liked and available everywhere.

*4 eggs; 25g **butter**; 200g **wild mushrooms**, well cleaned; 2 tbsp freshly grated
Parmesan cheese; salt, pepper.*

Break the eggs into a bowl, season with salt and freshly ground pepper.
Melt one-third of the butter in a saucepan, add the mushrooms, season
well and cook gently – let their juices run out and then evaporate again.
When the juices have concentrated to almost nothing, put the pan into
a larger pan of hot, but not boiling, water with the rest of the butter and
let it melt. Add the beaten eggs and stir over the hot water until you
have a smooth cream. Stir in the Parmesan. Spoon the eggs onto hot
plates. Serve either as a starter or as a light lunch with green salad and
toast. (Serves 2.)

Chapter Four

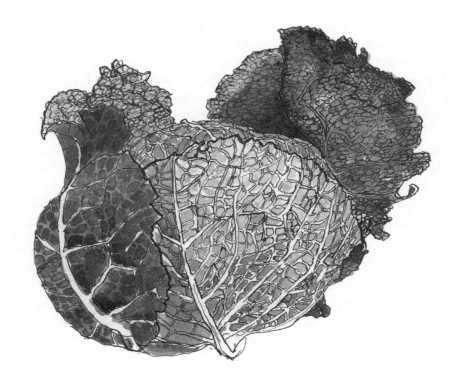

Soups, Winter and Summer

Sausage and Cabbage Soup
Potée d'hiver

The author of *La Cuisine Paléolithique* (Stone Age Cookery), Joseph Delteil, was born and brought up in the village of Pieusse, close to the Pyrenees, north of Limoux, a handsome medieval town where the most excellent, rich, dry and biscuity sparkling wine is made – Blanquette de Limoux. He states that as a child he only knew three dishes, soups, *fricassées* and roasts. Three – and that's it. In the spring it was dried broad bean soup, in summer green bean, and in winter, cabbage.

This sausage-based winter soup is a member of a universal tribe. The Haut-Languedoc version would include a large smoked boiling sausage of pure pork flavoured with white wine and garlic. A version from the *Pays catalan* might include *chorizo*. Any winter vegetables can be added to the soup except, perhaps, beetroot – pumpkin is good, as are celeriac and chard or spinach beet. Haricot beans can also be included.

The flavour will be at its best if you use a good home-made chicken or duck stock. For the sausage a French *saucisse de Morteau* is ideal, but any good boiling sausage, even Polish *kielbasa*, will do and if it is smoked that adds more depth to the flavour.

It can be served as two courses, soup first, then the sausage and vegetables with *gros sel*, but I like it all together.

> 3 small **onions**, chopped; 1–2 **turnips**, cut in pieces; 3 fat cloves of **garlic**, chopped; ½ tsp hot **chilli powder**; 2 **bay leaves**; 1 large **boiling sausage** weighing 250g–350g; 200g **salt pork**, diced, or lardons; 1½ litres good **stock**; 3 **potatoes**, peeled and cut in pieces; 1 small **green cabbage**, or 250 g **spring greens** or **kale**, cut in pieces, thicker stalks removed; slices of toasted **pain de campagne**; grated **Gruyère** cheese; **salt, pepper**.

Put the onions, turnip and garlic into a large pot. Add the chilli, bay leaves, sausage and salt pork, cover with stock, bring to the boil and simmer for 20 minutes.

Add the potatoes. Simmer for 20 minutes, until the potatoes are soft, then add the cabbage, greens or kale and simmer a further 10 minutes. Remove the sausage and slice it. Divide the soup between 6 ovenproof bowls, share out the sausage and salt pork between them. Place a piece of toast on top of each bowl, scatter the grated Gruyère on top and serve directly; or you can put under a hot grill, until the cheese is bubbling and starting to brown. (Serves 4–6.)

Escudella

It is hard to say if this dish is more popular in Andorra or in the *Pays catalan*. It is certainly mountain food and it can be beefed up to an even more filling level by the addition of white haricot beans. Cabbage is often preferred to *blette* (Swiss chard or spinach beet), but the earthy dark green beet leaves are my favourite. This is for 6–8 people.

> 450g **smoked poitrine fumée, pancetta** or **streaky bacon** in a piece; 1 **chicken** 1.5–2kg in weight; 2 **pig's trotters**, cut in pieces; 2.5–3 litres **water**; 2 **carrots**, cut in pieces; 2 **potatoes**, cut in pieces; 500g **blette (Swiss chard)** or **spinach beet**, leaves only, cut into manageable pieces; 1 **black pudding** weighing about 250g.

> *For the dumpling:*
> 1–2 slices **bread**, crusts removed; 400g **Toulouse sausage** or **butifarra**, casing removed, or **sausage meat**; 250g **minced pork**; 2 cloves **garlic**, mashed; 2 tbsp chopped **parsley**; 1 tsp **dried herbs** such as **thyme**, **savory** and **rosemary**; 1 **egg**, beaten; **flour**; **salt**, **pepper**.

Place the bacon, chicken and pig's trotters in a large casserole, cover with the water and bring to simmering point. Simmer for 1 hour, and remove the bacon and the chicken. Remove from the heat and let it cool.

While the chicken cooks, make the dumpling. Soak the bread in water and squeeze dry. Crumble it into a mixing bowl and add the sausage meat, pork, garlic, parsley, dried herbs and egg. Add a little salt and plenty of pepper and work together until thoroughly blended. Form into two large balls or a long cylinder shape. Roll the dumpling(s) in flour.

After removing the chicken and bacon put the carrots, potatoes, dumpling(s) and black pudding in the broth with the pig's trotters and bring back to simmering point. Simmer for 20 minutes, then put the chicken and bacon back in. Add the chard or beet leaves, pushing them into the liquid, and simmer for a further 10 minutes.

Some people eat *escudella* as two courses, the broth first, followed by the vegetables and meats. It is easier and more satisfying to eat everything at once. Slice the black pudding and bacon. The chicken looks good if it is left whole, to be carved at the table.

Put the whole chicken surrounded by the sliced bacon, trotters and black pudding on a platter for carving. The dumpling, on a separate dish, is cut into slices and the casserole is put on the table so that you can serve out the wonderful, fragrant broth and its vegetables. (Serves 6.)

Pumpkin and Chestnut Soup, from the Aveyron
Soupe au potiron et aux châtaignes aveyronnaise

300g fresh chestnuts peeled (see below) or use vacuum packed chestnuts; 3 tbsp olive oil; 1 small onion, chopped; ½ stick celery, chopped (keep the leaves); 3 strips lemon peel, chopped; 4 sage leaves; 1 leek, white part only, chopped; 500g pumpkin or acorn squash, peeled and diced; 1 bay leaf; 1 litre chicken stock; 250ml single cream or milk; salt, pepper.

To peel the chestnuts make a cut on the flat side with a sharp knife. Drop them into salted boiling water and boil for 10 minutes. Fish them out one at a time and peel off inner and outer skin while still hot. If this is all too fiddly, use some vacuum packed chestnuts ready to go.

Heat the oil in a large saucepan and soften the onion, celery, lemon peel and sage leaves, sprinkled lightly with salt, for 10 minutes without browning them.

Add the leek, pumpkin, chestnuts, bay leaf and water or stock. Season, bring to the boil and simmer for half an hour. Purée with a hand-held blender or food processor, or pass through a *moulin à légumes*. It will be rather thick; add the cream or milk and heat through.

Serve with a sprinkle of chopped celery leaves. (Serves 4.)

Pumpkin Soup with Sage
Soupe au potiron

5 tbsp olive oil; 1 onion, finely chopped; 1 leek, white part only, finely sliced; 750ml–1 litre chicken stock; 750g pumpkin, peeled and cut in chunks; 1 carrot, finely diced; 1 stick celery, finely sliced; 2 bay leaves; 4 tbsp cream; 8 sage leaves, sliced into little strips; salt, pepper.

Heat 3 tablespoons of the olive oil in a large pan and soften the onion and leek without letting them brown.

Pour in the stock, add the pumpkin, carrot, celery and bay leaves. Season with salt and pepper, bring to the boil and simmer for 30 minutes, covered. Extract the bay leaves.

Whizz briefly in a food processor or with a hand-held blender. (I think myself that the texture is better if the soup is puréed with an old-fashioned *moulin à légumes*, if you have one, more itself somehow, less fluffy and bland.)

While you reheat the soup, heat the remaining olive oil in a small frying-pan and fry the sage until crisp. Add more stock to the soup if it looks too thick.

Ladle the soup into hot bowls, spoon a little cream into the middle of each and on top scatter some strips of sage with the flavoured olive oil. (Serves 4–6.)

Chick Pea and Spinach Soup
Soupe de pois chiches et épinards

Golden chick peas, dark green spinach and russet red paprika, hot or sweet, is a harmonious combination and one that has a strong following across the Mediterranean, where chick peas are grown and enjoyed as often as beans. This marriage is particularly liked in the *Pays catalan* where chick peas are called *cigrons* (in Catalan, *becuda* in Occitan) and down the Rhône Valley, the home of this delicious soup.

> *500g tin of cooked* **chick peas** *or 150g of dried* **chick peas**, *soaked overnight and cooked;* 4 tbsp **olive oil**; 1 **onion**, *finely chopped;* 1 clove **garlic**, *finely chopped;* 100g **poitrine fumée** *cut in small pieces, or* **lardons**; 2 medium **tomatoes**, *peeled, deseeded and chopped;* ½ tsp **hot pimentón** *or* **piment d'Espelette**; 1 generous pinch **saffron**; 750ml **chicken stock** *or stock combined with the chick pea cooking water;* 400g **spinach**, *well washed, stalks removed; slices of* **French bread** *fried in olive oil (optional);* **salt, pepper**.

If you are using dried chick peas, soak them overnight and boil them in unsalted water until they are tender, 1–2 hours, drain and keep the cooking water if you want to mix it with the stock.

Heat the olive oil in a sauté pan and cook the onion, garlic and lardons over a low heat until transparent and melting. Add the tomato and cook until it has a jammy consistency, around 5 minutes. Add the paprika and saffron and stir into the mixture. Stir in the chick peas, add the stock, season with salt and pepper and simmer for 20 minutes.

Wash the spinach and, while it is still wet, put it into a large pan and cover it; after a minute or two turn it, and when it has all wilted, drain it, keeping the cooking liquid. When cool enough, chop the spinach coarsely and add to the chick peas. Cook for 5 minutes or more. Add enough of the spinach water to give the right consistency and heat through. Season again and serve with slices of fried French bread. (Serves 4–6.)

Winter Vegetable Soup with Black Pudding
L'ollada, also known as ouillade

The *olla* was a big black cauldron that hung over the fire in every kitchen fireplace. The soup made in this pot became the *ollada*.

Ollada podrida meant rotten pot; tradition held that keeping the cauldron going continuously for days on end, the soup could be resurrected with some new ingredient added each day, together with a bit more water. The flavour that developed was a popular one in the region – a slight rancidity, which is definitely not sought after today.

But a fresh *ollada*, almost a Catalan national dish, is a wonderful soup, especially if you are half way up a mountain and it is freezing hard outside – this is comfort food for cold days (and it certainly can be bitter in winter in the snowbound villages of the Vallespir in the Pyrenees).

The traditional flavour comes from *jarret de porc* or *garro* – pork shin with the bone in, cured in salt and smoked up in the rafters, then sawed into pieces. This is still available in some Languedoc pork butchers. Smoked bacon or any piece of salt pork, a pickled pig's foot or ear, or even a tail can all be added. The type of sausage used should preferably be an all-pork Toulouse-type of sausage rather than English breakfast sausages, which are really best fried.

Old grandmothers like to drink the water in which the cabbage has blanched, as they believe it is good for the health. Use unsalted stock as the bacon, salt pork, pig's feet and so forth can make it salty.

> *200g dried **haricot beans** or **chick peas**, soaked overnight; 200g **smoked bacon** or **salt pork** (see note above) cut into slices 2 cm thick, or use a **ham hock**, in which case leave it whole and slice it up when you serve the soup; 300g **carrots**, sliced across diagonally into thick slices; 1 **medium onion**, coarsely chopped; 1 **stick celery**, sliced into crescents; 3 **bay leaves**; 2 sprigs of **thyme** or ½ tsp **dried thyme**; 1.5 litres unsalted **chicken stock**; 1 **green curly cabbage** around 750g in weight, dark outer leaves removed; 1 **leek**, cut diagonally into large pieces; 1 **potato** cut into rough pieces; 150g **spinach beet** or **chard** (blette), cut into short strips; 150g **boudin noir** or **black pudding**; 150g **boiling sausage**; 4 tbsp **olive oil**; **slices of country bread**; **salt, pepper**.*

Boil the soaked haricot beans or chick peas in unsalted water until almost tender. Put the ham hock, smoked bacon and/or salt pork in a large casserole together with the carrots, onion, celery and herbs. Cover with the stock, bring to the boil, skim and simmer gently for 30 minutes.

While the pork simmers, quarter the cabbage and slice it into manageable pieces, throwing out the tough stalks. Bring a large pan of water to the boil and blanch it for 1–2 minutes. Drain and cool.

Add the cooked haricot beans or chick peas (depending on your choice of pulse), leek and potato to the soup and cook for a further 30 minutes. Slice the sausage and black pudding into thick pieces and fry in two tablespoons of oil until the sausage starts to brown. Transfer to a plate and set on one side.

When the soup has cooked for an hour altogether, stir it vigorously to release some of the starch from the beans and potatoes, then add the cabbage and the chard you have prepared and simmer for 5 minutes. On top, place the slices of sausage and black pudding, simmer for 5 minutes more, or until the cabbage and chard are tender, without disturbing. Add a couple of tablespoons of olive oil, if you like, season and serve with slices of country bread and a robust red wine. (Serves 4–6.)

Cheese Soup
Soupe au fromage aveyronnaise

Making this soup is a rewarding experience – the flavours are rich and so much deeper than a normal onion soup. It is also a good way to eat leftover bread, which in the general course of things in Languedoc is a vital ingredient rather than the embarrassment that we find it, and is never thrown away. This version is based on one from *Recettes au Pain Perdu* from the *Recettes Paysannes* collection, by Les Éditions du Curieux.

In another version, *soupe au cantal*, Cantal cheese is used, the casserole is rubbed with a clove of garlic, and the flavouring is thyme.

> 250g day-old or stale **bread**, country type or sourdough; small head **celery**; 6 **carrots**; **bouquet of herbs**, **parsley**, **sage**; 2 **bay leaves**; 2–3 **onions**; 2 tbsp **olive oil**; ½ **stock cube**; ½ **cabbage**, core removed, coarsely cut into shreds; 250g **Laguiole**, **Cantal**, **Salers**, **Cheddar** or **Leicester cheese**, grated; **salt**, **pepper**.

Heat the oven to 220°C. Cut the bread into slivers the size of a finger. Chop all the vegetables and put the celery, carrots, and herbs into a large pan, cover with 1.5 litres of water, add the stock cube and a little seasoning and cook for 30 minutes.

Fry the chopped onions in olive oil, stirring, until golden brown, but definitely not burned. Add the onions to the vegetable stock and cook for a further 20 minutes. Strain the stock and reserve. Blanch the cabbage in boiling salted water for 2 minutes and drain it.

In a heavy casserole put a layer of bread, followed by a layer of cabbage, and sprinkle a third of the cheese on top. Repeat the layers twice more, always finishing with cheese.

Add the stock to the casserole, then bake, uncovered for 30 minutes until the top is brown and crackling.

When you bring the soup to the table, stir it for a few minutes in front of the diners – the stock miraculously thickens – and hopefully, there is an appetizing crackling sound from the crunchy top. Serve it very hot. If you are using the customary Laguiole cheese, the strings of cheese are part of the gorgeous, gooey experience. (Serves 6.)

Languedoc Fish Soup
Bouillabaisse languedocienne

I was reminded of Connecticut chowder, – a fish soup with bacon and tomatoes – when I came across this rather magical dish. The Languedoc bouillabaisse is an aromatic Mediterranean fish soup containing garlic, saffron and fennel, but, unlike the Marseillaise version, this one shares the basic chowder theme of fish with bacon. André Bonnaure, the chef-author of *À Table, Petit Précis de Cuisine Occitane* and a world authority on cooking *foie gras*, prefers to use *jambon cru* for the dish, but I have found that lardons work better because ham, unless it is almost entirely fat, tends to go a bit hard and dry.

The choice of fish in the south of France includes lots of rock fish, and all sorts of things we cannot usually get, such as blennies, sand eels and *rascasse*. Away from the Mediterranean, it always depends on what is available on the day, but gurnard, monkfish, large red mullet and John Dory are suitable; ask the fishmonger to fillet all the fish and give you the bones. If clams are not to be found then use just mussels.

*2kg **mixed filleted fish**, including bones; 300g **clams**, well washed; 750g **mussels**, cleaned.*

For the fish stock:
*2–3 **leeks**, green parts, washed and sliced (keep white for the soup); 2 cloves **garlic**, sliced; fresh **thyme leaves**; 1 **bay leaf**.*

For the soup:
*large pinch **saffron**; 150ml **white wine**; 3 tbsp **olive oil**; 200g **lardons**; 3 cloves **garlic**, chopped; white part of the **leeks** (see above), halved lengthwise and finely sliced; 2 ripe **tomatoes**, skinned, deseeded and chopped; **aïoli** (page 91); 12–18 slices of toasted **baguette**; salt, pepper.*

Soak the saffron in the white wine. Cut the fillets of fish into manageable pieces. Put all the fish bones in a pan with the fish stock ingredients and 750ml of water, season and bring to the boil. Simmer for 20 minutes, then turn off the heat and allow to infuse for 15 minutes, then strain and keep the stock hot.

Heat the olive oil in a wide pan and add the lardons. Sauter for a few minutes then add the garlic and white part of the leeks. Sweat gently over a low heat, stirring from time to time, until very soft. Add the tomato and cook for a further 5–10 minutes, then add the saffron-infused white wine and simmer for 5 minutes more. It may be prepared in advance up to this point.

Make the aïoli as previously instructed (page 91).

Place the pieces of fish on top of the vegetable and white wine base. Season with salt and pepper. Add the raw mussels and clams as an uppermost layer and then pour over the hot fish stock. Bring to the boil, then cover and cook over a high heat for 5 minutes or until the mussels and clams have all opened. Serve with aïoli and slices of toasted *baguette*. (Serves 4–6.)

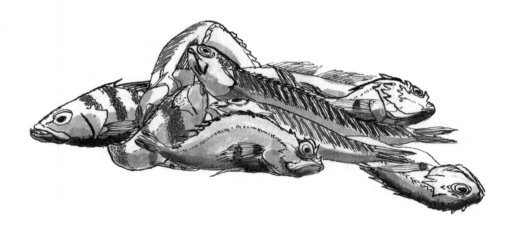

Monkfish Soup with Garlic, Sage and Fennel
Baudroie en l'aïgo boulido

To flavour and colour this aromatic soup, it is worthwhile finding powdered saffron, or you can use the favourite Spanish colouring Spigol which comes in tiny but potent packets in a bright red and yellow box. It has a warm, spicy taste and is used to give paella its characteristic tone and flavour; it is much cheaper than real saffron and gives a gorgeous golden yellow colour.

*500g **monkfish**, cut into medallions 1.25 cm thick; 750ml **chicken** or **fish** stock; 1 packet powdered **saffron** or **Spigol**; 1 whole head of **garlic**; 6–8 **sage** leaves; 5 sprigs of **thyme**; 10 sprigs of **fennel**; 2 **bay leaves**; 2 large **egg yolks**; 1–2 tbsp **double cream**; **aïoli** (recipe page 91, optional); slices of toasted **country bread**; **salt, white pepper**.*

Put the stock in a saucepan with the saffron, garlic, sage, thyme and half the fennel. Bring to the boil, lower the heat and simmer for 30 minutes. Keep the pan covered. Remove the garlic and press to extract the pulp from the skins. Discard the herbs. Poach the fish in the broth for 5 minutes. Keep warm.

In a food processor or a mortar, work the garlic pulp and egg yolks to a paste. Whisk in a ladleful of the fish broth and stir in the cream. Pour the emulsion back into the pan with the fish.

Taste for seasoning; warm over a low heat, stirring. Do not overheat or it will curdle. Chop the remaining fennel, scatter it over the soup and serve with toasted *pain de campagne* and, if you like, aïoli. (Serves 4.)

Crab Soup with Fennel and Saffron
Soupe de cranquettes

Sold as *cranquettes*, and also known as *crabes enragées*, these tiny crabs are furious, fierce little things – you find this out because they are sold live and when you get them home and tip them into the sink, they try to nip you with their spiky claws. The soup could be made with velvet swimming crabs or small crabs of any kind. This recipe is based on one from the fishing port of Gruissan, one of a wonderful collection of recipes given by the grandmothers of Gruissan, collected by Alain Delsol. The flamed Armagnac gives a specially heightened flavour.

*1kg live **crabs**; generous bunch of fresh wild **fennel** twigs or dried fennel twigs; 2 **bay leaves**; 2 sprigs **thyme**; 1 packet powdered **saffron** or **Spigol**; 300ml dry **white wine**; 4 tbsp **olive oil**; 1 **onion**; 1 **leek**; 2 cloves **garlic**; 2–3 tbsp **Armagnac** or brandy; 600g **tomatoes**, skinned, deseeded and chopped; 1 small or ½ large hot red **chilli pepper**; 750ml **chicken** or **fish stock**, fresh or made with stock cube; rounds of toasted **pain de campagne**; grated **hard sheep's cheese** or **Parmesan**; **salt, pepper**.*

You may want to put the crabs in the freezer for 30 minutes before starting to cook them, which makes them drowsy and means they do not suffer when they are cooked. Tie the herbs into a bundle. Put the saffron to soak in the white wine.

Put the olive oil in a heavy casserole large enough to take all the crabs, and put in the onions and leek. Allow to soften for 20 minutes over a low heat, stirring frequently. Add the garlic and continue to cook gently for a further 5 minutes.

Fill a basin with cold water and throw in the crabs. Swoosh them round with a wooden spoon to wash them clean. Tip the crabs into a colander and throw them on top of the leeks and onions, quickly put on the lid and steam for 5 minutes until they turn red. Add the Armagnac and let it bubble, set it on fire if you like, then scatter the tomatoes on top. Push in the bundle of fennel and herbs. Add the saffron-flavoured wine, chilli and the stock, and season with salt and pepper. Boil for 30 minutes.

Pour off the liquid part of the soup into a bowl and mash the crabs with a rolling pin or wooden pestle. Now the hard bit – put the the mashed crabs in a colander over a bowl, pressing them hard with a potato masher to extract every drop of juice from them. Throw away the debris and combine the juices with the liquid soup. You are aiming at essence of crab.

Taste for seasoning and serve with rounds of toasted country bread rubbed with raw cloves of garlic and, if you like, with grated *tome de brebis* – hard sheep's cheese – or Parmesan. (Serves 4.)

Catalan Mushroom Soup
Soupe de champignons

This is a splendid soup which can be made with mushrooms you have picked or with cultivated mushrooms. If you use foraged fungi, it will not matter too much if they are less than perfect specimens, the soup gains its rich flavour from the dried ceps.

> *175g fresh* **mushrooms**, *wild or cultivated, or a mixture of both, chopped into 2 cm pieces; 3 tbsp* **olive oil**; *2 small* **onions**, *chopped; 2 cloves* **garlic**, *chopped; 25g dried* **ceps**, *soaked in 500ml warm water for 30 minutes; 300g* **tomatoes**, *skinned and chopped; ½ tsp hot* **pimentón**; *750ml* **chicken stock**; *25g* **vermicelli**; *4 slices of* **country bread**, *fried in olive oil – or toast;* **salt**, **pepper**.

Heat the olive oil in a casserole and soften the onions for about 15 minutes. Add the garlic, cook a further 5 minutes, then add the fresh mushrooms and let them sweat gently with the onions, stirring often so that they cook evenly. Drain the dried ceps, keeping their soaking liquid. Squeeze the water out of the soaked ceps and chop coarsely, then add to the other mushrooms.

Add the tomato, paprika and salt, and continue to cook gently. All this has to be done slowly, but you can do other things at the same time, as long as you stir it from time to time, to make sure it does not catch.

When everything is soft and jammy, add the 500ml liquid from the dried ceps – leaving the last dregs, as this is full of dirt from the mushrooms – and the stock, bring to the boil and cook for 15–20 minutes. Throw in the vermicelli and cook until the pasta is tender, 10–15 minutes. Serve with slices of fried bread or toast. (Serves 4–6.)

Granny's Tomato Soup
Soupe de mamie

Joseph Delteil, the kitchen-sage, would approve of this dish. When making tomato soup, he advises, 'the tomatoes must not be over cooked – cheeks on fire, cool at heart.'

To be able to make such a good soup out of a tomato and a slice of bread is a bit of a miracle, handed down by the frugal cooks of an older generation. This is a version of one in a collection of recipes by the pupils of the Collège of the coastal town of Sigean – facing Gruissan across a wide *étang* that reaches the outskirts of Narbonne. I am sure that on the roads leading into town you will often see a sturdy lady or check-shirted man walking home from the *hortes* (allotments) with a basket filled with huge tomatoes, ready to make a similar dish.

The tomato has a season in Languedoc, and some people live on them throughout the summer. This is a tomato-glut dish. How substantial it is depends on the type of bread used, but red, sun-ripened tomatoes and well-flavoured stock are the key.

*8 ripe, red **tomatoes**, skinned; 4 thick slices of good **French bread** (8 if using baguette); 4 cloves **garlic**; handful of **basil leaves**, torn, or **fresh thyme leaves**; **bouillon** or **chicken stock** (or use **stock cube**); **olive oil**; **salt**, **pepper**.*

Grill or toast the bread. Cut the garlic cloves in half and rub with the cut sides all over the surface of both sides of the toast. Place the toast in four heated bowls.

Cut the tomatoes in half, squeeze to shake out the seeds, place cut side down on a board and cut into thin slices.

Arrange the tomatoes over the toast. Season well.

Sprinkle with basil or thyme.

Heat the stock and pour it into the four bowls. Drizzle copiously with olive oil and serve. (Serves 4.)

Creamy Garlic Soup
Aïgo boulido

When I mentioned the cooking of Languedoc to my friend Frances Fedden, whose mother lived in the Gard, and who has spent her life taking people for beautiful walks round the Mediterranean, her first thought was of the easy, creamy garlic soups, perfumed and supple, which can be made in so many styles and flavoured with so many different herbs. Some people favour thickening with cream, others pour their soup over thin slices of country bread. This version, based on one from the Hérault, is made by combining a herb and garlic bouillon with a simple mayonnaise. Serve it with toasted *pain de campagne* or with *croûtons* made with *baguette* or *ficelle*, thinly sliced.

> 5 cloves **garlic**, peeled; bunch **flat-leaved parsley** (25g); bunch **thyme** (25g); bunch **chervil** (25g); 2 good sprigs **tarragon**; 2 **spring onions**; 1 litre **chicken stock**, home made or made with ½ stock cube; 2 **egg yolks**; 125ml **olive oil**; **salt**.

Put the washed herbs, spring onions and cloves of garlic in a pan with 1 litre of stock and a pinch of salt, bring to the boil and simmer for 20 minutes. Remove from the heat and allow to cool and brew up a deep flavour. Fish out the cloves of garlic and set them aside. Strain the stock.

Meanwhile start a mayonnaise in your normal way, with the egg yolks and a pinch of salt. Mash the boiled garlic and work it into the egg yolk emulsion until it is smooth. Then whisk in the olive oil, a little at a time. This can all be done in advance.

Heat the herb-flavoured stock. When it boils, let it rest for 5 minutes then, in a separate bowl, mix a tablespoon of hot stock into a tablespoon of mayonnaise. Continue adding the rest of the stock and mayonnaise one or two tablespoons at a time, whisking all the time. You can make this in a food processor. Season well with salt.

The soup is now ready and can be served, with its croûtons or toast, straight away. If you want to keep it for later, reheat it carefully, stirring all the time and take great care not to let it even simmer, let alone boil. (Serves 4.)

Gazpacho

*400g ripe **tomatoes**, skinned; 150g day-old **bread**; 1 **onion**; 1 **red pepper**; 1 **cucumber**, peeled; 2–3 cloves **garlic**; 6 tbsp **olive oil**; pinch of **cumin**; 2 tsp of **ground almonds**; 2 tbsp **sherry vinegar**; 4 sprigs **basil**, chopped; **salt**, **pepper**.*

Cut the bread into little cubes and fry them in half the olive oil. Set them on one side. Cut the half the tomatoes, onion, red pepper and cucumber into tiny dice, as small and neatly as possible. Chop the other half of the vegetables roughly and put them with all the other ingredients, except the basil, into a food processor. Pulse until smooth. Chill until you are ready to serve the soup.

At that point, whisk the soup to distribute the oil evenly. Serve it with the croûtons, the jewel-like diced vegetables and the chopped basil in small bowls, ready for each person to scatter into their soup. (Serves 4–6.)

Chilled Tomato Soup with Cucumber

This alternative to gazpacho is lighter in style. If you want a more Catalan flavour, you can add small amounts of red pepper, cut into tiny dice, with the diced cucumber.

*1 large **cucumber**, peeled and seeded, cut in pieces; 1kg very ripe, red **tomatoes**, skinned and roughly chopped; 2 cloves **garlic**, peeled; ½ fresh **white onion**; juice ½ **lemon**; 200ml **single cream**; a few **basil leaves** (optional); **salt**.*

Peel the cucumber and cut it in half. Remove the seeds from one half and put the flesh in the bowl of a food processor. Add the tomatoes and their juice, the garlic and the onion and pulse until all is thoroughly liquidized. Push the mixture through a wire sieve into a bowl, using a wooden spoon or a pestle to extract every bit of liquid.

Season and leave covered in the refrigerator to chill for a few hours, or leave it overnight. Dice finely the remaining cucumber, salt it lightly and let it drain in a colander for 1 hour. Rinse and add to the soup, together with the lemon juice.

When you are ready to serve the soup, whisk the cream until very frothy. Divide the soup between soup bowls and finish with a spoonful of cream in each bowl. Scatter basil leaves on top, whole if they are small, otherwise shredded. (Serves 4.)

Chapter Five

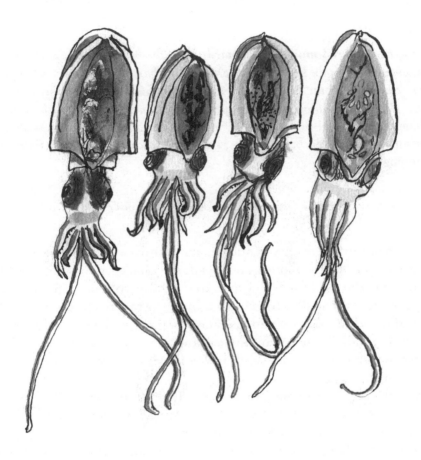

Fish and Seafood

Fish Soup with Aïoli and *sauce ardente*
Bisquebouille

This soup, originally from the Ermitage Restaurant in Les Angles, near Avignon, is a wonderful cross between a *bouillabaisse* and a *bourride*. It is a superb *pièce-de-résistance*, a golden, creamy broth, enriched with aïoli and chunks of fish. The original contained eels, which are in plentiful supply in the lagoons of Languedoc. Add them, if you like the rich taste of eel.

300g fillets of **red mullet** *or* **gurnard** *(keep the bones, heads, etc.); 300g* **monkfish** *(obtain the head if possible); 200g* **sea bass** *fillets, or use* **eel, conger eel** *or* **huss** *(keep the bones); 6* **crayfish** *or* **langoustines***, preferably raw; 4 tbsp* **olive oil***; 1* **onion** *finely chopped; 1* **leek***, finely diced; 1 stick* **celery***, chopped; ½* **fennel bulb***, chopped; 1* **banana shallot** *or 2 small shallots, chopped; 2 large pinches* **saffron***; ½* **chicken stock** *cube; 6 slices* **pain de campagne***, toasted.*

For the aïoli and sauce ardente:
2 large cloves **garlic***, crushed; 2* **egg yolks***; 250ml* **olive oil***; 1 tsp* **harissa***;* **salt***.*

Cut the fish into 5 cm pieces and season lightly with salt. To make the fish stock, put all the bones and heads in a large pan with 1.5 litres water. Heat the oil in a frying-pan and gently soften the onion, leek, celery, fennel and shallot for 10–15 minutes. Transfer to the pan of fish bones and add the saffron and chicken stock cube. Season with salt and bring to the boil. Turn down the heat and simmer for 20 minutes. Taste and season, then strain the stock into a bowl, pressing with a spoon to extract all the juices.

Make the aïoli according to the instructions on page 91. Divide it between two bowls and add 1 teaspoon of harissa to one half, to make the *sauce ardente* (hot sauce). Toast the bread.

Ten minutes before you want to serve the soup, return the strained stock to the pan and bring to the boil. Add the monkfish, huss or sea bass, red mullet or gurnard and langoustines. Cover the pan and simmer 5 minutes. Remove from the heat and allow to cool for 3 or 4 minutes.

Carefully transfer the fish and langoustines to heated bowls. Stir one ladleful of the soup into the plain aïoli, whisk until it is very smooth and then pour this mixture back into the pan of soup and mix it in. Swirl and gently shake the pan to distribute it evenly. Reheat without boiling. Do not boil the soup once the aïoli is added, or it will curdle. Ladle out the soup into bowls, each served with a piece of toasted country-style bread spread with the *sauce ardente*. (Serves 6.)

Bourride from Sète
La bourride à la sètoise

Sète is the Venice of the Sud de France. When I first saw this dish, in one of its many quayside restaurants, the tables in cool reflected light from the sunny buildings across the water, I thought there was something wrong with the way it looked and tasted. They had added chopped carrots and tomatoes to the sauce. Oh well, if that is how they prefer it, but it is subtler and more delicate if you keep to a palette of pale green vegetables.

> *750g* **monkfish** *(ask for the head or other white fish bones);* **aïoli** *(made as on page 91); 2* **leeks***, white parts cut into fine dice, keep the green for the stock; ½* **chicken stock cube** *(optional); 3 tbsp* **olive oil***; 1* **onion***, finely chopped; 2* **sticks celery***, chopped into fine dice; ½* **head of fennel***, cut into fine dice; 2 cloves* **garlic***, finely chopped; bouquet of* **thyme** *and* **bay leaf***;* **salt***,* **pepper***.*

First make the aïoli in the usual way. Then, put 350ml water in a saucepan, add salt and the green parts of the leeks, and the monkfish head or fish bones if you are using them (if not, add a half stock cube). Simmer for 20 minutes. Strain through a colander and reserve.

In a large pan, heat 3 tablespoons of olive oil over a very gentle heat, then put in the diced vegetables and the bunch of herbs. Let them soften slowly, without colouring, for 20 minutes, stirring occasionally. Add the garlic and 250ml of the stock and cook for a further 15 minutes.

Slice the monkfish into medallions and place in the pan on top of the vegetables. Season with salt and pepper, cover the pan and cook for 7 minutes, until the fish is just cooked. Remove the fish to a deep, heated dish and keep it hot.

Mix 2 tablespoons of the fish broth into the aïoli, then 2 more, and stir this mixture into the fish broth in the pan. Taste for seasoning, remove the bunch of herbs and heat gently, stirring, until hot, but stop before the sauce starts to simmer, or it will curdle. Pour this sauce, complete with its vegetables, over or round the fish. (Serves 6.)

Catalan Fish Stew
Bouillinade

This is the fish stew you will encounter in fishing villages such as Matisse's favourite, Collioure, close to the Spanish border. Once a fisherman's dish, often cooked on board the boats, it is also known as *suquet*. It should be clean and simple and will include any local fish such as larger rock fish, including weaver and blennies, monkfish, gurnard, John Dory, sea bream and if it is available, *rascasse* – scorpion fish. You can add prawns or mussels if you like. It is a particularly easy fish stew to prepare and cook.

> *1 kilo **assorted fish**, cleaned and cut into thick slices; 300g **raw prawns** or **mussels**, or a mixture of both (optional); 4–5 tbsp **olive oil**; 2 **medium onions**, finely chopped; 4 cloves **garlic**, coarsely chopped; 2 fresh **green or red chillies**, seeds removed and chopped; 3 ripe **tomatoes**, skinned and chopped or 3 tbsp tinned chopped tomatoes; ½ tsp **fennel seeds**; ½ tsp dried or fresh **thyme** leaves; 3–4 **bay leaves**; 1 litre **fish stock**, or 750ml **water** and 250g **white wine**; 500g small **potatoes** in their skins, thickly sliced; freshly chopped **parsley**; **salt, pepper**.*

Soften the onions and garlic slowly in the olive oil. When they are tender but not brown, add the chillies, tomato and the fennel, thyme and bay leaves and cook for a further 5 minutes, until the tomatoes are just starting to fall apart.

Add the stock or water and wine and the potatoes, season, and simmer until the potatoes are tender, 20–30 minutes, stirring occasionally.

Add the pieces of fish, pushing them under the liquid, and cook for 2 minutes. Add the prawns or mussels, taste for seasoning, cover the pan and simmer for 5 minutes more.

Serve in heated soup plates, sprinkled with chopped parsley, with a drizzle of olive oil. (Serves 4–6.)

Shellfish Paella with Monkfish
Petites lottes au riz

I was given the idea for this recipe by a shopper standing next to me in the fish queue in Saint-Chinian market. Everybody was exclaiming on how perfect the baby monkfish were, the size of a fat finger, pearly, with red tassels on their tails. Most people in the queue, including the fishmonger, said that they ate them fried, some with egg and crumbs and some with garlic, but my favourite suggestion was to eat them with rice *'en paella'*. If you do not have a paella pan, use a very large frying-pan and cover it with foil. In this area paella is cooked covered, whereas in southern Spain it is always uncovered.

> *600 grams skinned and filleted baby **monkfish** or large monkfish, cut into 3 cm pieces; 4 tbsp **olive oil**; 18 **mussels**; 12 large raw **prawns**; 2 large pinches **saffron**; 150ml **white wine**; 150g **green beans**; 300g **Calasparra rice** (from Murcia in Spain, best for paella); 300g **tomatoes**, skinned, deseeded and chopped finely; 1 tsp medium-hot **pimentón**; 600ml **stock** made from the mussels and prawn shells, plus **chicken stock cube** and **water**; **salt, pepper**.*

Sauter the monkfish in half the olive oil for 2 minutes on each side, in a paella or other wide pan, until pale golden. Transfer to a plate.

Put 300ml water in a large pan to boil. Throw in the mussels, cover and shake the pan over the heat. Let the mussels cook until they are all open. Any that refuse to open should be rejected. Keep the cooking liquid. Remove most of the mussels from their shells, keeping a few in the shell for decoration.

Shell half the prawns and cook the shells in the mussel liquid for 5 minutes. Mash them and then strain the liquid into a bowl. Taste for salt, it may be very salty.

Soak the saffron in the white wine. Cook the green beans in boiling salted water for about 8–10 minutes until just tender (not crunchy).

Add more olive oil to the paella pan, heat it and stir in the rice. Let it cook, stirring, for a few minutes then add the tomatoes. Cook a few minutes more and add the wine and saffron, let it bubble and add the paprika and the boiling hot mussel liquid and stock – enough to almost cover the rice. Season with salt, if needed, and pepper. Cook very gently, covered, without stirring, for about 20 minutes, until half the liquid has been absorbed, then arrange the monkfish tails, the peeled prawns and the shelled mussels on top and slightly push them down into the rice. Decorate the top with the unshelled mussels and prawns and the green beans.

Cook, covered, 5 minutes more or until the rice is tender and juicy, then leave to settle, in a warm place, for 5 minutes. Serve with aïoli (see page 91). (Serves 6.)

Seafood Paella with Toasted Noodles and Aïoli
Fideuà with aïoli

This is an exotic looking dish, even more so if you heighten the red-golden colour with a packet of paella spice mix (Spigol). I first came across *fideuà* in the Casa Sansa Restaurant in Perpignan; it is a seafood paella made with noodles.

Fideu – a kind of vermicelli – are probably a legacy from the Arab world, where they are called *rishta,* or *reshteh,* rather than from Italy. Fine noodles have been eaten in the Middle East, for example with a paste of basil and pistachios *(pesteh)* and in pastries soaked in honey with nuts, since earliest times.

If you cannot find *fideu* use spaghettini broken into very short pieces

> *250g **fideu** No. 2 or spaghettini, broken into short pieces; 500g fish bones to make 500ml **stock** or use chicken or fish stock cube; 300g **clams**; 8 large raw **prawns** in their shells; 300g raw **squid**, cleaned and cut into rings; 2 large pinches **saffron**; 200ml **white wine**; 5–6 tbsp **olive oil**; 1 **onion**, finely chopped; 1–2 cloves **garlic**, finely chopped; 1 tsp smoked sweet **pimentón**; 1 red **chilli**, finely chopped; 2 **tomatoes**, skinned, deseeded and chopped; **salt** – very little as the clams are salty; **aïoli** – optional (see page 91).*

Wash the clams several times in clean, cold water and leave them to soak. Make the fish stock by boiling fish bones in unsalted water for 20 minutes, or by using a stock cube if no bones are to hand. Remove the bones and bring the stock to the boil; put in the clams and cover the pan, cook just long enough for them to open. Scoop them out and set them aside. Taste the stock for salt.

Soak the saffron in the white wine. Shell the prawns and chop the shells and heads into rough pieces. Heat 2 tablespoons of olive oil in a paella pan and fry the prawn shells, mashing them down. Remove the shells and discard them.

Add another tablespoon of olive oil to the pan and fry the noodles in two batches, turning them all the time, until they turn hazelnut brown. Do not let them burn. Set aside, leaving as much oil as possible in the pan. Soften the onion for 10 minutes in the same oil, adding more if necessary.

As the onion just starts to turn brown add the garlic, paprika and chilli, cook for a couple of minutes and then add the tomatoes. Cook for a further 5 minutes. Add the white wine, let it reduce for 3–4 minutes until the sauce is almost jammy, then add the noodles, stirring them into the *sofregit.*

When they are well coated, add enough boiling hot stock to almost cover the noodles (you may not need all of it) and bring it back to the boil. Push the squid into the mixture, cover and cook for 10 minutes, then add the prawns and cover again, cook for 3 minutes. Lastly add the clams and cook for 1–2 minutes, until they are hot. The noodles take about 15 minutes to cook, or a little more. Keep an eye to see that they do not dry up and add more stock if needed; the texture is succulent and silky and the dish has a rich, reddish colour.

Serve with an aïoli. (Serves 4–6.)

la Galère

This is the mantis shrimp (Squilla mantis), known in Spanish as galera *and in proper French as* squille. *Found all round the Mediterranean, it is often used in fish soups in Languedoc. The tail sports a pair of false eyes, and the front claws are in fact an extension of the mouth, as in a praying mantis.*

Clams in Tomato Sauce
Sauce de clovisses

This sauce can be made with *clovisses,* the stripy clams abundant in the Bassin de Thau which many people will know as *vongole*, or with the larger *palourdes.* Another excellent clam is the *amande* or dog cockle. Lastly there is the *praire* or venus clam, ridge-shelled and much enjoyed in Languedoc. *Clovisses* have beautifully marked deep purple and fawn shells, are about 2 cm across, and feel satisfyingly heavy in your hand. Locally they are made into this rich *fricassée* to serve with rice or pasta.

To keep clams alive, which they must be until you cook them, take them out of their plastic bag, wrap them in a wet cloth, put them in a bowl, cover it lightly with a disc of cling film laid on the cloth to keep them from drying out, and keep them in the refrigerator. Cook them on the day of purchase if at all possible.

> *500g medium-sized **clams**; 1 **small onion**, chopped; 3 tbsp **olive oil**; 500g ripe **plum tomatoes**, skinned, seeded and chopped or 400g tinned tomatoes, chopped and drained; 3–4 sprigs **thyme**; 2 cloves **garlic**, chopped; 2 tbsp chopped **parsley**; 1 tsp **sugar**; little **salt**, ½ tsp ground **black pepper**.*

Wash the clams thoroughly in cold water. Put them in a saucepan with 2 tablespoons of water, cover the pan and place it over a fairly high heat, shaking the pan once or twice, until the clams have all opened. Any that do not open should be discarded. Drain in a colander placed over a bowl to catch their cooking liquid. Set aside to cool while you make the tomato sauce.

Soften the chopped onion very gently in the olive oil, which takes 15–20 minutes. Add the tomatoes to the pan, together with the thyme. Season with pepper and a teaspoon of sugar and cook for 15 minutes (or longer for fresh tomatoes) until the sauce is thick. Add 150ml of the clam liquid, which is quite salty, then taste for seasoning. Add the garlic and parsley and cook a few minutes more. Add the clams to the sauce and heat through.

Serve with rice or pasta; a lot of pasta is eaten in the region, particularly noodles. (Serves 4.)

Mussels with Ravigote Sauce
Moules, sauce ravigote

The most herbaceous and refreshing way to eat mussels on a hot day is this dish, served at the excellent L'éstagnol restaurant, next door to Narbonne's magnificent daily covered food market, the Mecca of all the Aude's gourmets and cooks. We like to buy all the ingredients we need and then enjoy some oysters from one of the seafood stalls inside the market hall; they are opened on the spot and served at one of the many busy zinc bars. Expertly opened and bedded in ice, with a glass of delicious local wine, they provide a good moment to take in the scene and the large and generous humanity of the well-lived-in faces. Then, for lunch, a table at L'éstagnol, with fish soup or these lightly chilled, bright-flavoured mussels.

*1.5kg **mussels**, cleaned and beards removed.*

For cooking the mussels:
*250ml white wine; ½ **banana shallot** or 1 large **shallot**, chopped.*

For the sauce:
*75g **shallots**, finely chopped; 1 tbsp finely chopped **cornichons**; 1–2 tbsp finely chopped **capers**; 2 tsp **mustard**; 3–4 tbsp **crème fraîche**; 1 tsp chopped **parsley**; 1 tsp chopped **tarragon**; 1 tsp chopped **chives**; 3 tbsp **olive oil**; **salt**, **pepper**.*

Start with the mussels; bring the white wine and shallot to the boil in a large pan. Simmer for 5 minutes then add the mussels and cover the pan. Cook, shaking the pan occasionally, for two or three minutes, or until the mussels have opened. Let them cool – I usually put the pan outside.

To make the ravigote sauce, put the shallots, cornichons and capers into a bowl, stir in the mustard and then whisk in the *crème fraîche*. Add the herbs and lastly the olive oil, trickling it in slowly and whisking continuously. Season with salt and pepper.

Remove the upper shells of the mussels, and cover each mussel with a spoonful of ravigote sauce. Divide them between four plates, arranging them in a circle. They are best served lightly chilled. (Serves 4)

Mussels with Sausage Sauce
Moules farçies au gras

This rich dish is very popular in the coastal villages of Languedoc and I have based my recipe on a version recommended by the Association de Femmes du Bassin de Thau (their equivalent of the Women's Institute). I have also seen one which claims the recipe's origins to be the 'cowboys' of southern Tuscany. They ask you to tie up each mussel with thread to keep the stuffing in, but that is very fiddly and in any case I think it tastes more succulent when some of it is allowed to escape into the sauce.

*400g **sausage-meat**; 2 **eggs**, beaten; 100g yesterday's **bread** made into breadcrumbs; 1 clove **garlic**; bunch **flat parsley**, chopped; 2kg **mussels**, cleaned, beards removed; 200ml **white wine**; 4 tbsp **olive oil**; 2 **onions**, finely chopped; 100g **lardons** or **bacon** (poitrine fumée) cut into small dice; 2 large **tomatoes**, skinned, deseeded and chopped; 2 tsp **tomato purée**; **salt**, **pepper**.*

Mix the sausage meat in a bowl with the eggs, breadcrumbs, garlic and chopped parsley.

Heat the white wine to boiling point in a large pan, throw in the cleaned mussels, cover the pan and cook for 2–3 minutes, shaking the pan a couple of times, until they have just opened their shells. Let them cool and strain them, catching the liquid in a bowl. Stuff a teaspoon or less of the sausage meat mixture into each mussel.

Heat 2 tablespoons of olive oil and gently fry the onions and lardons until the onions are melted and tender and just beginning to turn golden brown. Add the chopped tomatoes and continue to melt everything together into a jammy sauce. Now add the mussel cooking liquid and the tomato purée, and simmer until well reduced. Taste for seasoning

In a large pan, heat the remaining olive oil and gently sauter the stuffed mussels for minute or two, turning them over once or twice. Do not worry if some of the stuffing falls out.

Add the sauce, stir it in, cover the pan and simmer gently for 30 minutes, stirring occasionally. The stuffing must be cooked, with bits of it melting into the sauce. The mussels themselves will have a different, creamier texture from the long cooking

This is messy to eat, but truly delicious. Serve with a grand bowl for the shells and another full of hot water for dipping your fingers.

(Serves 4–6.)

Wedge shell clams or tellines, *smaller than but similar to* clovisses.

Mussels in Saffron Sauce
Moules au sauce safran

*1kg **mussels**; large pinch **saffron**; 250ml **dry white wine**; 4 tbsp **olive oil**;
1 large **onion**, finely chopped; 5 ripe red **tomatoes**, skinned, deseeded and
chopped; 1–2 **bay leaves**; a few sprigs of **thyme** or large pinch **dried thyme**; 1
red chilli, deseeded and chopped or large pinch dried flakes; **salt** – possibly.*

Scrub and beard the mussels. Put them in a large pan with 2 tablespoons
of water, place over a fierce heat and cover. Cook for 2–3 minutes,
shaking the pan once or twice, until the mussels have opened. Drain their
liquid, which is added to the sauce. Soak the saffron in the white wine.

Heat the olive oil in a large pan and sweat the onions over a low heat
for 10–15 minutes, until they are soft and golden. Add the tomatoes, bay
leaf, herbs, chilli, saffron and wine, and the liquid from the mussels.

Reduce the sauce for 10 minutes, taste for seasoning, then add the
mussels and cover the pan. Cook for, at most, 4–5 minutes and serve
very hot. (Serves 4.)

Grilled Crawfish or Lobster with Garlic Butter
Langouste ou homard grillé à l'ail

*2 live **lobsters** or **crawfish**, each weighing 600g; 100g softened **unsalted butter**; 1 large clove **garlic**, finely chopped; 2 tbsp **parsley**, finely chopped; **salt**, **pepper**.*

For the light mayonnaise (optional):
*125ml **mayonnaise** (page 90); 3 tbsp **crème fraîche**; 2 tsp **lemon juice**; **salt**, **pepper**.*

If you are serving the shellfish with mayonnaise, make it as usual and stir in *crème fraîche* and a little lemon juice.

Heat the overhead grill. Mix the butter with the garlic and parsley and a little salt and pepper. Split the live lobsters or crawfish in half lengthwise with a very large, sharp knife, starting at the middle of the head shell. Remove the intestinal veins. Crack the claws: try a few blows with a mallet, but not hard enough to crush them completely, or use the back of a cleaver.

Line a roasting tin with foil, put in the lobsters, cut side up, and spread them with the garlic butter. Grill for 10 minutes and serve immediately – a plain green salad is all you need to partner it. (Serves 4.)

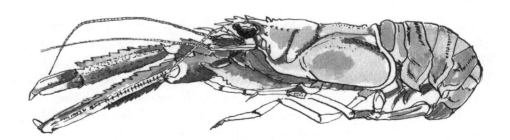

Langoustine *or Dublin Bay prawn.*

Fresh Lobster with *sauce rémoulade*
Homard, sauce rémoulade

In Languedoc you would be more likely to get crawfish, *langouste,* than lobster, and the sauce would be equally good with their wonderful, firm-fleshed but still moist large prawns called *gambas.*

*2 **lobsters** – medium size, each weighing 750g (you can use raw or cooked lobsters).*

For the sauce rémoulade:
*2 **egg yolks**; 1½ tbsp **mustard**; 3 **anchovy fillets**, mashed; 375ml **sunflower oil**, or **olive oil**, or a mixture; 2 tsp **white wine vinegar**; 2 tbsp chopped **capers**; 2 tbsp chopped **parsley**; 2 tbsp chopped **basil**; 2 tsp chopped **tarragon**; 6 **gherkins** finely chopped; 3 tbsp **crème fraîche**; salt, **pepper**.*

It is possible to enjoy a ready-cooked lobster that has spent some time in a fridge, but a freshly boiled lobster, cooled to room temperature, is easily the best – more succulent and better flavoured.

To cook a live lobster, bring an enormous pot of quite heavily salted water to the boil. Drop in the lobster, leaving the bands on its claws, and put on the lid. Boil gently for 12–15 minutes for a medium-sized lobster, then remove to a dish and allow to cool. Cook the lobsters one at a time. The same suggestions apply to crawfish.

To make the *sauce rémoulade,* start just as if you were making a mayonnaise, but you can add the oil faster at the outset. Stir the egg yolks and mustard together with a pinch of salt, add the mashed anchovies and slowly add the oil(s), stirring after each addition. I use a small whisk. When the sauce thickens a little, add the vinegar and then finish adding the oil(s). Stir in the capers, herbs and gherkins and, lastly, the *crème fraîche*. Taste for seasoning; the anchovies are quite salty.

Cut the cooked lobsters in half. I do this by turning them on their backs and cutting lengthwise through the softer under-shell with strong scissors. Cut through the division in the underside of the head. Now with a large heavy knife cut through the flesh and then, using strong scissors again, cut through the top shell, keeping the lobster on its back. If you prefer to use a knife, position it along the middle of the back shell and strike the back of the knife with a wooden mallet. Crack the claw shells with the mallet.

Serve the lobsters with a herb salad and the sauce. (Serves 4.)

Grilled Baby Cuttlefish or Squid with *chorizo*
Petites seiches grillées à la soubressade

This is made with little cuttlefish called *seiches*; I first encountered the dish at L'éstagnol restaurant in Narbonne's main square, a place of plane trees and gushing water, through which a procession of barges and pleasure boats make their way along the Canal du Midi.

Squid and cuttlefish are often sold already cleaned, which is just as well as they are fiddly to prepare. You can also use squid for the dish. The other ingredient, *soubressade*, is pork sausage meat flavoured with paprika. A good substitute is *chorizo*.

*16 little **cuttlefish** or 8 small or 4 medium **squid**, cleaned but with sacs kept whole, keep the tentacles; 150g hot **chorizo** or **soubressade** (pimentón-flavoured fine sausage meat); 1 **onion**, finely chopped; 2–3 tbsp **olive oil**; aïoli (see page 91); **salt**.*

Clean the cuttlefish or squid sacs in plenty of running water, turning them inside out to remove any sand. Remove the head, beak and guts as well as the internal bone or shell. Leave to drain in a colander. Chop the tentacles finely and put them on one side.

Remove the skin from the *chorizo* and crumble the meat, or crumble the *soubressade*. Heat a tablespoon of olive oil in a frying-pan and soften the onion for 10 minutes, without browning. Add the crumbled sausage and fry gently for 3–4 minutes, turning it over regularly so that it cooks evenly, breaking up any larger lumps into small pieces. Add the tentacles and cook, stirring constantly, for 5 or 6 minutes until the tentacles are just cooked. Leave to cool in the pan for 10 minutes.

Pat the outside of the squid sacs dry with kitchen paper if necessary, and put them in a bowl with a teaspoon or so of olive oil and a sprinkling of salt. Turn them over with your hands, so that they are evenly coated.

With a teaspoon, stuff each squid sac with the *chorizo* mixture, dividing it equally between them. Skewer the opening of each one with a cocktail stick to keep them secure. Press down each sac lightly so that two sides are flattened.

Heat a ridged grill pan or griddle and grill the squid for 3–4 minutes on each side, flattening them gently with a spatula as they cook.

When they are completely opaque, serve them with a bowl of aïoli, and some fresh olive bread.

Squid or Cuttlefish With Garlic, Saffron and White Wine
Encornets ou blancs de seiche au vin blanc

Squid and cuttlefish come in all sizes, from 2 cm long to half a metre or more. They are one of the staple fish of the Mediterranean (and, incidentally, the Adriatic) and can be bought on the markets already beautifully prepared, or whole and swimming in their own ink – I would be inclined to buy the prepared ones for this dish. It is fragrant, quick and simple and offers the warm, deep flavour of a southern fish stew with very little trouble.

*1kg (4 or 5 large) prepared **squid** (10 cm), or 800 grams **cuttlefish** pieces (or 2 whole cuttlefish weighing 650g each); 3 large pinches **saffron** or a packet of powdered saffron; 250ml **dry white wine**; 4 tbsp **olive oil**; 2–3 cloves **garlic**, finely chopped; 3 **bay leaves**; ½ tsp dried **thyme** or 2–3 sprigs fresh thyme; 4 medium or 2 large **tomatoes**, skinned deseeded and diced; **salt**, **pepper**.*

Prepare the squid as before. Cut each sac across into four pieces – if you can make these roughly diamond-shaped they will look more elegant. Cut the tentacles into short pieces. If using cuttlefish the same applies.

Soak the saffron in the white wine for at least 20 minutes.

Heat the olive oil in a large pan and sauter the squid or cuttlefish pieces for 2–3 minutes until they lose their translucence and become white and opaque. Add the wine, garlic, bay leaves, thyme, and tomatoes. Season and cook gently for 12 minutes. Serve with country bread to mop up the juices and a green salad. (Serves 4.)

Squid à la plancha with Preserved Lemons
Encornets à la plancha au citron confit

Cooking à la plancha first beguiled me in Catalonia where, to the sound of the guitar, the chef at the Bar Madame Zozo could be seen – and heard – sizzling the most magnificent prawns on the plancha, a flat, iron griddle heated over a wood fire. There was dancing, flaming sambuca and the smell of prawn whiskers scorching – a great education in the art of joie de vivre.

All along the Mediterranean seashore, from Montpellier to the Spanish border, à la plancha is a favourite way of cooking – you can choose from prawns and squid, local vegetables such as sliced peppers, courgettes and aubergines, lamb cutlets and beef steak. This is an adaptation of a recipe by Montpellier's exceptionally talented twin chefs, the Pourcel brothers.

*750g small, fresh **squid**; 1 tbsp **olive oil**.*

For the dressing:
*1 or 2 **lemons** preserved in brine, rinsed and drained; 1 **tomato**, skinned, deseeded and diced into small dice; 1 tbsp chopped **spring onion** or chives; 1 tbsp chopped **parsley**; juice of ½ **lemon**; 3 tbsp **olive oil**; salt, pepper.*

Clean and prepare the squid. Rinse well to remove any sand, particularly from the tips of the sacs and the legs, then drain. Carefully make a little slash along each side of the body pockets, so that they fold flat when they are grilled. If you like the look of it, you can also slash the body pockets with diagonal slashes in both directions, to form a diamond pattern, but do not cut right through.

Remove the flesh of the preserved lemons and discard it. Cut the peel into small dice. Mix all the dressing ingredients, including the lemon peel, in a bowl. Taste for seasoning, adding more oil if necessary.

Heat a griddle or a large heavy frying-pan over a high heat and rub it over with a very little olive oil, I do this with kitchen paper. When it is hot, put on a few of the squid and brown them rapidly, the bodies on both sides, and the legs on all sides. They will take about 4 minutes altogether. Transfer them to a dish. Continue to sear the squid in batches. Serve hot or cold, with the confit lemon dressing. (Serves 4.)

Prawns *à la plancha*
Gambas à la plancha

The scorching and blackening of the fragile bits of shell on the *plancha* gives the prawns a heady, smoky flavour – the very essence of the Mediterranean.

Buy large juicy raw prawns, grill them on a heated, lightly oiled griddle as in the previous recipe, and let people peel them themselves. Serve with aïoli and quartered lemons.

Cuttlefish with *rouille*
Seiches à l'aiguemortaise

According to Alan Davidson, an excellent version of this recipe, containing brandy and pastis, was invented by Rémi Rigal of l'Escale in Aigues-Mortes. Mine, leaving out the snort of alcohol, is a traditional *rouille*, a splendid cuttlefish (or you can use squid) dish found everywhere in the region, *rouille* incidentally also being the name of the hot sauce that flavours the dish. Davidson accurately describes it as having 'a very special smack of the Midi'.

For the cuttlefish:
*1kg cleaned **cuttlefish**, cut into strips; 3 large pinches **saffron**; 250ml **white wine**; 3 tbsp **olive oil**; 2 **onions**, chopped; 3 cloves **garlic**, chopped; bouquet of **thyme**, **bay** and **fennel**; 1 strip **orange peel**, dried or fresh; 2 **tomatoes**, skinned, deseeded and diced; 1 small **red chilli**; 600g **potatoes**, peeled and sliced; **pain de campagne**, sliced and toasted; **salt, pepper**.*

For the rouille:
*1 large **potato**, peeled and boiled until soft; 1–2 tsp **harissa**; 2 cloves **garlic**, mashed to a paste; 2 **egg yolks**; pinch **saffron**; 100ml **olive oil**; coarse salt.*

To make the *rouille* sauce, while the potato is still hot, mash it well with a fork; set it aside to cool completely. Put the harissa, garlic, egg yolks, a large pinch of coarse salt and a pinch of saffron in a mortar and work them together. Add the potato, and work it together with the egg yolks until you have a paste. Gradually drip in the olive oil, working it into the mixture as if you were making mayonnaise.

To cook the cuttlefish, soak the saffron in the white wine. Heat the olive oil over a gentle heat and sweat the onion and 2 cloves of the garlic in 3 tablespoons of olive oil until soft. Add the herbs, orange peel, tomato and the whole chilli. Cook over a medium heat, until soft and jammy, then add the white wine, let it bubble, and reduce to the consistency of a thick sauce. Add the cuttlefish and the sliced potatoes, almost cover with water, add a little salt and simmer very slowly for 30–40 minutes, stirring from time to time to release the starch from the potatoes.

Toast the *pain de campagne* and rub the slices with the third clove of garlic, then cut into croûtons. Give everyone a spoon and serve the fragrant soup-stew very hot in heated soup bowls. Hand the rouille round in a bowl. This golden fish stew with a tablespoon of red sauce on top is a beautiful sight. (Serves 4–6.)

Chipirons *or baby cuttlefish.*

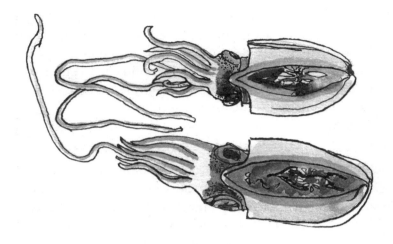

Cuttlefish or Squid With Green Olives
Seiche à la mode d'Estaque

*1 kilo **small cuttlefish** or **large squid**, cleaned and prepared; 125g **green olives**, preferably Lucques; 2 large pinches **saffron**; 300ml **dry white wine**; 3 tbsp **olive oil**; 4–5 cloves **garlic**, crushed and cut in half; 600g **tomatoes**, skinned, seeded and chopped; large bunch **fennel twigs**, folded up and tied with string; 3 **bay leaves**; 2 tsp **harissa**; 3 tbsp **tomato paste**; salt, **pepper**.*

Cut the cuttlefish or squid roughly into 2 cm pieces.

Shave the flesh off the olives with a knife so that it comes off in little slices (this is optional, you can also add them whole).

Soak the saffron in the white wine.

Heat the olive oil in a sauté pan with a lid. Put in the cuttlefish or squid, together with the garlic and let it fry for 2–3 minutes, then add the tomatoes. Cook for about 5 minutes, until the tomatoes are beginning to break up, then add the saffron-infused white wine, the fennel twigs and bay leaves. Bring to the boil, stir in the olives, harissa and the tomato purée, season and cover the pan. Turn down the heat and simmer until the cuttlefish is tender, about 30 minutes for very small cuttlefish and squid; for larger fish allow 45 minutes to 1 hour. (Serves 4.)

Squid with Chard
Encornets aux blettes

This is a truly simple, clean-tasting affair, freshened with plenty of lemon. The chard stalks are not needed for the dish, but can be used in a gratin (see page 277). If chard is not available, use spinach, preferably large mature leaves, as baby leaves are too fragile.

*10–12 medium **squid**, about 1kg before cleaning; 1kg **chard**; 3 tbsp **olive oil**; 2 **lemons**; **salt**, **pepper**.*

Clean the squid, if they are not already cleaned, and cut the bodies into rings about 1–2 cm thick. Cut the tentacles into smaller, manageable pieces.

Bring a pan of salted water to the boil. Wash the chard, remove the leafy parts and shred them. Cook them in boiling water for about 5 minutes or until tender. Drain well, the chard should be as dry as possible.

Heat the oil in a large frying-pan. It should be hot enough to cook the squid briskly without their juices escaping. Fry, stirring, for 3–4 minutes, until the pieces are opaque. Add the chard and cook, stirring, for 2–3 minutes, until very hot. Squeeze on the juice of one lemon and season well with salt and pepper. Serve quarters of lemon with the squid. (Serves 4–6.)

Salt Cod with Tomatoes and Peppers
Morue campagnarde

There are hundreds of ways of cooking salt cod and I believe that most of them involve olive oil and garlic. This one has the added bite of green peppers and the mellow sweetness of tomatoes.

*500g **salt cod** previously soaked for 24–36 hours in frequently changed water; 4–5 tbsp **olive oil**; 1–2 tbsp **flour**; 4 cloves **garlic**; 750g ripe red **tomatoes**, skinned, cut in pieces and drained or 400g chopped tinned tomatoes; 1 tsp dried **thyme** or 3 sprigs fresh thyme; 2 pinches **sugar**; 2 **red onions**, sliced; 200g small **green peppers** (piquillos or other) or 1 large one, roasted in the oven, skinned and cut into strips; 1 **lemon**; **pepper**.*

Cut the soaked cod into 3–4 cm pieces with a saw-toothed knife. Put the pieces in a pan of cold water and bring slowly to the boil. As it reaches boiling point remove the pan from the heat and cover it at once. Let it sit for 5 minutes, then lift out the pieces and leave to drain and cool. Skin the fish and remove any bones.

Heat half the olive oil in a large non-stick frying-pan. Dip the pieces of cod in flour and fry gently until golden on all sides. They may stick, so turn them carefully with a spatula, without breaking them up too much. Remove them to a plate, keeping the pan with its oil.

Heat the remaining olive oil in a separate pan, fry the cloves of garlic until they turn a pale golden colour and give off an aromatic smell, then put them with the cod. In the hot, fragrant oil fry the tomatoes, seasoning them with thyme and pepper and two pinches of sugar.

Fry the sliced onions in the pan in which you cooked the cod, adding more oil if necessary. After 5 minutes add the green peppers and continue to fry until tender and soft, about 10 minutes. Add the tomatoes and the cod to the frying-pan and heat through, distributing the cod carefully through the tomatoes and onions. Taste for seasoning and serve with quarters of lemon. (Serves 4–6.)

Salt Cod with Leeks
Morue aux poireaux

A Lenten standby (except for the chicken stock used as a cooking medium) – simplicity itself, some salt cod from the *cave*, a few leeks from the garden, a bit of olive oil and you have a meal. Best for this is the thinner fillet that can easily be cut into pieces before cooking. Another version adds potatoes to the dish before it goes into the oven.

> *400g fairly thin fillets of* **salt cod***, cut into 5–6 cm pieces and soaked for 24–36 hours; 30g* **flour***; 4 tbsp* **olive oil***; 600g* **leeks***, white part only, finely sliced; 100ml* **chicken stock***;* **salt, pepper.**

Poach the cod briefly, as in the previous recipe. Heat the oven to 200°C. Dip the pieces of cod in flour, heat half the olive oil in a frying-pan and fry the cod until golden brown on both sides, adding more oil if necessary. Place the pieces of cod in a gratin dish.

Heat the olive oil and soften the leeks over a low heat until they are tender and wilted. Place them on top of the cod, sprinkle with plenty of pepper and baptize with the chicken stock, then bake for 20 minutes. Serve with potatoes mashed with olive oil and milk. (Serves 4.)

Salt Cod Marseillan Style
Brandade de morue comme à Marseillan

Marseillan, facing the port of Sète at the other end of the Bassin de Thau, is a charming holiday fishing town, with one or two lively dockside restaurants. It is still home to the Noilly Prat vermouth factory. Made here for 200 years, herb-flavoured Noilly Prat is known as the Rolls Royce of dry vermouths. Vermouth does not have to be made into martinis, it makes a cooling pre-dinner drink in a tumbler with ice and lemonade.

I like the local *brandade* of salt cod, a very good rustic version of the more famous *brandade de Nîmes*, and about as easy to make as mashed potatoes. The joy of this recipe is the abundant parsley flecked through the white purée, which gives a new lift to the dish.

> *200g middle cut of **salt cod**, soaked for 24–36 hours in frequently changed water, or buy ready-to-cook salt cod; 2 **bay leaves**; 2 medium **potatoes**, peeled; 8 tbsp **olive oil**; 2 cloves **garlic**, chopped; 6 tbsp of chopped **flat parsley**, stalks removed; 50g **butter**; 5–6 tbsp **milk**.*

Put the previously soaked cod in a pan of cold water, together with the bay leaves, and bring slowly to the boil. As it reaches boiling point remove the pan from the heat and cover it at once. Let it sit for 5 minutes for a medium thick piece of cod, 15 minutes for a thick piece, then lift it out and cook the potatoes in the cod-poaching liquid until they are very soft. Skin the cod and remove any bones.

In a separate pan, heat 3 tablespoons of olive oil and gently soften the chopped garlic and half the parsley, without browning.

Away from the heat, flake the cod into the garlic and parsley mixture. Crush the cod lightly with a fork, then place in a food processor with a little warm olive oil and pulse it to make a *pommade*.

Purée the potatoes as if you were making mash, and add the cod, together with the remaining parsley, butter and milk. Taste and add pepper and salt if it is needed. Stir until smooth and serve lukewarm with slices of grilled *pain de campagne*, one half trickled with olive oil. (Serves 4.)

Salt Cod Sète Style
Morue sètoise

*400g **salt cod**, cut into pieces 6 cm across and then soaked for 24–36 hours; 6 tbsp **olive oil**; 2 **onions**, finely chopped; 2 cloves **garlic**; 1 large **tomato**, skinned, de-seeded and chopped; 2 **bay leaves**; 4 medium **potatoes**, peeled and sliced; 75g **black olives**; 75g **green olives**; 1 tbsp chopped **parsley**.*

For the batter:
*125g **plain flour**; 1 large **egg**; 125ml **cold water**; 2 tsp **olive oil**.*

Make the batter by putting the flour in a bowl, drop in the egg and start to work it into the flour, adding a few teaspoons of water at a time, and eventually beating the mixture until smooth. Beat in the olive oil and allow to stand.

Poach the fish according to the recipe for *brandade de morue*. Discard the skin and bones and place the cod in a colander to dry off.

Heat half the olive oil in a pan large enough to hold the fish. Soften the onions, garlic and tomato over a low heat until soft and jam-like. Add the bay leaves, potatoes and olives. Just cover with water, bring to the boil and cook until the potatoes are tender. Taste for salt, but remember the cod will be salty too.

Heat 3 tablespoons of olive oil in a second frying-pan. Make sure the pieces of cod are dry, whisk the batter, dip in the pieces of cod and fry them, turning them carefully so they do not break.

When they are nicely browned, transfer them to the pan with the potatoes, heat through, scatter on the parsley and serve hot. (Serves 4.)

Bigorneau *or winkle.*

Salt Cod Fritters
Accras de morue

These little fritters can also be made with any fresh white fish – do not spare the cayenne, they are best if they are quite spicy. They can be eaten *en apéritif,* with drinks.

> *500g **salt cod**, soaked for 36 hours; 2 tbsp **olive oil**; 2 **shallots**, finely chopped; 1 clove **garlic**, finely chopped; 1 **red chilli**, finely chopped; bunch of **chives**, snipped; 2–3 pinches **cayenne pepper**; **oil** for deep frying, 1 lemon.*

> *For the fritter batter:*
> *250g **flour**; 2 **eggs**, yolks and whites separated; 1 tbsp **olive oil**; 60ml **cold water**; pinch of **salt**.*

To make the batter, mix the flour, egg yolks and olive oil in a bowl, gradually adding the water, and beating until it is nicely smooth. Keep the whites on one side.

Poach the cod as explained in the recipe for *brandade de morue*, above. Flake it and pulse it in the food processor until finely chopped.

Heat the oil in a pan and soften the shallots and garlic until just tender. Drain and stir into the salt cod mixture. Add the chilli, chives and cayenne to the mixture.

When you are ready to cook the *accras*, whisk the egg whites to a soft peak and fold them into the batter. Then fold in the cod mixture as lightly as possible.

Heat the oil in a deep pan so that it is hot but not smoking (around 180°C). If you fry one as a test, it should rise to the surface unaided if the oil is hot enough. Fry teaspoonfuls of the batter, a few at a time, until they are golden brown. Turn them over once. Remove with a slotted spoon and drain on kitchen paper.

Serve hot with sliced lemon, or aïoli. (Serves 4.)

Roasted Cod with Caper Sauce
Morue fraîche aux câpres

Although there is nothing more appetizing than a magnificent cod, with its white flesh coming away in succulent flakes, this dish can equally well be made with a whole hake or with cod or hake fillets. The sauce is light and refreshing with a bit of a tang.

*1 fresh **cod** or **hake** weighing 2kg, cleaned and gutted, fins and tail trimmed, head removed or 1kg filleted hake or cod; 1–2 **shallots**, chopped; 3 tbsp **olive oil**; a few sprigs and stems of **flat parsley**; 100ml **white wine**; **salt, pepper.***

For the caper sauce:
*100g **capers**; 2 large cloves **garlic**, peeled and chopped; 2 **shallots**, peeled and chopped; 2 strips **lemon zest**, chopped; 8–10 sprigs **flat parsley**, chopped; juice of ½ **lemon**; 2 tbsp **olive oil**; 250ml **crème fraîche**; a little **salt, pepper**.*

To make the sauce, put the capers with a teaspoonful of their vinegar, the garlic, shallots, lemon peel and parsley in the food processor and pulse until the pieces are the size of split lentils. Add the lemon juice and the olive oil with the motor still running. Lastly, add the *crème fraîche*. When the sauce is homogeneous, turn it off and transfer it to a bowl. Leave in the refrigerator.

Heat the oven to 200°C. Line a roasting tin with foil, scatter in the chopped shallots, sprinkle with olive oil. Season the inside of the cod with salt and put in the parsley. Lay the cod on top of the shallots. Season again and sprinkle with the remaining olive oil and the white wine.

Place a piece of foil lightly over the fish. Roast the cod for 25–30 minutes (14–16 minutes if using fillets) until the flesh comes away from the backbone when separated with a knife.

Serve hot or cold, with the refreshing caper sauce. (Serves 4–6.)

Tartare of Grey Mullet
Tartare de muges

South and west of Narbonne lies Bages, a pretty fishing village over-
looking one of the many blue salt lagoons of Languedoc and a perfect
place for lunch. Here, a number of families combine their fishing
activities with wine-making, and they supply both their daily catch and
their wine to Le Portanel, a comfortable restaurant perched above the
water.

As well as eels, which are its signature dish, the restaurant serves bass
and grey mullet, trapped in the lagoon in triangular nets called *trabacs*,
which are visited by the fishermen once a day. Grey mullet, or *muge* or
lisse, like mackerel, should be eaten very fresh. Happily they know how
to deal with it at Le Portanel, serving it smoked – they do this in-house –
side by side with their own smoked eel, or in a tartare which they serve
with oysters from Gruissan nearby.

Recent research has shown that mullet live entirely on a diet of
plankton, the same food eaten by anchovies and herrings; their preferred
habitats are estuaries, lagoons and harbours. *Poutargue*, pressed mullet
roe, is known as Mediterranean caviar in the south of France. This is
my version of the mullet tartare; you can make it with raw salmon too.

*2 fillets of **grey mullet**, around 400g, skin removed by the fishmonger; 1
whole **cucumber**, peeled, seeds removed; 150 g **bulb fennel**; 3 tbsp of **olive
oil**; 1 **lemon**; 10 leaves of **basil**, cut into strips; **fine salt, pepper**.*

Chill the mullet in the freezer for 30 minutes to firm the flesh for dicing.
Cut the chilled mullet into tiny dice – 5 mm or less. Season the fish with
fine salt and several turns of the peppermill; it should be well seasoned.

Peel the cucumber and halve it lengthwise, remove the seeds with a
teaspoon and cut into cubes of the same size as the fish. Dice the fennel
similarly. Mix the fish with the cucumber and fennel. Pour on the olive
oil, mixing it in well. Chill.

Twenty minutes before serving, squeeze quarter of a lemon onto the
fish and mix the juice in carefully to distribute it evenly. Divide the
mixture between plates, scatter with basil and serve with a slice of
lemon.

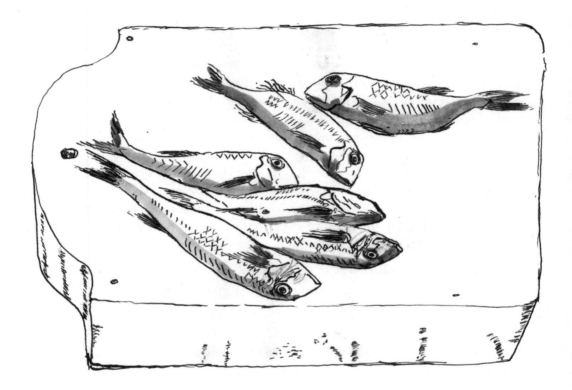

Small red mullet.

Red Mullet from Algiers
Rouget à l'algérienne

When *rouget* is combined with tomato and saffron the red skin transforms to golden-pink, making these beautiful fish even more vivid, and the deep scents of saffron and fennel always seem to bring a happpy mood to the table.

This and the recipe that follows are among the many recipes in Languedoc with Moorish connections. It is a dish with a long history. An early English recipe I once came across gives instructions for Red Mullet Arabienne, in which the fish is cooked with tomatoes, onions, saffron and 'curry powder', a stand-in for freshly ground spices – coriander and cumin are two that were associated with saffron to flavour fish in the medieval Islamic kitchen. They might be a good addition to this recipe.

> *6 fine red mullet (rougets) each weighing 200g; 3–4 pinches of saffron threads; 150ml dry white wine; 6 tbsp olive oil; sprinkling of flour; 3 cloves garlic, finely chopped; ½ tsp fennel seeds, crushed in a mortar; 600g large ripe tomatoes, skinned, deseeded and cut into small dice; salt, pepper.*

Scale the fish, or ask the fishmonger to do this, and cut off the fins and tips of the tail with scissors. You can keep the livers inside the fish – they add to the delicate flavour. Sprinkle the fish with salt. Heat the oven to 180°C. Soak the saffron in the white wine.

Heat the olive oil in a sauté pan. Flour the fish lightly and fry them, in batches, for 2 minutes on each side until lightly browned. Remove them to a dish, turn the heat to very low and let the pan cool for a minute or two. Put the garlic into the same oil. Let it stew gently for 2–3 minutes, add the fennel seeds and after 30 seconds add the tomatoes. Simmer for 5 minutes, stirring gently without breaking up the tomatoes too much. Add the white wine, season with salt and pepper, and cook 5 minutes more. Tip the mixture into a large oval gratin dish, spreading it out so that it covers the bottom. Place the *rougets* on top and roast for 20 minutes. Serve with a green salad.

This dish is also stunning served at room temperature, especially when eaten outside, in the shade of a trellis, on a hot day. (Serves 6.)

Roasted Red Mullet with Black Olives
Les rougets barbets au four

This recipe, perfumed with basil, is from the Béziers district. Local writer Joseph Delteil says this creation, the famous red mullet with black olives, burst up out of the seafoam ready-formed, like Venus.

In Languedoc red mullet are plentiful, but are always treated with great respect, I think partly because of their iridescent cardinal red colour. These fish are sometimes cooked whole and ungutted, as the liver is a delicacy to be savoured, but the guts can be horribly gritty. I prefer to clean the inside of the fish and then put the liver back inside, rejecting the rest.

*4 large **red mullet**, around 200g each – called femelles on the market of Béziers – have them scaled and gutted, but leave the livers inside if possible; 2 **onions**, finely chopped; 4–5 tbsp **olive oil**; 1kg ripe **plum tomatoes** skinned, seeded and chopped; 50g **black olives**, stones removed; 100ml **dry white wine**; generous handful of **basil leaves**, torn in your fingers and a few whole leaves for serving; **salt, pepper**.*

Heat the oven to 200°C. Season the fish inside and out with salt and coarsely ground pepper. Soften the onions in 2–3 tablespoons of olive oil with a pinch of salt, until tender and transparent. Add the tomatoes and half the olives and season with salt and pepper. Cook over a medium heat until much of the liquid has evaporated, around 10 minutes.

Put the mixture in an oval or rectangular gratin dish and lay the fish on top. Sprinkle them with white wine, the remaining olive oil, salt and pepper.

Roast for 15 minutes, turn the fish carefully and roast for a further 10 minutes, until the flesh is quite firm when pressed with your thumb. Remove from the oven and scatter with fresh basil leaves and the remaining olives. Serve hot or cold. (Serves 4.)

Grilled Monkfish with Aïoli
Saupiquet de baudroie

This is one of the simplest and best ways to cook monkfish: soaked in a marinade cleanly flavoured by fennel and lemon, then grilled. The fish, with its sweet, bone-free flesh of pearly whiteness, is served with a pungent golden aïoli. A true *saupiquet* of monkfish, a Narbonnais dish, would incorporate the monkfish liver, which is white and exudes a great deal of bright orange oil when cooking; it tastes impressively strong.

If you like the flavour, monkfish roe can also be eaten, first soaked in a brine before frying with a scattering of garlic and parsley, or seasoned and cooked under a weight in a terrine, then cooled and served cold in slices with a salad.

*1kg **monkfish** – four good fillets, ask the fishmonger to remove the greyish membranes and extraneous bits; 60ml best **olive oil**; 2 **lemons** thickly sliced; 1 tsp **fennel seeds**, bruised.*

*For the **aïoli**:*
*2 **egg yolks**; 2–3 decent sized cloves **garlic**; 200ml **olive oil**.*

*For the **lemon sauce**:*
*250ml **white wine**; 4 cloves **garlic**; 4 bruised **allspice berries**; **salt**.*

At least 2 hours before the meal (or, preferably, overnight), cut slashes on opposite sides of each fillet, to prevent them from curling up while they cook. Put the clean white fillets in a bowl with the olive oil, sliced lemons and fennel seeds. Leave in a cool place to absorb the flavours. Make the aïoli as described on page 91.

Heat a ridged grill pan until you judge it to be medium-hot, not smoking. If you don't have a grill pan, a flat griddle will do. If it cooks too fast the fish will curl up and even split; not hot enough and the juices will run out.

Grill the fillets for 6–10 minutes on each side depending on their thickness. If they do start to curl you can hold them down straight with two wooden spatulas.

While the fish is cooking, take the lemon slices used in the initial marinade and boil them in white wine with the cloves of garlic and the allspice, until they are tender. Serve the fish hot and juicy with the drained, cooked slices of lemon and the golden aïoli. (Serves 4.)

Monkfish with Swiss Chard
Bourride aux blettes

This dish has a beautiful simplicity. Swiss chard, called *blettes* in the south, is a huge favourite and continues to appear on the markets throughout the winter. The stalks are flat, thick, succulent and white, the green leaves positively billow when freshly picked. It has a flavour reminiscent of spinach tinged with seaweed. Spinach can be substituted, but has less body and tends to disintegrate.

> *700g **monkfish**; 1kg **Swiss chard** or **spinach beet**, thick stalks removed, or use spinach (not so much, as it doesn't have the large stalks); 2 **egg yolks**; 250ml **double cream**; 2–3 tbsp **olive oil**; 3–4 cloves **garlic**, finely chopped; **salt, pepper**.*

Heat the oven to 190°C. Remove any grey membranes adhering to the fish – the flesh should be white. If the monkfish is large, remove the backbone so that you have two fillets. Smaller fish should be left on the bone. Slice into medallions 2 cm thick and season with fine salt.

Mix the egg yolks and cream together, seasoning well with salt and pepper.

Wash and strip the spinach beet or chard and chop roughly. This recipe uses only the leaves, the stalks can be served in a gratin at some other meal (see page 277). Drain, but place in a pan with some water clinging to the leaves, and with half the olive oil and the garlic. Cover the pan and let the leaves wilt over a low heat until soft and tender, turning them from time to time. Remove the lid from the pan and continue cooking until they are almost dry. Remove from the heat, transfer to a gratin dish and allow to cool a little.

Mix the cream and egg yolk liaison with the leaves. Place the slices of monkfish on top and cover with foil. Bake in the oven for 20 minutes, remove the foil and, just before serving, spoon some of the sauce over the top of the fish. (Serves 4.)

Sea Bass Fillets with Tapenade Sauce
Filets de loup de mer, sauce tapenade

The idea for this robust black olive sauce came from the great American writer about wine and food Richard Olney, who documented the cookery of his friend Lulu Peyraud, proprietor of the Domaine Tempier, producers of the most wonderful vin rosé from Bandol. The estate is in Provence, but olive sauces are very much a Languedoc taste. I make the sauce with tapenade and serve it with fish, while Lulu made it from scratch with stoned black olives and served it with poultry.

*4 large **sea bass** fillets; 50g **flour**; 125ml **milk**; 3–4 tbsp **sunflower oil**; salt, pepper.*

For the black olive sauce:
*100g **black olive tapenade**; 2–3 cloves **garlic**, chopped; 8 **anchovy fillets**, chopped; ½ tsp dried **thyme**; 3–4 tbsp **olive oil**; pinch **cayenne pepper** or **chilli powder**; salt, pepper.*

Start by making the sauce. If you are making it by hand, mash the garlic and anchovies to a paste with a fork or the flat blade of a knife. Mix the paste with the black olive tapenade, stir in the thyme and gradually add the olive oil, stirring as if you were making salad dressing or mayonnaise. It will probably separate, but that does not matter. If you are making it in a food processor, purée the anchovies and garlic, add the tapenade and the thyme and then add the olive oil in a steady stream. Season with pepper, cayenne or chilli and a pinch of salt if necessary – anchovies and olives are both salty.

To fry the bass, mix the flour with a little salt and pepper and spread on a large plate. Put the milk in a wide, shallow bowl. Heat 4 tablespoons of oil in a large frying-pan. While it is heating, dip the fillets into the flour to coat them, then dip them in milk. Lastly dip them again into flour and place them carefully in the hot oil over a high heat. Cook for 2 minutes on each side, until nicely browned. Transfer to kitchen paper to rid them of any excess oil, then to hot plates. Serve with the black olive sauce and plainly cooked new potatoes. (Serves 4.)

Roasted Sea Bass with Fennel and Thyme
Loup grillé comme dans les calanques

Les calanques are the deep salt water creeks one sees from the train, as it slides between the Mediterranean and the marshes close to the salty vineyards of Listel (where a good vin rosé is made) on the route from Montpellier to Béziers. If you have time to do the preparation an hour or two before you cook the fish, the flavours will permeate the flesh, making it even more fragrant.

> *2 **large** or 4 **small sea bass** (about 1 to 1.5kg altogether) scaled and cleaned; 1 tsp **dried thyme**; 1 tsp **fennel seeds**; 1 tsp **sea-salt** crystals; ½–1 tsp cracked **pepper**; handful of dried or fresh **fennel stalks** or 1 head of **bulb fennel** cut into strips; 3 tbsp **olive oil**; 1 **lemon**.*

Heat the oven to 220°C. Make incisions in the bass, cutting 2–3 diagonal slashes down each side, and cutting through to the bone. Grind the thyme, fennel seeds, salt and pepper in a pestle and mortar.

Line a roasting tin with foil. (I do this because it makes it much easier to wash up, and I don't have a roasting tin that smells of fish.) Lightly oil the foil, preferably with a brush – oil the sides as well.

Put the fennel stalks or sliced fennel in the belly of each fish. Place the fish in the roasting tin. Rub the herb mixture into the cuts on both sides of the fish. Sprinkle olive oil all over, then turn them over and sprinkle the second side. Roast the fish for 15–20 minutes, 20–25 minutes if they are larger.

Drizzle the fish with fresh olive oil before bringing them to the table. Serve with slices of lemon. (Serves 4.)

Sea snail..

Sea Bass with Crab Sauce
Bar au sauce de cranquettes

The original sauce is made from *cranquettes*, small swimming crabs, full of flavour but a bit short on meat, and therefore perfect for making into a sauce. Our large crabs taste a little less pungent, but still work well in this dish, adapted from one I tasted at the restaurant which sits amongst the vineyards surrounding the Domaine Gayda between Carcassonne and Limoux.

This can also be made with red mullet, in which case I like to leave the livers in the fish while they cook, and then remove them when they are cooked through and incorporate them with the sauce.

> 4 **small sea bass** weighing 200g–250g each; 100g brown and white **crabmeat** or 1 x 250g **female crab**, cooked; 2 **egg yolks**; 1 tbsp **harissa**; squeeze of **lemon juice**; 100ml **olive oil**; extra **olive oil** for cooking the fish; **salt, cayenne pepper**.

If using a whole crab, remove the claw meat, brown meat and the red roe from the body. Otherwise, rely on your fishmonger to do the hard work and buy the meat ready-processed.

In a mortar or the bowl of a food processor, combine crabmeat, egg yolks, harissa and a squeeze of lemon juice. Combine and mash or pulse long enough to remove any lumps, then trickle in drops of the olive oil, incorporating them a little at a time, as you would if making mayonnaise. Add a total of 100ml oil. Warm the sauce through, but do not boil or even simmer it. Taste for seasoning, adding salt and plenty of cayenne pepper.

Place the fish on a board – it is a good plan to put newspaper underneath, so that the board does not smell of fish afterwards. You will have bought them scaled and gutted, but now trim the fins and tails with a pair of scissors. Some people also like to remove the gills.

With a sharp knife cut along the sides of each fish, following the line that runs from gills to tail. Sprinkle with fine salt and trickle olive oil into the cuts and over the fish. Heat a little olive oil in a large heavy pan and fry the fish for about 5 minutes on each side, until cooked through.

Serve with the hot crab sauce. (Serves 4.)

Sea Bream with Tomatoes and Olives
Daurade aux tomates rôties

This is a Mediterranean classic, with the added intensity of slow-roasted tomatoes. The idea derives from the twin brothers Jacques and Laurent Pourcel, who reign over their hotel le Jardin des Sens near Montpellier. It certainly improves beyond all recognition the flavour of sad, pale tomatoes, grown without the sunshine of the Midi, that we sometimes have to buy in Britain.

4 fillets of **black bream**, *500–600g altogether;* **salt, pepper;** **olive oil** *for frying.*

For the roasted tomatoes:
2 large **tomatoes;** *80ml* **olive oil;** *1 tsp* **sugar;** *generous sprinkling* **salt;** *15 stoned* **black olives.**

For the vinaigrette sauce:
200ml good quality **sherry vinegar;** *200ml best* **virgin olive oil;** *5 sprigs fresh* **mint,** *finely chopped;* **salt, pepper.**

Season the bream fillets on the flesh side with salt and freshly ground pepper, pressing it in with the palm of your hand. Allow to rest in the refrigerator while you roast the tomatoes.

To make the roasted tomatoes, preheat the oven to 120°C. Skin the tomatoes by dipping them briefly in boiling water. Cut them into quarters, remove all the seeds and the central pulp.

Put half the olive oil in a small roasting tin and sprinkle with half the sugar and a few pinches of salt. Put the tomatoes on top and scatter over the remaining oil, sugar and salt. Roast for 2 hours. Allow to cool and then remove from the roasting tin and chop coarsely. Mix with the black olives, and set aside.

Whisk the vinaigrette ingredients together in a bowl.

To cook the fish, heat 2–3 tablespoons of olive oil in a large frying-pan and cook the bream for 2–3 minutes on each side, turning up the heat to crisp the skin side.

Arrange the bream on plates, drizzle with the vinaigrette and put the slow-roasted tomato and olive mixture on the side. (Serves 2.)

Red and Gold Sardines
Sardines sang et or

Sardines are very much on the menu in the Mediterranean, and they do make a splendid meal grilled on the barbecue or cooked in the oven. The flavours of sweet peppers, tangy sea salt and sharp vinegar perfectly compliment the richness of the fish and the colours – red, yellow and silver – give the dish that touch of the Midi.

I adapted this recipe from one of Stéphane Bachès' beautifully produced series of reproduction cook books, *Cuisinière Catalane*. The publisher has cleverly created a book that might have been discovered in a grandmother's kitchen, with handwritten recipes of family favourites.

*16 **sardines**, scaled and gutted; 2 **red peppers**; 2 **yellow peppers**; **red wine vinegar**; **olive oil**; **sea salt**.*

Lay the fish in a porcelain dish and sprinkle with sea salt. Turn them and sprinkle the second side. Leave in the fridge for 3 hours.

Heat the oven to 200°C and grill the peppers for 25 minutes until the skin has blackened. Remove from the oven and drop them into a plastic bag. When cooled, remove the skins and stalks, together with the seeds, and cut the peppers into wide strips. Keep warm.

Heat the grill.

Have ready a large round dish at least 30 cm across.

Remove the sardines from their dish and place on a rack in a roasting pan. I line the pan with foil to prevent it from smelling of fish afterwards. Grill the sardines for 4–5 minutes on each side, until crispy and brown.

Lay them quickly on a dish, placing them like spokes of a wheel, heads to the middle. Rapidly place the strips of pepper, alternately red and yellow, between the fish. Sprinkle with red wine vinegar and olive oil. Serve immediately, while the fish are burning hot, and with some crusty bread and a crisp green salad. (Serves 4.)

Fried Fresh Anchovies
Anchois frais frits

This is how the ladies of Saint-Chinian enjoy their anchovies on a Sunday
– they buy them fresh on the market, and they take them straight home
(anchovies are best when very fresh). You could equally well use this
recipe for fresh sprats or small sardines. You can tell the difference as
anchovies have a thinner, lighter body and larger mouth than sardines.

*400g fresh **anchovies**, 10–15 cm long is a good size; **milk; flour; sunflower
oil** for frying; 2 **lemons; salt, pepper**.*

As soon as you get home from fish shop or market, put the anchovies in
the fridge. When you want to eat them, transfer them to a colander and
pour milk over them. Give them a shake and leave to drain for a minute.
Put the flour on a plate and season it with salt and pepper. Mix the
seasoning in well and then spread the flour out over the whole plate.

Heat the oil in a wide frying-pan – use a fair quantity so that it will
reach almost halfway up the sides of the anchovies when you place them
on their sides in the pan.

Coat the anchovies with flour on both sides – I use my fingers to pick
them up, dip them, turn them and transfer them immediately to the hot
oil. I then wash my hands and use tongs to turn them in the oil.

Fry in batches until nicely browned and crisp on both sides, about 2–3
minutes per side, and remove them to a dish lined with kitchen paper to
drain the surplus oil. Serve with halved lemons. (Serves 4.)

Monsieur Olmo's Snails in Tomato and Garlic Sauce
Petits gris (escargots)

M. Olmo is a master-builder who specializes in traditional roof-tiling, he is also a mustard-keen forager and cook. For this dish, he collects the snails himself, after it rains, and he gets them ready to eat in a very specific way, as described earlier on page 66. He cooks them in a rich tomato, ham and garlic sauce. The ham he uses is from the knuckle end of a *jambon sec* or *jambon cru* – literally dried ham, it is an uncooked country ham from Lacaune, which is *ranci* (aged), and has the special taste beloved in the area. You can substitute lardons or buy pieces of Serrano ham knuckle, which is similar, from the Spanish shop, Garcia, in Portobello Road.

> *100 prepared **snails** (see page 65); bunch of **parsley**, stalks removed, leaves chopped; 5 cloves **garlic**, chopped; 4 tbsp **olive oil**; 2 thick slices of **fatty jambon cru**, cut in small cubes or 75g **lardons**; 1 tube of **tomato paste**; 250ml **water**; a bowl of **aïoli** (see page 91); **salt, pepper**.*

Mix together the chopped parsley and garlic to make a *persillade.*

Heat the olive oil in a large, wide, heavy-bottomed pan and put in the snails. Fry them for a few minutes. Add the ham or lardons and brown a little, then add the *persillade*.

Mix the tomato paste with the water and pour it over the snails, season, and turn down the heat. Simmer gently for half an hour. Taste for seasoning and serve with a bowl of aïoli on the side. (Serves 6–8.)

Chapter Six

Poultry and Other Birds

Fried Chicken
Poulet à la Barthelasse

La Barthelasse is a small island in the Rhône, near Avignon, on the very border of Languedoc. On Sundays everyone used to make their way across the river to a small restaurant, la Bagatelle (now a hostel), to eat the sautéed chicken, because they did it so well there and it is so pleasant to arrive by boat and eat by the river. This is the simplest dish, but is delicious. The recipe can be varied by using dry white vermouth, preferably Noilly Prat, which is made in Marseillan, close to Agde.

> *1 free-range **chicken**, cut into 8 pieces; 120ml **olive oil**; 5 **bay leaves**; 200ml **dry white wine** or **vermouth**; 2–3 large cloves **garlic**, mashed with a fork; bunch **flat parsley**, chopped; **salt**, **pepper**.*

Season the pieces of chicken generously with salt and coarsely ground black pepper. Heat the oil in a wide shallow pan with a lid. When it is very hot, put in the chicken pieces and brown them for 4–5 minutes on each side.

Pour off half the oil and add the wine or vermouth and the bay leaves. Cook for 2–3 minutes to let the the wine give off its alcohol, turning the pieces of chicken. Add 3 tablespoons of water, turn down the heat, season well, cover the pan and simmer 4 minutes. Remove the pieces of breast to prevent them drying out, turn the remaining pieces of chicken and continue to simmer, covered, for a further 6 minutes.

Return the breasts, sprinkle everything with well-mashed garlic and parsley and let it cook for a further 2 minutes until the breasts are just done. Serve from the pan. (Serves 4.)

Roasted Baby Chickens in Cream
Coquelets à la crème

This is an easy recipe for those meals when you have to cook for large numbers. Our view of the Mediterranean diet is all about olive oil, garlic, tomatoes and fish, but not according to Jean-Claude le Masson, who made a collection of recipes from the French Mediterranean called *La Cuisine littorale de nos aïeules* (The Coastal Cuisine of our Ancestors). He includes a surprising number based not on olive oil but on *crème fraîche,* insisting that along the coast from the Italian frontier to the Spanish border, and even in Corsica, there are herds of cows kept in a traditional, non-intensive way. Their milk, he says, produces cream with an incomparable taste. *Crème fraîche* is certainly available everywhere.

> 2 large **poussins**, up to 450g in weight; 1 tbsp **olive oil**; 1oz **butter**; 2 cloves **garlic**, peeled and crushed; 300g **chestnut mushrooms**, or **chanterelles**, sliced if large; 100ml **dry white wine**; 150ml **chicken stock**; 3 tbsp **crème fraîche**; 1 **egg yolk**; salt, pepper.

Pre-heat the oven to 220°C. Put the olive oil in a small roasting pan and roll the poussins round in it. Put butter and a clove of garlic inside each one and season them with salt and pepper.

Roast for about 25–30 minutes, until just cooked and nicely golden, basting once or twice. Remove them to a dish, having poured the garlic-infused juices from their insides into the roasting tin.

Heat the pan juices over a moderate heat on the top of the cooker and add the mushrooms. Let them cook until their juices start to run, about 3–4 minutes, then add the wine and let it bubble until reduced by about half.

Add the stock to the pan and let it simmer for 5 minutes, and then add the cream. Continue cooking to reduce the sauce a little then turn off the heat.

Put the egg yolk in a cup and, away from the heat, stir in 2 tablespoons of the mushroom sauce; return this to the rest of the sauce and stir it in to thicken it. You can thicken it more, if necessary, by putting it back on the heat, but take great care not to let it boil as it will curdle.

Serve the chicken with the mushrooms and their sauce and a green salad, scattered with some chopped herbs – mint, basil and chives is a good combination.

The original recipe cuts the poussins open along the back, removes the backbone and roasts them spatchcocked (flat). They are then cut in half along the breastbone and served on pieces of grilled *pain de campagne.* This would then serve four people but the sauce would lose out on the flavour from the juices. (Serves 2.)

Chicken with Green and Black Olives
Poulet aux deux olives

The sumptuous colours – the colours of the *Pays catalan* – red, gold, green and black, and the sweetness of the red peppers against the sharp saltiness of the olives, give a great lift to this dish.

It appears to be complicated, with a long list of ingredients, but most are simple things that we tend to have to hand. The peppers I prefer are the long, thinner-skinned ones as they are more delicate, but the thick, square peppers are also good for making a mellow and harmonious dish.

1 x 2kg free-range **chicken** *cut in 8 pieces or 4 chicken thighs and 4 drumsticks; 4 tbsp* **olive oil***; ½ tsp* **paprika** *or* **sweet pimentón***; ¼ tsp* **cayenne pepper** *or* **hot pimentón***; 3* **onions***, finely chopped; 4 cloves* **garlic***, peeled and halved; 200ml* **dry white wine***; 2 tsp* **tomato purée***; 2* **bay leaves***; 1 tsp dried* **thyme***; 3* **red peppers** *or 6* **long red peppers***, roasted, skinned and deseeded as in the recipe for red peppers with tomatoes on page 271; 150g stoned* **black olives***; 150g stoned* **green olives***;* **salt***,* **pepper***.*

Heat the olive oil in a wide, shallow casserole. Season the pieces of chicken with pepper and salt and fry, in batches, on both sides over a moderate heat, until they are a deep golden brown. Remove the pieces to a dish and season with paprika and cayenne.

Soften the onions and garlic in the same oil, adding more if needed. Stir from time to time. When they are soft and melting, after 15–20 minutes, add the white wine, tomato purée and herbs. Return the chicken, cover the pan and cook for 10 minutes, turning the chicken once or twice. Add a little water or stock if necessary.

Cut the peppers into strips and add them with the olives to the casserole, pushing them down into the juices. Taste for seasoning and cook for a further 10 minutes.

Serve with *pain de campagne* and a green salad. (Serves 4–6.)

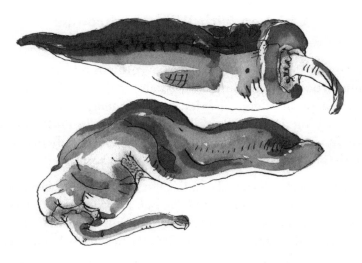

Chicken with Sherry Vinegar and Tomato
Poulet au vinaigre de Jerez

This version of *poulet au vinaigre* uses delicious sherry vinegar. If you use the sweet and sharp red Banyuls vinegar instead, which is not so easy to find, you may need less or no sugar.

> *1 free-range* **chicken** *cut into 8 pieces, or 4 drumsticks and 4 thighs; 3 tsp* **butter***; 3 tbsp* **olive oil***; 400g ripe red* **tomatoes** *(in Languedoc this could mean one enormous tomato), skinned, seeded and chopped; 2 cloves* **garlic***, chopped; 6* **anchovy fillets***, chopped; 150ml* **sherry vinegar** *or* **red wine vinegar** *from Banyuls; juice ½* **lemon***; ¼* **chicken stock cube***; 1 tsp* **sugar** *(optional);* **salt, pepper***.*

Season the pieces of chicken on both sides with salt and freshly ground pepper. Heat the butter and olive oil in a large sauté pan. Brown the pieces of chicken over a medium heat, turning them over from time to time. When they are golden all over add the tomatoes and let their juices evaporate, continuing to turn the pieces of chicken from time to time. When the tomatoes have turned into a thickish sauce, add the garlic, anchovies and vinegar. Stir them together with the tomatoes and chicken, adding lemon juice and stock cube and sugar. Season and continue to cook, turning the chicken pieces occasionally, until the juices and liquids have reduced once more to a rich consistency.

Serve with French beans cooked with garlic, see page 264 for a recipe. (Serves 4.)

Chicken with Wild Mushrooms
Poulet forestière

If you are using cultivated mushrooms, you can add the extra flavour of wild mushrooms by adding a few dried ceps, previously soaked in water, or a teaspoon of cep powder, *poudre friande*, which you can make yourself by drying a quantity of dried *cèpes*, *morilles* and/or *mousserons* a little more, in a very low oven, until they are completely crisp, and then pounding them to a powder with a pestle and mortar.

> *8–12 **chicken** thighs, drumsticks and wings; 1 **onion**, finely chopped; 5 tbsp **olive oil**; 1 large **tomato**, skinned and chopped; 1 tbsp **flour**; 750g mixed fresh **mushrooms**, button, chestnut, and portobello or any edible wild mushrooms, in 1 cm slices; 250ml **dry white wine**; 250ml **chicken stock**; salt, pepper.*

Cook the chopped onion gently in 3 tablespoons olive oil until soft, stirring occasionally. When it turns golden, turn up the heat a bit and add the tomato and stir; simmer until it becomes jammy, but take care it does not burn. Coat the pieces of chicken with all of the flour, mixed with salt and pepper.

Heat the remaining oil in a casserole large enough to hold all the mushrooms. Fry the pieces of chicken on each side, a few at a time, removing them as they turn golden.

When they are all browned, return them to the casserole with the mushrooms. Add the white wine. Simmer for 5 minutes, then add the stock. Lastly add the tomatoes and onions and season with salt and pepper. Cover and simmer gently for 15 minutes, and then for a further 10 minutes, uncovered, until the chicken is cooked and tender, and the juices are rich and velvety. (Serves 4–6.)

Chicken with Lemon and Pine Nuts
Poulet à la catalane

I love the Catalan combinations of sweet and sharp, fruit and meat; both are in evidence in this recipe with the pairing of lemons, complete with peel and pulp, and sweet wine, for a heavenly chicken dish. Lemon trees, dripping with fat yellow fruit, can be seen in the streets of the fishing port of Collioure, while along the coast they are nurtured in sheltered gardens, frost-free throughout the winter. Picked fresh, they are more perfumed and oily and taste more vibrant than the shop-bought ones. Above this coast, between Collioure and the Spanish border, on the vertiginous terraces where the Pyrenees end their plunge into the sea, grow the vines producing Banyuls, a sweet, but not too sweet, fruit-laden wine. Banyuls, pronounced *bunyoose*, really is nectar if you can find it, but use any well-made sweet white wine if you can't. This is a simplified version of a recipe from Éliane Thibaud-Comelade, a well-known French Catalan food-writer who is also the director of the Ateliers de Cuisine Catalane Traditionelle.

*1 free-range **chicken** weighing 1.5–2kg, cut into 8 pieces or 8 chicken wings and drumsticks; 2 unwaxed **lemons**; 1 head fresh **garlic**; 2 tbsp **flour**; 3–4 tbsp **olive oil**; 1 **onion**, finely chopped; 1 thickish slice raw **ham** – Lacaune or Serrano or 50g lardons; 100ml **sweet wine** (preferably Muscat – St-Jean de Minervois or Banyuls); 2 tbsp **pine nuts**; 100ml **chicken stock**; 8 small rounds of **baguette** and 1 fat clove **garlic**, peeled; **salt, black pepper**.*

Put the lemons and the whole head of garlic into a pan of boiling water and bring to the boil. Cook for 5 minutes and drain. Slice the lemons into rounds, return to the pan, cover with fresh boiling water from the kettle and simmer gently for a further 2–3 minutes. Drain once more. Set the lemon and garlic on one side.

Season the pieces of chicken liberally with salt and pepper and dredge them with flour all over. Heat the olive oil in a wide, heavy casserole with a lid. Fry the pieces of chicken, a few at a time, until brown on both sides and remove them to a dish. This will take about 10 minutes for each batch. Turn the heat down very low.

In the same oil, with more added if necessary, soften the onions with the ham or lardons and the cloves of boiled garlic, until pale golden (at least 10 minutes). Add the white wine, let it bubble for a minute, then add the chicken, slices of lemon and pine nuts. Add the stock, season lightly, cover the pan and cook for 10 minutes, turning the pieces of chicken once. Remove the garlic and place the lid back on the pan.

Press or squeeze out the garlic pulp, removing the skins, return the pulp to the sauce, stir it in and let everything bubble once or twice over a low heat. Serve with rounds of crunchy *baguette*, rubbed with garlic and fried to a golden brown. (Serves 4.)

Chicken with Thyme
Le poulet au thym

This basic and rustic dish can be rustled up quickly and has simple ingredients. It is a real Languedoc standby, described by Albin Marty, the food-writer from Béziers, as a dish from the *garrigue*, and it is made with highly aromatic wild thyme, which grows freely everywhere. Clustering by the sides of the road in any rocky place, the twisting stems barely hang onto life during the hot summer days, and the leaves darken to a metallic grey. They return to a soft grey-green with the autumn rains. In spring, when they flower profusely, they attract crowds of bees and you can buy thyme honey. I cannot think of anything more special. The taste of the leaves is warm and earthy, an essential flavour of the Midi.

> *4 **chicken thighs** and 4 **drumsticks**, preferably free-range; 1 tbsp **goose** or **duck fat** or **olive oil**; 8–12 unpeeled cloves of **garlic**; 100ml **marc** or **Armagnac**; 2 tsp **dried thyme** or **fresh thyme leaves and flowers**, stalks removed; 1 tsp cracked **black pepper**; 1 tbsp **flour**; 250ml **dry white wine**; ½ **chicken stock cube; salt.**

Fry the pieces of chicken in the fat or oil over a medium heat, with the unpeeled cloves of garlic, turning everything from time to time, until golden on all sides – continue for at least 12 minutes, but remove the garlic when it starts to get too brown. Pour on the marc or Armagnac and flame it.

Add the thyme and pepper, a little salt and the flour. Add the white wine, stir it round until you have a smooth sauce, add the stock cube, cover the pan and simmer until the chicken is just cooked through, about 10 minutes. (Serves 4.)

Chicken with Garlic and Anchovies
Poulet à la languedocienne

You can still hear cockerels crowing in most Languedoc villages, although the young people are less keen on keeping rabbits and poultry than their grandparents. This simple recipe would originally have included the whole chicken, cut in eight pieces, but you can make it with just the legs as the breasts tend to get a bit dry in the oven. I have added a small quantity of cream to the rather short *jus*, but it is also good without.

*4 **chicken drum sticks** and 4 **chicken thighs**; 2–4 cloves **garlic**, peeled and chopped; 8 **anchovy fillets**, chopped; juice ½ **lemon**; 4 tbsp **olive oil**; 3–4 tbsp **single cream**, whisked to a foam; **coarse salt, pepper**.*

Heat the oven to 220°C. Pound the garlic and anchovies to a paste in a pestle and mortar (adding a bit of coarse salt makes this easier), or pulse them in the small bowl of a food processor. Add the lemon juice, pepper and then gradually mix in the olive oil.

Put the pieces of chicken, skin side up, in a roasting tin and roast for 20 minutes. Lower the heat to 180°C.

Whisk the anchovy mixture and spread it over the pieces of chicken. Return them to the oven and cook for a further 10 minutes. If the skin of the chicken starts to look too dark, lower the heat. The lemon juice tends to blacken if overcooked, but it will still taste good.

When they are cooked through, put the meat in a heated dish to rest while you make the *jus*. Heat up the pan juices and add the cream, whisking it in. If there does not seem to be enough sauce, add a few tablespoons of chicken stock and more cream and cook a few minutes more. Pour the juices over the chicken and serve with a green salad. (Serves 4.)

Chicken with Dried and Fresh Mushrooms
Poulet à la roussillonnaise

The depth of flavour of this excellent dish depends on the quality of the chicken, on incorporating the mushroom soaking water and on the flavour of the tomatoes – it is also worth buying good quality dried ceps, as the cheap ones can be gritty and tough.

When buying poultry in France, the magic word to look for is *fermière* or *fermier,* meaning from a farm that cares about its poultry and raises it in a traditional way. If you can find a *Chapon fermier* or a *Poularde fermière,* these are chickens raised by hand for local distribution, a far cry from factory-farmed poultry – look out for *Poularde Fermière du Languedoc,* or *…des Cévennes, …d'Oc, …des Garrigues* or *…du Lauragais,* then you will know that you are getting a bird with a decent flavour and texture.

> *1 really good quality, large* **chicken** *cut in 8 pieces, or 8 chicken drumsticks and thighs; 30g dried* **ceps***; 1* **onion***, finely chopped; 1 clove* **garlic***, chopped; 50g* **lardons***; 4–5 tbsp* **olive oil***; 125g fresh* **button mushrooms***, cleaned and sliced; 4 tbsp* **tomato sauce** *(page 98) or tinned passata (sieved) tomatoes; 1* **clove***; 1 tsp* **tomato purée***; 12–18 stoned* **green olives***, sliced lengthwise into quarters if large; 125ml* **dry white wine***; 500ml* **chicken stock** *or use chicken stock cube (if no chicken stock available);* **salt, pepper***.*

Soak the ceps in 150ml of warm water for 20 minutes. Fry the onions, garlic and lardons carefully in 2 tablespoons of olive oil until soft and nicely browned. Make sure they do not catch, as black bits of onion will ruin the dish. Add the sliced fresh mushrooms, season with pepper and a little fine salt and allow to cook gently for 10 minutes, so that their juices run out and then reduce.

Lift the soaked dried mushrooms out of their juice and squeeze gently. Place them on a board and chop the larger pieces in half. Add them to the pan and stir them in well, then add the tomato sauce or passata, the clove and the tomato purée. Add the green olives for flavour.

Pour in the wine and stir, scraping the bottom of the pan to combine the browned juices with the liquid. Cook gently for 10 minutes until reduced. Strain the soaking liquid from the mushrooms into the pan, then add the stock, season and simmer for 10 minutes.

Season the chicken with salt and freshly ground pepper all over, and fry in the remaining olive oil until well-browned on both sides. Put the legs and thighs into the mushroom sauce and simmer, covered for 10 minutes. Add the chicken breasts and wings, if using them, and cook for a further 7–8 minutes, until chicken is just cooked but still very juicy. If the sauce is too liquid, remove the chicken, and simmer the sauce down until it is a bit more concentrated, taste for seasoning, return the chicken, heat through and serve. (Serves 4.)

Ragoût of Chicken Wings and Giblets
Ragoût d'escoubilles

This little stew from the Aude, made with chicken wings and gizzards or a mixture of the two, is typical of Languedoc. Using the lesser bits of the bird together with plentiful vegetables, it makes something very tasty out of little. If you could add fresh ceps that you had just picked in the mountains (which cost you nothing), it would be a strikingly good as well as a cheap dish. Chicken giblets are available at some halal butchers. Some say that gizzards are unacceptably tough and suggest parboiling them for over an hour before finishing. I have recommended extending the cooking time if you use them. Another remedy is to parboil them for a short time on their own then marinate them in oil, vinegar and herbs to break down the tissue.

> *500g **chicken wings** and/or cleaned and skinned **gizzards** (you can also add necks); 1 tbsp **goose fat**; 1 tbsp **olive oil**; 2 small **onions**, finely chopped; 2 **carrots**, finely diced; 1 large stick **celery**, finely diced; 250g **mushrooms** – button mushrooms or ceps, sliced; 100ml **white wine** or water; 2 **tomatoes**, skinned and chopped; 20 stoned **black olives**; 2 sprigs **thyme** or ½ tsp dried thyme; chopped **parsley**; **salt, pepper**.*

Heat the goose fat and olive oil in a large sauté pan, add the onions and let them soften for 10 minutes, over a low heat, stirring from time to time. Turn up the heat a little, add the chicken wings and gizzards and cook for about 5 minutes, turning them over to colour lightly. Add the carrots and celery and continue to cook for another 5–10 minutes, turning, then add the mushrooms. Cook for a little longer, until the mushrooms are cooked, and add the wine or water, tomatoes, olives and thyme. Season well and cover the pan; simmer for 45 minutes for chicken wings on their own, 1 hour 15 minutes if using gizzards. Stir occasionally and add more water if it is drying out. Sprinkle with parsley before serving. (Serves 4.)

Chicken Stuffed with *chorizo* and Black Olives
Poulet au chorizo et aux olives

This is a beautiful way to serve a chicken. The stuffing and the small amount of sauce in which it braises keep the bird succulent and give the juices a mellow, satisfying taste. Guinea fowl, which can be a trifle dry, is most enjoyable cooked like this.

1 free-range **chicken** *or* **guinea fowl** *weighing about 1.5kg.*

For the stuffing:
100g hot **chorizo sausage**; *1* **chicken liver** *and* **heart**, *if available, chopped; 2 tbsp* **olive oil**; *1–2 fresh pork* **sausages**, *skins removed; 1 slice* **white bread**, *crusts removed, torn into small pieces; 2 tbsp stoned* **black olives**, *chopped; 2–3 sprigs of* **thyme**.

For the chicken:
2–3 tbsp **olive oil**; *1* **onion**, *chopped; 2 cloves* **garlic**, *chopped; 1 large* **tomato**, *skinned and chopped or 200g canned* **tomatoes**; *2* **bay leaves**; *2 sprigs* **thyme**; *200ml* **dry white wine**; *100ml* **chicken stock**; *salt,* **pepper**.

Remove any yellowish or greenish bits from the chicken liver. Chop it and the heart into small pieces.

To make the stuffing, skin the *chorizo* sausages and slice them lengthwise, then across, to make small chunks. Heat a little olive oil in a frying-pan and add the pieces of *chorizo*, the chopped liver and heart, the crumbled pork sausage and the torn-up bread. Sauter for 4 minutes, over a medium heat. Mix in the olives and a pinch or two of thyme, allow to cool a bit, tipping the pan to let the oil run out of the stuffing.

Heat 2 tablespoons of olive oil in a casserole large enough to take the bird, or you can use the reddish oil from the stuffing. Brown the chicken all over until it is golden and then remove it to a dish.

Using a spoon, push the stuffing inside the bird. (Any left over can go into the sauce with the tomatoes and herbs.)

Soften the onion and garlic in the oil in the casserole, then add the tomato and herbs (you are making a *sofregit*). Let them cook for 3–4 minutes, then add the white wine and simmer for 2–3 minutes before adding the chicken stock. Season with salt and pepper and replace the chicken. Cover the pan and simmer for 1 hour 10 minutes (1 hour for a guinea fowl, 1 hour 20 for a large chicken), basting the bird with the juices once or twice, adding a little stock if it becomes too dry.

When it is done, turn off the heat and let it rest for 10 minutes. Remove the bird to a carving board. If you like you can spoon off some of the reddish-gold fat in the pan, but it tastes delicious; pour the sauce into a bowl to serve as gravy.

Give each person some stuffing with their chicken and bread to mop up the juices. (Serves 4–6.)

Chicken with Almonds and Pine Nuts
Poulet aux Pyrénées

Comforting, warm and easy-going food, simple to cook and a good way to cheer up chicken.

> *4 **chicken thighs** and 4 **chicken drumsticks**, preferably cut into 16 small pieces; **flour** for dusting; 3–4 tbsp **olive oil**; 1 **large** or 2 small **onions**, chopped; 200ml **dry white wine**; 150ml **chicken stock** or water and stock cube; 1 tsp fresh **thyme**, stalks removed, or ½ tsp dried thyme; 2–3 cloves of **garlic**, mashed; 2 tbsp **pine nuts**, toasted pale brown; 50g **blanched almonds**, toasted pale brown; 1 bunch **flat parsley**, chopped; **salt**, **pepper**.*

Dust the pieces of chicken with flour. Heat the olive oil in a casserole or sauté pan and brown the pieces of chicken all over. Remove them to a dish and soften the onion slowly in the same oil for 15–20 minutes, adding more oil if necessary. Let it brown very lightly.

Toast the pine nuts and blanched almonds in a medium oven, or by dry frying them. Ensure that they do not burn.

Add the wine to the onions and let it bubble for 5 minutes, then add the thyme, garlic and toasted nuts.

Return the pieces of chicken, add the stock, season well and cover the pan. Simmer for 35 minutes, adding more stock if necessary, until the chicken is cooked and the juices have blended into a creamy, velvety sauce. Allow to rest for 5 minutes, sprinkle with chopped parsley and serve. (Serves 4.)

To Roast a Duck
Caneton rôti

Une canette is a young female duck, *un caneton* is a young male duck and *un canard* is an adult drake.

To roast the duck, preheat the oven to 200°C, put sage, garlic and salt inside the duck and place it – as it is, no oil or salt on the skin – in an oiled roasting tin. Let it roast, undisturbed, for 30 minutes. Then turn the heat down to 180°C and continue to roast (undisturbed) for a further 1½ hours.

Remove the duck to a hot dish and allow to stand in a warm place (e.g. the oven turned off, with the door open) for 15 minutes. Spoon all the fat off the roasting tin (which can be kept in the refrigerator for roasting potatoes) and use a little of it to fry the duck liver until just firm.

Make the gravy by deglazing the roasting tin with wine and orange juice (or you could use vinegar and honey) and a bit of stock, stirring in half a tablespoon of flour to thicken it. Cook the flour, taste for seasoning and serve in a bowl or sauce-boat.

Carving

Ducks never seem to get any easier to carve; it helps to know that the top thigh joints are tucked away right underneath the bird and you have to pull the whole leg outwards with your fingers to expose them, then feel for them with the tip of a smallish knife, wriggle it into the ball and socket joint and twist the knife to cut through. When carving the breast, it is best to remove the curved wishbone first, and to take off each breast in one piece. It can then be more easily sliced.

Serve with fried apples (see how to cook them in the next recipe) and a salad of endive.

Duck Breasts with Fried Apples
Magrets de canard aux pommes

In the west of the Aude, where geese and ducks are reared in quantities for *foie gras* or as roasting birds, many in the traditional way, look out for the ones described as *Volailles Grasses du Fermier* or *Volailles du Lauragais*, they have a fine flavour and a succulent, firm texture. The juicy duck breasts from the region are twice the size of ours, and a single one can easily feed two people.

*4 **duck breasts** or 2 large **duck breasts**; 3 large **dessert apples**, peeled and cut into eighths; 2–3 tbsp **white wine vinegar**; 2–3 tbsp **dry white wine**; 2–3 tbsp strong **chicken stock**; **salt crystals**, **pepper**.*

Heat the oven to 200°C. Slash the duck breast fat in a diamond pattern, without cutting through to the flesh.

Heat a dry frying-pan and cook the breasts, fat side down and, after 3 minutes for small breasts, 5 minutes for large, pour off the fat into a bowl. Repeat this twice more then, when the skin is nicely browned, turn them over and brown the flesh side for 3 to 5 minutes, according to their size.

Remove them from the heat, transfer to a roasting tin, season with salt and pepper, and continue to cook them in the oven for 8 minutes for small breasts, 10 minutes for large. Remove them and allow to rest.

While the breasts are cooking in the oven, transfer some of the duck fat from the bowl to the frying-pan; you will need about 2 tablespoons.

Put the pan over a medium heat and put in the pieces of apple. Fry gently on all sides until lightly browned (about 10 minutes) and put them in the tin with the duck breasts. Sprinkle them with salt crystals for a sweet and salty taste.

Pour off any remaining duck fat from the frying-pan and deglaze with the vinegar. Let it bubble for a couple of minutes, then add the white wine and stock. Let this mixture reduce by half and keep it hot, ready to pour over the duck breasts. It does not produce lots of gravy, just some rather mouth-watering juices. Serve the duck cut into nice, pink slices, with the pan juices and the salty, golden apples alongside. (Serves 4.)

Duck Breasts with Honey and Vinegar
Magrets de canard au miel de l'Aude

*4 small **duck breasts** or 2 large **duck breasts**; 2 tbsp clear **honey**; sprinkling of **thyme leaves**; 4 tbsp **red wine vinegar**; salt, pepper.*

Heat the oven to 200°C. Warm the honey so that it becomes very liquid. Slash the duck breast fat in a diamond pattern, without cutting through to the flesh. Cook them in a dry frying-pan to reduce the fat content as in the previous recipe.

Remove them from the heat, transfer to a roasting tin, brush them generously with honey, sprinkle with thyme, season with salt and pepper and continue to cook them in the oven for 8 minutes for small breasts, 10 minutes for large. Transfer them to a hot plate.

Pour off the fat, then deglaze with vinegar, stirring up the juices with a wooden spatula. Slice the duck breasts, pour the juices over the slices and serve hot ; the duck breasts should be pink and moist inside. (Serves 4.)

Duck with Olives
Canard aux olives

It would be surprising not to notice that duck is a fundamental ingredient in Languedoc, often appearing in the form of duck breasts or *confit*. They also enjoy a whole duck cooked with olives; I first encountered this dish in Paris, at Chez Allard in the Rue de l'Éperon on the Left Bank. This was alchemy; tender duck, yes, but duck with character, bathed in a ravishing sauce of tomatoes, olives, anchovies and white wine.

*2.5kg **duck**, with its giblets.*

For the sauce:
*1 tbsp **duck fat**; 1 tbsp **olive oil**; 1 small **onion**, coarsely chopped; 500ml **dry white wine**; 500ml **chicken stock**; 2 **bay leaves**; 2–3 sprigs **thyme**; 2–3 sprigs **savory**.*

For the duck:
*6–8 **anchovy fillets**; 1 tbsp **tomato paste**; 200g stoned **green olives**; 1 tsp grated **lemon rind**; 1 tbsp **cornflour**; salt, **pepper**.*

To make the basic sauce, heat the duck fat and olive oil in a saucepan and fry the duck giblets, neck, gizzard and heart, until golden brown all over. Add the chopped onion and sauter gently until tender and transparent, then add the white wine. Boil for 5 minutes and add the stock and herbs. Season with salt and pepper and simmer for 1 hour. Strain and reserve. This stage can be done in advance.

To cook the duck, preheat the oven to 200°C. Prick the fatty parts of the bird with a skewer to let the fat run out. Put it in a roasting pan and roast it for 50 minutes. Spoon off the fat and add the basic sauce, the anchovies and tomato paste. Reduce the heat of the oven to 160°C. Cover the roasting pan with foil and cook for a further 30 minutes, then add the olives and lemon rind and cook for a further 20 minutes.

Now you should finish the roasting by crisping the skin. Turn the oven up to 220°C and cook uncovered for 20 minutes or so. Remove the duck to a warm dish and leave it to rest while you skim as much fat as possible from the sauce in the tin.

Slake the cornflour with 2 tablespoons of water in a cup, and stir it into the sauce; let it simmer, stirring, over a low heat. When it has thickened and turned transparent, taste for seasoning and keep hot.

Carve the duck, put the pieces onto a deep dish, pour over the olive sauce and serve hot. (Serves 4–6.)

To Cook Duck Confit
Confit de canard

In order to have confit that is hot, crisp and juicy, a traditional Toulouse way of cooking it is to steam the confit in the top of a *couscoussier* (a steamer would do as well) for 10 minutes. This heats it through, keeps it tender and succulent and removes the excess fat. The confit can then be cooked in some of its own fat in a frying-pan until crisp and golden on the outside.

A second way is to heat the oven to 220°C. Place the pieces of confit in a heavy iron pan, fat side up and roast, uncovered, for 20 minutes, turning them over once. Take care when you turn the pieces as they are inclined to stick.

A third way is simply to fry it, skin side first, in its own fat (no need to add any more) until deep brown, then turn the pieces carefully and fry the second side. In all cases, keep the fat for frying potatoes later.

Serve it with *pommes paillasson* (page 253) or with green or brown lentils.

Duck Giblets with Fennel
Poêlée de gésiers de canard au fenouil

The correct giblets to use are *gésiers de canards confits*; these are made with duck gizzards, round and plump, and are preserved in duck fat after long simmering which makes them meltingly tender; the same method is used for *confit de canard* which is made with the legs and wings. *Gésiers de canard* are usually served fried, burning hot on a crisp green salad made with frizzy endive or leaves of lettuce. In this recipe from Pierrette Chalendar's *La Cuisine de l'Aude* they are cleverly combined with the cooked bulb of Florence fennel.

*250g jar of **gésiers de canard**; 2 small **fennel bulbs**, weighing altogether 500g, trimmed and quartered; 150ml **chicken stock**; 1 tbsp of **duck fat**; **salt**, **pepper**.*

Warm the jar of giblets in a *bain-marie*. Lift out the pieces and drain them on absorbent kitchen paper. Slice them into thirds and fry them in their own fat until lightly browned. Remove them from the pan and put them on one side.

Blanch the fennel in boiling salted water for 5 minutes and drain well. Put the fennel into the pan in which you fried the giblets, add the stock and a small nut of duck fat. Season with salt and pepper. Bring to a simmer and add the giblets. Braise, covered, for about 10 minutes until tender. Serve very hot with slices of country bread. (Serves 4.)

Duck with Muscat, Peaches and Hazelnuts
Canard au pêches

A nice plump duck cooked with ripe peaches, the roasting juices flavoured and thickened with sweet wine and a *picada* of nuts and cinnamon, is a sumptuous dish, which is based on Éliane Thibaut-Comelade's version, in her book *Ma Cuisine Catalane*. She recommends using slightly under-ripe fruit to counteract the richness of the duck.

In the Catalan country between Perpignan and the Spanish border, several delicious sweet wines are made – Banyuls, Rivesaltes and Maury are three of the best. Their use in cooking adds a deep, sweet musky flavour.

*1 large **duck**, remove the giblets and leave the duck uncovered in the refrigerator for 24 hours; 4 **fresh peaches** skinned and halved, stones removed (to skin peaches, cook 3 minutes in boiling water); 3 cloves **garlic**, peeled and halved; 2–3 tbsp **olive oil**; 30g or 1 slice of **country bread**, crusts removed, cut in cubes; 50g **hazelnuts**; ½ tsp **ground cinnamon**; 125ml **sweet muscat wine**; 250ml **chicken stock**; salt, pepper.*

Heat the oven to 200°C. Place the duck in an oiled roasting tin, season with salt and pepper and roast for 1½ hours, turning down heat to 180°C when it is golden brown and crisp. No need to baste it – it bastes itself. After 1½ hours pour off some of the fat and add the peaches. Continue to cook until well done – about 30 minutes more.

Meanwhile, lightly brown the cloves of garlic in 1 tablespoon of olive oil. Remove them and fry the bread in the same pan, adding more oil.

Toast the hazelnuts in a dry frying-pan over a moderate heat until brown. Put the garlic, its oil, the toasted hazelnuts, cubes of bread and cinnamon in a pestle and mortar or food processor and grind to a paste. Set aside.

Remove the duck and peaches to a plate; pour all the fat from the roasting tin and keep it for cooking roast vegetables. Put the roasting pan on a low heat and add the sweet wine, bubble for 2–3 minutes then add the boiling-hot stock. Reduce for 5–10 minutes while you carve the duck and put the pieces on a hot plate. Then add the hazelnut *picada* to the duck gravy. Stir and allow to thicken to a creamy sauce. Divide between four plates, smoothing it flat if it is thickish. Place the duck on top of the sauce, and make sure that everyone gets a juicy peach. (Serves 4–6.)

Guinea Fowl with Pig's Trotter and Turnips
Pintade aux navets

The French love guinea fowl, and they are indeed charming birds, if a bit
flighty and noisy. They have spotted feathers, Egyptian-shaped heads
and, I found when I tried keeping a few, they can run like the wind and
like to roost overnight in the trees. So mine were skinny and tough.
But in Languedoc they really know how to rear poultry – traditionally
a poultry yard was a good way for a housewife to earn a little money –
and their guinea fowl are tender and succulent. They taste very slightly
gamier than chicken and the meat is darker.

Use belly pork if you cannot get a pig's trotter.

> 1 **guinea fowl** (about 1.25kg) cut into four pieces (keep the carcass); 1 **pig's
> trotter**, cut into four pieces by the butcher, or 250g belly pork; 1 **onion**, cut
> in quarters; 1 **carrot**, cut in large pieces; 1 **leek**, cut in large pieces; 1 stick
> **celery**, coarsely sliced; 1 bouquet of **bay leaf**, **parsley** and **thyme**; 300g small
> **turnips**, peeled; 2 tbsp **olive oil**; 120ml **dry white wine**; 4 slow-roasted
> **tomatoes** (page 186, optional); **salt, pepper**.

Place the carcass of the guinea fowl, pig's trotter or pork belly, the
vegetables (other than the turnips) and herbs in a large pan and cover
with water. Season and place over a medium heat. Bring to simmering
point, skim, cover and simmer for 1½ hours, until the meat is falling
off the trotters. Allow to cool enough to handle. Remove the trotters or
pork belly and then strain the stock. Cut the turnips into chips if they
are large, otherwise keep them whole and cook them in enough stock
to cover for 20 minutes, or until tender, adding more stock if needed.
Drain and keep stock and turnips separately. Remove and dice the meat
from the trotters or cut the belly pork into neat pieces. Set on one side.

Heat the olive oil in a sauté pan and fry and brown the pieces of guinea
fowl thoroughly on both sides, cooking them in two batches. Remove
them to a plate, pour the white wine into the pan and scrape up any
juices, then add 350ml of the stock. Let it simmer, taste for seasoning,
and return the legs of the guinea fowl. Cook, covered, for a further 10
minutes or so, then add the turnips, the breasts and the trotter meat
or belly pork. Place the tomatoes on top, if using them, and cook for
a further 10 minutes. Cover the pan for 5 minutes to let the flavours
mellow, then serve with baked potato halves. Rather than the tomatoes,
you could scatter a *persillade* of garlic and parsley at the end. (Serves 4.)

Partridge or Quails with Garlic, Almonds and Orange
Perdrix ou cailles à la catalane

This recipe relies on two Catalan essentials, a *sofregit*, which is in this case a rich and complex tomato and vegetable sauce, and a *picada* to hold the sauce together. A *picada* is 'one of the bookends of Catalan cuisine,' according to Colman Andrews, author of *Catalan Cuisine*. I love the word *picada* – it isn't quite a sauce in itself, unless you think of bread sauce perhaps, it is a luscious paste of bread or fried bread, plus nuts, olive oil, spices or herbs all pounded together.

Authentically, and most enjoyably, this is done with a large pestle and mortar and the sweat of the brow, but it can be made more quickly in a food processor – keep pulsing for a long time or the texture of the nuts will not be smooth enough. The *picada* is a useful tool – it is used as a thickener, but it also adds heart and a whole spectrum of deep flavours to any dish.

*4 **partridge** or 8 **small quails** (4 if they are large); 3–4 tbsp **olive oil**; 5 cloves **garlic**, blanched in boiling water for 1 minute.*

For the sofregit:
*2–3 tbsp **olive oil**; 1 large **onion**, finely chopped; 2 **tomatoes**, skinned deseeded and chopped; 1 **carrot**, finely chopped; 1 **fennel bulb**, finely chopped; 50g **lardons**; 1 **bay leaf**; 3 sprigs **thyme**; 2 strips **orange peel**, blanched for 1 minute; 250ml **sweet white wine**; 2 pinches **pimentón**; **salt, pepper**.*

For the picada:
*1 slice or 50g of **country bread**, crusts removed; 40g **almonds**, toasted; sizeable bunch **flat parsley**, chopped; **salt, pepper**.*

Do this in three stages. First, make the *sofregit* or sauce. In a deep, heavy frying-pan or sauté pan with a lid, heat a tablespoon of oil and soften the chopped onions, seasoned with a little salt, until golden brown. Then add the chopped tomatoes, carrot, fennel, lardons, bay leaf, thyme and chopped orange peel. Season with salt and pepper and *pimentón*. Cook gently for a further 15 minutes, or until the tomatoes have cooked down and the mixture has started to thicken. Add the wine, season well and reduce for a few more minutes. Remove the thyme stalks and the bay leaf.

Next, season the birds generously with salt and pepper. Heat the oil and fry the blanched cloves of garlic. Remove them when they are golden brown, and keep them for the *picada*. Brown the quail or partridge in this oil on all sides. Set them aside.

To make the *picada*, cut the bread into cubes, fry it lightly until golden in the same oil as the birds, then put it into a mortar together with the almonds, toasted in a dry frying-pan to a light brown (not burnt), the chopped parsley, the fried cloves of garlic, salt and pepper. Grind to a fine-textured paste. (You can do this in a food processor.)

Now place the birds on their sides on top of the sauce, cover the pan and cook for 8 minutes. Turn them over and cook for a further 10 minutes over a very low heat. Make sure the sauce does not dry out, add a little wine or water if necessary. Stir in the *picada* and allow to bubble gently into the sauce. If necessary add enough hot water or stock to make the sauce as smooth as velvet. It is ready, with all its layers of flavour.

This dish is sometimes served with slices of orange – peel a couple of oranges, removing all the pith, and boil them whole until soft. Slice with a sharp serrated knife. Place the slices around the birds. (Serves 4.)

Grilled Quails with Garlic and Parsley
Cailles grillées

A simple recipe but a good one: hot, juicy quails bathed in buttery, garlicky juices. Eat them with your fingers. Trussing the birds helps keep the stuffing from falling out during cooking.

> 8 **small quails**, or 4 if large; **olive oil**; 4 cloves **garlic**, sliced; large handful **flat parsley**, chopped; 80g **butter** at room temperature; **salt**, **pepper**.

Sweat the sliced garlic for 3–4 minutes in olive oil over a gentle heat. Remove the garlic, leaving the oil to cool.

Chop the garlic and mix it with the parsley and the butter; work in a little salt and pepper. Divide this mixture between the birds, stuffing it into their insides. Stick a toothpick through the flaps of the cavity and tie a short length of string around the drumsticks, fastening it to the toothpick.

Roll the quails in the garlicky olive oil and season the outsides with pepper.

Grill the quails under a heated grill, putting them in an oven dish or a grill pan to catch the juices, for about 15–20 minutes, turning frequently with tongs, until the meat starts to feel firm when poked with your finger.

Remove from the heat and allow to rest in a warm place for 5–10 minutes, serve with watercress and *pommes frites* or lentils or be more extravagant and serve them with *tartiflette* (page 120) and a salad of endive, best of all of red endive, with a mustard dressing. Give people paper napkins and finger bowls as they will make a mess when they demolish the quails. (Serves 4.)

Chapter Seven

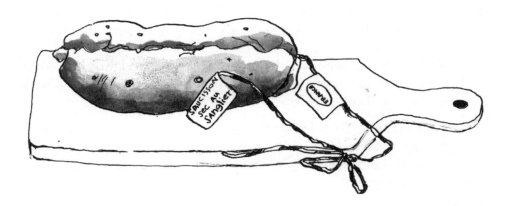

Meat

Rancher's Beef
Gardiane de taureau

These ranchers are the guardians of the black bulls of the Camargue, a breed of cattle reared in the wild salt marshes, prized for their meat as well as for their bravery in the bullring. Descended from the bulls of ancient Rome, they take part in the non-bloodthirsty French *course de taureaux* and the Spanish *feria* of the arenas of Béziers and Nîmes.

In the *course*, the bulls are heroes, entering and leaving the ring at a fierce gallop, usually, if they have been brave, to loud fanfares. They are not killed; the game is to remove cockades from their horns. They need no encouragement to charge the *razeteurs* – athletic young men dressed in white whose job is to snatch the cockades from their heads. The boys have to leap and twist out of the way to avoid the sharp horns, the crowd goes mad with excitement, the bulls do their best to get over the barriers and into the crowd and no one is badly hurt (although human blood may be drawn).

This *daube* is the traditional dish of these bulls' *gardianes*, fine horsemen all. Elizabeth David suggested you add brandy and serve the dish with croûtons, but this is often served with Camargue rice.

> *800g **shin of beef**; 1 litre **red wine**; 3 **onions**, sliced; 2 tbsp **vinegar**; 3 **cloves**; 3 sprigs **thyme**; 3 **bay leaves**; 3 sprigs **rosemary**; 2 strips **orange peel**; 3–4 tbsp **olive oil**; 2 tbsp **flour**; 12 **green** and 12 **black olives**; **salt** and coarsely ground **black pepper**.*

Cut the beef into large (5cm) pieces, place them in a dish and cover with red wine, onions, vinegar, spices, herbs and orange peel and a tablespoon of olive oil. Mix it round and marinate for 24 hours to tenderize and flavour the beef. Drain off the liquid, keeping the marinade for cooking the beef. Pat the meat dry with kitchen paper.

Heat the remaining olive oil in a casserole, coat the meat with flour and brown very thoroughly, in batches, a few pieces at a time, adding a tablespoon of oil after each batch. Pour the marinade over the meat, add the olives and season with a little salt and masses of pepper. Simmer gently for 2–3 hours. If there is too much sauce, remove the lid and simmer for a further 15–20 minutes.

Like all *daubes* this one will taste better and better if kept for a day or two. (Serves 4.)

Beefsteak with Green Olives and Anchovies
Bifstek Mirabeau

For much of his life Mirabeau – one of the French Revolution's earliest statesmen, and a child of the Midi – lived and worked as a politician in Aix; famously louche and extravagant, incapable of managing his finances, he was locked up for a time in the infamous Chateau d'If in Marseille harbour. A well-known gourmand in his day, he is quoted as saying, 'Frenchmen should dine generously and, under no circumstances, never less than four times a day.'

The ingredients of this dish, supposedly invented for him, are in the spirit of Languedoc: green olives, anchovies from Collioure, and plenty of garlic.

> *4 **entrecôte**, **fillet** or **rib-eye steaks**; 8 branches **tarragon**; 12 **anchovy** **fillets** in oil; 4 cloves **garlic**, mashed; 75g **unsalted butter**, softened to room temperature; 4 tbsp stoned **green olives**; 1 tbsp **olive oil**; **salt**, **pepper**.*

Pour boiling water over the tarragon and drain well. Separate the leaves from the stalks, pat them dry and chop them.

Drain the anchovy fillets, keep half aside, and chop and mash the rest together with the garlic. Mix into the butter. Add the tarragon, and combine everything together. This butter keeps well, developing its flavour.

Put the olives in a bowl and pour boiling water over them. Leave for 5 minutes, then drain well and chop them roughly. Keep them in a warm place.

Brush the steaks with oil and season with plenty of coarsely ground black pepper. Grill, preferably over wood or vine prunings, for 2 minutes on each side, perhaps a little longer if you are cooking thick fillet steaks or rib-eye steak.

Put the steaks on heated plates and put a lump of anchovy butter and some chopped olives on each one, let it melt over the hot steak and serve very hot. (Serves 4.)

Mariner's Sauce for Beefsteak
Bifstek marinière

These *mariniers*, tough men with pigtails, were the boatmen of the Rhône, who had the river in their blood. They plied up and down from Arles to Lyon with their barges heaved upstream by teams of struggling horses, mules or donkeys, up to sixty strong, each team with its *équipe* of riders and walkers or whipmen.

The boats were then rowed back downstream, carrying passengers and loaded with donkeys, grain and bundles of fabric.

It is easy to imagine that, rather than beef, the boatmen enjoyed a lot of horsemeat – whenever a horse injured itself, the tough meat could be made into all kinds of strong-tasting, long-cooked stews, laden with vinegar, wine, anchovies and garlic. There is still a very strong demand for horsemeat in the area, with regular weekly market stalls selling nothing else.

However the anchovy and garlic combination works beautifully with beef. Here it is used in a sauce that has the same powerful flavours as the stews, but it accompanies the more tender parts – T-bone or rump steak.

> 50g **butter**; 1 tbsp **olive oil**; 4 **onions**, *finely sliced into crescents*; 4 cloves **garlic**, *chopped*; 1 tsp of **flour**; 4 tbsp **water**; 12 **anchovy fillets**, *chopped*; 4 tbsp **white wine** or **sherry vinegar**; 8 tbsp **sherry**; 3 tbsp *finely chopped* **parsley**; **salt, pepper**.

Soften the onions and garlic in butter and olive oil for 15–20 minutes over a low heat, sprinkling lightly with salt – the anchovies will add more – and a few grindings of pepper and stirring to prevent blackening the onions – they should be just brown. Stir in the flour and let it cook for a few minutes.

Sprinkle with 4 tablespoons of water and cook a further 5 minutes, then add the anchovies, vinegar and sherry, and cook 5–10 minutes more, stirring the while. Add the parsley and keep the sauce hot as you cook the steaks in the normal way. (Serves 4.)

Another Version of Mariner's Beef
Filet de boeuf nautes

This is traditionally much enjoyed by the hunters or *chasseurs*. The beef is slapped into split *baguettes* and eaten standing up, boots on feet and guns on shoulder. Probably a shot of *marc* would go well with it early in the morning.

> 1 **beef fillet** weighing 500–750g; 5 tbsp **olive oil**; 1 **onion**, *finely chopped*; 2 cloves **garlic**, *finely chopped*; small bunch **parsley**, *finely chopped*; 4–5 **anchovies**, *finely chopped*; 6 **cornichons**, *finely chopped*; **salt, pepper**.

Heat 2–3 tablepoons olive oil in a saucepan and cook the onion gently for 10 minutes. Remove from the heat and allow to cool. Mix with all the other ingredients except the beef. Set this mixture aside.

Heat the oven to 200°C. Coat the fillet with olive oil and season well with freshly ground pepper. Oil a frying-pan with a tablespoon of oil and heat it until smoking; put in the fillet and brown it for 1 minute on each side. Transfer to a roasting pan and roast for 10 minutes, turn down the oven to 180°C for a further 10 minutes, then remove the fillet, transfer it to a deep plate and cover it lightly with foil. Let it rest for 10 minutes, then slice the meat into thick slices – a lot of juice should have run out by now. Mix the chopped mixture into the juices and muddle the slices of beef in this gravy. Serve with chunks of bread or in *baguette* sandwiches. (Serves 4–6.)

Braised Ox Cheeks with Thyme
Joues de boeuf braisées au thym

The head of any bull that has gone several rounds in the bullring is proudly presented by the butcher on a piece of fake grass or surrounded with little carnations. If you ever come across one, these *taureaux* take longer to cook than conventional butcher's beef, but are worth the time it takes as they are big on flavour. Ox cheek is a favourite piece of meat for braising, giving off a velvet-textured, rich *jus* with deep relish.

> *4 **ox cheeks**; 1–2 tbsp **flour**; 3 **onions**, chopped; 3 sticks **celery**, stalks and leaves, chopped; 3 cloves **garlic**; 3 tbsp **olive oil**; 2 tsp **tomato purée**; 1 bottle **red wine**; **chicken stock**; ½ tsp of dried **orange peel**, soaked in water and cut in slivers, or one strip fresh orange peel; 1 tsp dried **thyme** or one bunch fresh thyme; **salt, pepper**.*

Mix the flour with salt and pepper on a chopping board. Cut the ox cheeks into very large pieces, at least 6–8 cm across, and roll them in the seasoned flour until they are well coated. Heat the oven to 150°C.

Heat the olive oil in a casserole and fry the pieces of ox cheek until they are well browned on all sides. Remove them to a dish, turn down the heat and soften the onions, celery and garlic in the same oil, adding more if necessary. When they are well softened, stir in the tomato purée, then pour over the red wine, and let it bubble for 5 minutes.

Add the ox cheek and push it well down, then pour in enough stock to barely cover the meat – it should not be too wet. At this point you may want to throw in a bit more flour – not much – to keep the sauce the consistency of thin cream.

Season with more salt and pepper, the orange peel and thyme, cover and bring to a very slow simmer on the top of the stove. Let it barely simmer for 10 minutes and then transfer it to the oven and forget it for 3 hours. Test the meat with a knife-point, it should now be meltingly tender and bathed in rich, dark gravy. If it feels tough, turn the pieces of meat over and continue cooking for another hour. You can make this a day ahead – the flavours mellow if allowed to mature. (Serves 4–6.)

Cowhand's Oxtail with Fennel and Anchovies
Queue de boeuf des gardianes

The white horses of the Camargue and their riders, the *gardianes,* which roughly translates as ranch hands or cowboys, have had a certain magnetism for me since I first saw the beautiful film *Crin Blanc* (White Mane), which appeared in 1953. These cattlemen are serious horsemen whose job is to rear and manage the fine black cattle on the *manades* of the Rhône delta, and to bring them to the arenas for the bullfights, run them through the streets in summer, during village fêtes, or bring them in for breeding or the butcher. Many are exported to Spain.

The men dress in black felt hats, bright coloured shirts and chaps or jeans, and embroidered Spanish riding boots, while their bosses are proper dudes in black corduroy jackets, sporting string ties with silver clasps.

The horses are smallish and fast, with lifted, plumy tails. They are ridden hard and rough with large western saddles and cruel bridles. Their riders, of course, love to eat beef – the strong flavours and long, tenderizing cooking time of this *estouffade* go with the tough territory, the salt flats of the Camargue.

> *2kg* **oxtail***, trimmed and cut into pieces; 3–4 tbsp* **olive oil***; 2 large* **Spanish onions***, finely chopped; 150g* **poitrine fumée** *or* **pancetta***, cut into lardons; 2 bulbs* **fennel***, chopped; 8* **anchovy fillets***, chopped; 2 tbsp* **tomato purée***; 1½ tbsp* **flour***; 750ml robust* **red wine** *such as a Côteaux du Languedoc; 150g stoned* **black olives***; bouquet of* **thyme, bay leaf, parsley***;* **salt, pepper***.*

Heat the olive oil in a large frying-pan and sauter the pieces of oxtail, a few at a time, until they are well browned all over.

Remove them to a large casserole and continue to brown all the pieces. Lightly brown the onions and the lardons in the frying-pan, adding a little more oil if necessary. After 5–10 minutes add the chopped fennel and the anchovies and spoon or two of tomato purée. Cook, stirring, until the fennel is wilted and slightly softened. Stir in the flour, let it brown, then add the wine, stirring well. Transfer everything to the casserole. Season with a little salt – you already have salty bacon and salty anchovies and you will be adding olives – and plenty of pepper.

Put in the olives and the bouquet of herbs and bring to a simmer. Cover, lower the heat and cook gently, either on top of the stove or in a cool oven at no more than 180°C, for 3½ hours, or until the meat is coming off the bone. If you have time, let it cool in a cold place or the refrigerator, remove the fat from the top, and let it sit, covered, overnight to develop its flavours. Serve with country bread and a salad of bitter leaves such as frizzy endive and chicory. (Serves 4–6.)

Tripe from Abeilhan
Tripat à l'abeilhannaise

Abeilhan is a traditional, circular village near the sea between Montpellier and Béziers – originally, as in so many medieval Languedoc villages, the houses would all have been clustered around the château, with circular ramparts all the way round and an entrance gate with a door that was firmly shut and bolted at sunset. Those feudal days were bloodthirsty times, what with wars between nobles, marauding wolves and wild boar, not to mention neighbours, and this wall protected the villagers and their animals at night.

This is their method of making tripe, a popular dish which is sold ready to eat in most butchers. It is fairly typical of many southern tripe recipes. In the mountains, they use a pig's foot or two instead of a calf's foot, which can be harder to obtain, and I follow this practice. Traditionally, this dish is eaten at Carnival and is washed down with a strong red wine.

> *750g prepared* **honeycomb tripe**; *2* **pig's trotters**, *each cut into four pieces; 1 tbsp* **olive oil**; *200g* **lardons**; *2 tbsp* **flour**; *1 tbsp* **tomato purée**; *250ml* **white wine**; *2 whole* **onions**, *skinned and stuck with 1 or 2* **cloves**; *2* **carrots**, *sliced; 1 whole head of* **garlic**; *1 glass (100ml) of* **marc, cognac** *or* **Armagnac**; *bunch of* **thyme, parsley** *and* **bay leaves**; *2 pinches* **saffron**, *or a packet of powdered saffron or Spigol; 1 tsp* **hot pimentón** *or chilli flakes;* **salt, pepper**.

Cut the tripe into pieces about 6 cm square. Put them in a pan of cold water, bring them to the boil for 5 minutes, then drain them well.

Heat the olive oil in a casserole and add the lardons, cooking them gently, without browning, until the fat runs out. Stir in the flour and then add the tomato purée and the white wine and let it bubble for a minute or two. Add the tripe together with the onions, carrots and garlic. Pour in the marc or brandy. Put in the trotters and barely enough water to cover. Add the bouquet of herbs, saffron and *pimentón* or chilli and season well. Cover and simmer very gently for 2 hours, check to make sure there is enough liquid from time to time. It is at its best if you allow it to sit in a cool place overnight to develop its flavours. (Serves 6.)

Catalan Spiced Meatballs
Boles de picolat

For the meatballs:
500g finely minced **beef** *or* **veal**; *250 g finely minced fatty* **pork**; *250 g well seasoned, pure pork* **sausage meat**; *10 cm day-old* **baguette**; *5 tbsp* **olive oil**; *1* **onion***, finely chopped; 3 cloves* **garlic***, mashed with a fork; 2 tbsp chopped* **parsley***; 1 large* **egg***; ½ tsp* **cinnamon** *(use more if you like);* **flour** *for dusting; 1 tsp* **salt, pepper.**

For the sauce:
20 g **dried ceps***, soaked in 250ml warm water; 2–3 tbsp* **flour***; 150 g crushed plum* **tomatoes***; 3 small* **dried chillies***, crumbled or ½ tsp* **chilli flakes***; 1 tsp* **pimentón***; 150 g stoned* **green olives***; 225ml* **stock; salt.**

Start by soaking the ceps in 250ml warm water for 30 minutes. When they are all soft, remove them from their soaking water, but keep it for making the sauce. Cut larger pieces of cep in half.

Soak the bread in a cup full of water and when it softens, squeeze it dry. Heat 2 tablespoons of olive oil and soften the onion and garlic gently until soft and turning golden. Put the minced meats and sausage in a bowl with the crumbled bread, half the cooked onions and garlic, the parsley, egg, cinnamon and salt and pepper. Mix everything together thoroughly with your hands. If you have time to let it stand, this improves the flavour.

Take an egg-sized piece of the mixture and roll it into a ball. Continue until all the mixture is used up. Put the flour on a board and roll the meatballs to coat them well. Heat 3 tablespoons olive oil in a large frying-pan over a high heat. When it is smoking hot, fry the meatballs on all sides to brown them.

To make the sauce, heat the remaining onions and garlic in a large frying-pan, stir in the flour and let it brown, then add the tomatoes and chillies and *pimentón*. Stir together, put in all the meatballs and add the water from the mushrooms and 250ml stock (or water with half a stock cube dissolved in it). Season lightly with salt.

Heat, cover and simmer for 30 minutes. Taste the sauce and add a teaspoon of sugar if needed, but no salt at this stage. Add the olives and mushrooms and more water if the sauce is getting too thick, there should be plenty of it. Simmer for a further 30 minutes, taste for seasoning and enjoy the deep flavours of this magnificent dish. (Serves 4–6.)

Slow-roasted Shoulder of Lamb with Fresh Herbs
Épaule d'agneau aux herbes de garrigues

This is adapted from a dish served at Au Bonheur des Tartes, a tiny restaurant in Montpellier – little more than a hole in the wall, with tables outside in good weather. They specialize in the traditional cooking of the south-west. It makes a very impressive main course, especially when served with a gratin of potatoes. Try to get a shoulder that is not too fatty, lamb in the south has much less fat, and marinate it overnight if you can.

*1 shoulder of **lamb**, around 2.5kg in weight, shank removed; 8–10 sprigs of **thyme**; 4–5 sprigs of **rosemary**; 8–10 **sage leaves**; 3–4 **bay leaves**, crumbled; 3 **fat** cloves **garlic**, crushed or finely chopped; 3 tbsp **olive oil**; 300ml **dry white wine; salt, pepper**.*

Trim the lamb of any excess fat and put it in a large roasting tin with the flesh side facing up. Chop all the herbs and mix them in a bowl with the garlic and oil, and plenty of black pepper. Rub all over the lamb, trying to cover every bit of flesh. If there isn't enough to cover it completely, chop more herbs, mix with more oil, then cover the remaining bits. You should leave the lamb to marinate overnight if you can, but it is still good if it goes straight into the oven.

Heat the oven to 180°C. Pour the half the wine into the roasting pan and season the lamb with salt. Cover with foil and put in the oven, not too close to the top, then immediately turn down the heat to 150°C. Roast for around 4 hours, until the lamb is meltingly soft, topping up the wine if it is boiling away (or just use water). Slice down to the bone for serving, making sure that everyone gets a good taste of the herb-scented coating. (Serves 4–6.)

Braised Shoulder of Lamb with Garlic
Épaule d'agneau en pistache

I am including this well-known recipe since, according to Robert Ledrole, author of *Cuisine du Languedoc*, it is deeply embedded in the food memories of Languedoc and Catalonia.

It is also here because the whole is so much more than the sum of its parts, and it is a truly splendid, meltingly appetizing dish. For a thicker sauce, add some breadcrumbs to give more body to the juices.

The French name may imply the use of pistachios, but *pistache* in this case refers to the colloquial or argot phrase *avoir sa pistache*, to be drunk. *Pistache* was originally a drink derived from mastic and seems to have entered the language on account of its similarity to the word (again slang) *pitancher*, to drink. The lamb is thought drunken because of the wine used in its cooking. My comment in the preceding recipe about not having too much fat on the joint applies here too.

> *1 shoulder of **lamb**, boned, rolled and tied; 3 tbsp **olive oil**; 1 **onion**, finely chopped; 250g **tomatoes**, skinned, deseeded and chopped; 250ml **dry white wine**; 2 **bay leaves**; several sprigs of **marjoram**; 40 cloves of **garlic**; **salt**, **cayenne pepper**.*

Heat the oven to 150°C. Heat the olive oil in a casserole and brown the shoulder of lamb all over. Remove it to a plate and cover it with foil to keep it hot. Turn down the heat and add the onion, let it soften and turn light golden. Add the tomatoes, and after 3–4 minutes pour in the white wine. Let it bubble for 3 minutes, then add the herbs, salt and cayenne pepper and put the lamb back in the pot. Cover and put in the oven for 3 hours, turning it once or twice. If the liquid is evaporating too much, add a little more water or white wine.

Bring a pan of water to the boil and blanch the cloves of garlic for 3 minutes. Drain and add to the casserole and continue to cook for another hour.

If you object to a lot of fat, cook the lamb the day before and let it get cold over night. Spoon off the fat and reheat slowly. The meat is soft and the garlic mild and smooth. (Serves 6.)

Lamb Daube
Daube de mouton

*1kg boned shoulder of **mutton** or **lamb**; 1 **pig's trotter** cut into four pieces (optional).*

For the marinade:
*1 **onion**, sliced; 1 large **carrot**, sliced; 1 **leek**, sliced; 1 strip **dried orange peel**; bunch **bay leaf**, **thyme** and **parsley**; 1 small glass **marc**, **Armagnac** or **cognac**; 1 bottle **white** or **red wine**; 1 tbsp **olive oil**; 10 whole **black peppercorns**.*

For the sofregit:
*150g **lardons**; 2 tbsp **olive oil**; 3 **onions**, finely chopped; 4 cloves **garlic**, finely chopped; 500g ripe **tomatoes** skinned, deseeded and chopped; **salt**.*

It is preferable to start marinading the meat the day before you intend to cook it, but a few hours is better than nothing. Trim the fat off the outside of the lamb, cut the meat into large pieces and remove any large seams of fat. Place the lamb or mutton and trotter in a bowl with the vegetables, herbs, orange peel, marc or brandy, wine, olive oil and peppercorns. Leave in the refrigerator or in a cool place overnight or for several hours.

When you are ready to start cooking, heat the oven to 150°C. Make the *sofregit* by sautéeing half the lardons in the olive oil and adding the onions. Cook gently until the onions are soft and the lardons beginning to brown, about 10–15 minutes. Add the garlic, let it cook for a minute and then add the tomatoes, season with pepper and cook until reduced to a sauce.

Place the remaining lardons in the bottom of a casserole, lift the meat and trotter out of the marinade and place on top of the lardons. Season with pepper and a little salt. Put the *sofregit* on top and strain the marinade over everything.

Cover the casserole and cook for 2 ½–3 hours or until meltingly tender. (Serves 4.)

Lamb Sautéed with Green and Black Olives
Sauté d'agneau aux deux olives

This is a recipe from the Gard; the lamb of the region is pastured on the *causses* or limestone plateaux which produce meat that is lean and full of the flavours of wild herbs.

*1 shoulder of **lamb**, boned; 1–2 tbsp **flour**; 3 tbsp **olive oil**; 200g **lardons**; 2 large **onions**, finely chopped; 2 large cloves **garlic**; 2–3 **tomatoes**, skinned or 300 g tinned **tomatoes**; 3–4 sprigs of **thyme**; 1 **bay leaf**; 175ml **dry white wine**; 150g stoned **green olives**; 150g stoned **black olives**; **salt, pepper.***

Trim the outside fat off the meat, then cut it into large pieces. If it is fatty, remove any large seams of fat. Roll the pieces of meat in the flour. Heat the olive oil in a large casserole and brown the meat, a few pieces at a time. Remove to a plate and keep on one side. If the bottom of the pan is too burned, wipe it out and add more oil. Put in the lardons, onions and garlic and let them soften for about 15 minutes over a gentle heat.

Return the meat, season with salt (not much as the olives are salty), add the tomatoes and herbs and wine and bring to a gentle simmer, season with pepper and cover the casserole. Turn the heat down a little more and cook slowly for 1 hour. Add the olives and continue to cook until the lamb is very tender, about another 20–30 minutes. Taste for seasoning and serve very hot, with bread to mop up the rich juices. (Serves 4–6.)

Shoulder or Leg of Lamb with Potatoes
Épaule ou gigot d'agneau brayaude

The Auvergnat word, *brayaude* is rather poetically derived from the Gallic word for breeches, *braia*. Evidently Gauls fought their wars against Caesar wearing baggy pants, and dishes from this region bear their name (think of Astérix). This recipe is appreciated in northern Languedoc where the Auvergne meets up with the high *causses* of the Lozère and the Aveyron.

> *1 small shoulder or gigot of **lamb**, well trimmed of fat; 750g **potatoes**; 4 tbsp **olive oil** for frying; 4–6 cloves **garlic**; 4 sprigs **rosemary**; 2 **bay leaves**; 300ml **chicken stock**; 150ml **white wine**; 2 tbsp **olive oil**; 50g **butter**; salt, pepper.*

Heat the oven to 200°C. Coat the bottom of a roasting dish with olive oil. Slice the potatoes thinly, heat some olive oil in a large frying-pan, and sauter the potatoes in several batches, turning them so that they are just translucent and starting to brown.

Arrange them in layers in the roasting dish, interspersing them with the herbs, salt and pepper and cloves of garlic. Pour on the stock and the white wine. Place the lamb on top of the potatoes, anoint it with olive oil and butter, and roast for it for between 1 hour 30 minutes and 1 hour 40. Baste the lamb occasionally. Let the dish rest, covering the meat with foil, for 15–20 minutes. Remove the joint to carve it, and dish out succulent potatoes from the roasting tin. Serve on very hot plates. (Serves 4–6.)

Lamb's Liver with Onions
Foie d'agneau à la cévenole

This is reminiscent of the Venetian dish, *fegato di vitello alla Veneziana*, and if you want to try calf's liver using this recipe, it will be superb.

If you can obtain large sweet onions, they are perfect for this, which should have a luxurious texture and a piquant sweet and sour flavour.

> 500g **lamb's liver**, well trimmed and cut in thin escalopes; 1 tsp fresh **thyme** leaves or ½ tsp dried thyme; 3–4 tbsp **lard** or **olive oil**; 3 **onions**, thinly sliced; 1 tbsp **flour**; 250ml **white wine**; 250ml **chicken stock**; juice of 1 **lemon**; **salt, pepper**.

Sprinkle the slices of liver with the thyme and grind on plenty of black pepper. Put the fat or oil in a large frying-pan and place over a high heat. When the fat is hot but not smoking, fry the liver in batches just long enough to colour it lightly on both sides – as little as 30 seconds per side. Remove the browned slices to a plate and continue until all the pieces are done.

Turn the heat down to medium and let the pan cool down for a minute or two. Put in the onions and fry till they are brown and tender (this takes at least 10 minutes). Stir in the flour, season with salt and more pepper, and continue cooking for another few minutes. Add the wine and let it bubble for a couple of minutes, then add the stock. Continue cooking until the onions are fully cooked (around 10 minutes more).

Return the liver to the pan and heat for a minute or two – don't cook too long or the liver will dry out. Squeeze on the lemon and serve very hot; greens sautéed with garlic make a good accompaniment. (Serves 4–6.)

Braised Wild Boar
Sanglier en estoufffade

My neighbour at my first Languedoc house, in the top wine-making village of La Livinière, half-way between Carcassonne and Béziers, was a great hunter. M. André Galy went out with his syndicate, all old friends, twice a week in the hunting season, accompanied by his two charming dogs – fawn-coloured, with rough coats and long floppy ears, who couldn't wait to get into his van on hunting days.

He gave me a piece of one of the boars he shot, a cut from the hind leg; it was as intractable as a tree trunk, and covered on one side in dense, dark, hairy fat that no knife could penetrate. He advised me to cook it in the oven in white wine. What he forgot to tell me was to marinate it for several days first, and to cook it for three or four hours.

Fortunately, although most wild boar recipes require red wine, I found one using white wine, which comes from Valleraugue in the Tarn. I based my version on this, which was first published by Prosper Montagné, the originator of *Larousse Gastronomique*, in his *Trésor de la cuisine du bassin méditerranéen*, a wonderful little book from 1937 containing the original and splendid recipes of no less than seventy French doctors.

2kg **wild boar**, *cut into large pieces.*

For the marinade:
1 bottle **white wine**; *500ml* **water**; *12* **shallots**, *peeled; 1 tbsp of* **peppercorns**;
1 big bouquet of **bay, parsley, leek leaf, thyme**; **salt, pepper**.

Put the pieces of meat, trimmed of rind and most of the fat, in a bowl with the white wine, sliced shallots, peppercorns and bouquet of herbs. Cover and place in the refrigerator for at least 2 days.

Heat the oven to 150°C. Place the meat in a casserole with the marinade, add salt and pepper and cook gently in the oven, covered, for 4 hours, until tender. Remove the bouquet and serve hot. Simple and good.

You can add 500g of wild mushrooms, *morilles* or *cèpes*, or sliced open cap cultivated mushrooms, half an hour before the end of cooking. (Serves 8.)

Fréginat or *Fricassée de Limoux*

At pig-killing time in the Aude, participants (*les voisins du porc*) were regaled with a dish cooked outdoors in a big cauldron, called *frésinat* or *fréginat,* which was made with the neck or *goula* and the organs that go off quickly – liver, kidneys and so forth – and trimmings, all held together by stirring eggs and vinegar into the juices.

When it was tender and melting, after about 2 hours, potatoes were added and, at the end, a *persillade* – chopped garlic and parsley. Although the Aude is better known for lamb, it also rears excellent porkers. If your idea of fun is a Mass for animals or pig-racing, you will find it in Puichéric in the Minervois, at the January Pig Fair, where they serve *fréginat,* together with a robust local wine, in the street, to all-comers.

> *800g shoulder or neck of **pork**, trimmed and off the bone; 2–3 **pig's kidneys**; 125g **pig's liver**, or use calf's liver if this is not available; 4–5 tbsp **olive oil**; 2 **yellow onions**, sliced; 4 cloves **garlic**, peeled and chopped; 3–4 **bay leaves**; 100ml good **white wine vinegar**; 20ml **white wine**; 100ml **stock** – chicken or vegetable will do; several sprigs **thyme**, stalks removed; 200g **mushrooms** (wild or cultivated), sliced; 2–3 tbsp chopped **parsley**; 4 **cornichons**, diced; **salt, pepper.***

Cut the pork into pieces (about 2 cm across). Slice the kidneys into escalope-like slices about 1 cm thick, then cut these in half, removing the tough white centres of the kidneys. Slice the liver in the same way.

Heat a tablespoon of the olive oil in a casserole over a low heat and lightly brown the pieces of pork all over, a few at a time, adding more oil if necessary. Remove to a dish and brown the diced and trimmed kidney and then the liver in the same oil, but keeping them separate. Remove them to a dish and fry the onions, sprinkled with a little salt to stop them sticking, until lightly browned, about 10 minutes.

Add half the garlic and sweat for a few minutes without allowing to brown. Return the pork and kidneys, together with the bay leaves, and add the vinegar, letting it bubble for a moment to make it less harsh, before gradually adding the wine, stirring and scraping the bottom of the pan with your spoon. Add the stock and thyme, season with salt and pepper, cover and simmer gently for 50–60 minutes or until tender. The *fréginat* can be cooked in advance to this point.

Heat a tablespoon or two of olive oil in a frying-pan, throw in the mushrooms, sprinkle with salt and fry for 2–3 minutes, until the mushrooms start to throw off liquid. Add the chopped parsley and remaining garlic and fry 2 more minutes, just long enough to get the garlic fragrant. Add them to the pork together with the liver and simmer for 5 minutes. Beaten egg yolks may be stirred in at this point, but try it without. It already has a velvet texture and tastes richly savoury.

Serve scattered with cornichons. (Serves 6.)

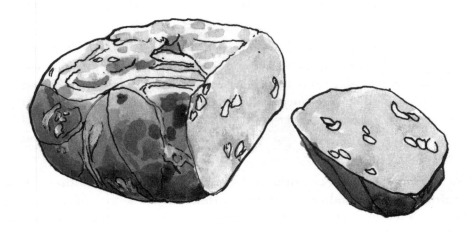

Fricandeaux

A typical dish from the Cévennes, *fricandeaux* are made with minced pork, both fat and lean, rolled into balls and wrapped in pieces of caul (the fatty membrane that holds the intestines and other organs within the body cavity of a pig, sheep or cow – you may be able to order caul fat from your butcher). The mixture may at times contain pork liver and also green chard leaves, finely chopped. The fist-sized balls are placed side by side in a dish and baked in the oven.

The *fricandeau* can be eaten hot, with fried onions like a meatball, or cold, with cornichons and a green salad, like a *pâté*. Accompany them with good bread and a bottle of red wine, says Marc Béziat, author of *Recettes Paysannes du Gard.* This recipe is adapted from his version, which comes from the small village of Saint-Paul-la-Coste, in the wild mountains of the Cévennes.

> *1 sheet of **caul fat**; 600g **pork belly**, complete with skin, minced; 4 pinches **quatre-épices**, or pinches of **cinnamon, ginger, cloves** and **nutmeg** (alternatively season them with **allspice**); 100ml **dry white wine**; 10g **salt**, plenty of freshly ground **pepper**; **olive oil**.*

Heat the oven to 220°C. Soak the caul fat in a bowl of lukewarm water to soften it. Mix the minced pork with the spices and seasoning and roll the mixture into six balls, each weighing 100g.

Spread out the caul and cut six large squares. Wrap each meat ball in a piece of caul and place them side by side in an oiled roasting tin. Sprinkle with white wine, a tablespoon of water and a trickle of olive oil and roast for 1 hour, sprinkling with a little water every now and then. (Serves 4–6.)

Black Pudding with Mushrooms
Boudin noir aux champignons

Open-cap cultivated mushrooms have enough flavour to make a good substitute for the local favourite milk cap mushrooms, *lactaires délicieux* (see page 38), or ceps. The most divine-tasting black puddings come from Asturias in Spain, rich with smoke and a touch of paprika, but any good quality black pudding will be fine, as long as it is not too fatty, as this turns out to be a very rich dish.

> *3 tbsp* **olive oil**; *1 medium* **onion**, *finely chopped*; *1* **bay leaf**; *½ tsp dried* **marjoram**; *200g* **black pudding**, *casing removed, cut into chunks*; *500g* **wild mushrooms**, *or* **open-cap chestnut**, **portobello** *or other cultivated mushrooms, cleaned and thickly sliced*; *2 tbsp* **flat-leaved parsley**, *finely chopped*; *3–4 cloves* **garlic**, *chopped*; **salt, pepper**.

Heat the oil and soften the onion together with the bay leaf over a gentle heat for 10–15 minutes, without browning. Add the herbs. Season with salt and freshly ground pepper and cook five minutes more. Add the black pudding and continue to cook for about 5 minutes, until crispy and crumbling, then add the mushrooms. Continue to sauter over a low heat for about 10 minutes, until the mushrooms start to turn golden. Taste for salt. Scatter on the parsley and garlic and mix thoroughly. Cook for a minute more, taste for seasoning and serve with toast, or with boiled or puréed potatoes. (Serves 4–6.)

Spare Ribs and Sausages with Lentils
Porc aux lentilles

*4 very meaty **spare ribs** (500g) cut into short lengths by the butcher, or 500g lean **belly of pork** cut into large pieces; 4 large **pure pork sausages** or 1 **boiling sausage** (to weigh 500g); 3–4 tbsp **olive oil**; 1 **onion**, finely chopped, about 100g; 1–2 **carrots**, finely diced; 2 cloves **garlic**, finely chopped; 1 **leek**, finely diced; 1 **bay leaf**; ½ tsp dried **thyme** or 1 tsp fresh thyme leaves; 1 tbsp **tomato purée**; 500ml **chicken stock** (or use chicken stock cube); 150g **green lentils** (lentilles de Puy); **salt, pepper**.*

Heat 1 or 2 tablespoons of olive oil in a casserole and brown the spare ribs or pork belly and sausages all over. Remove them to a dish and soften the onion and carrots in the same oil for 10 minutes. Add the garlic, leek and herbs and cook gently for a further 5 minutes.

Dissolve the tomato purée in the stock.

Stir the lentils into the meat pan and when they are well coated with oil, pour on the stock. Put in the spare ribs and sausages, pushing them into the lentils, season lightly, cover the casserole and simmer until the lentils are done; it will take 40–60 minutes, depending on how chewy or soft you like them. If there is too much liquid, continue to cook with the lid off until you have a thicker texture. (Serves 4.)

Loin of Pork with Red Wine Vinegar
Porc campagnarde au vinaigre et vin rouge

To the west of the Aude lies a district called the Quercorb – a place of deep valleys, oak trees, acorns, pigs and fine *jambon de pays*. Pigs are often raised in the traditional way. Recently, forty or so farms producing their own mature and sizeable pigs as well as artisanal charcuterie have formed a co-operative. Look for *saucissons secs* and *saucisses sèches* labelled with the words 'Aude – Pays Cathare', and try the amazingly good fresh sausages – butchers everywhere here make the finest, all pure pork without any padding.

Roast pork in the Aude is sometimes *cochon de lait* or sucking pig, which is boned and rubbed inside with aromatic sage, wild thyme and savory – pounded in a mortar with salt or mixed with butter. I have adapted the idea for a loin of pork.

> *2 lbs boned **loin of pork**, rind removed, but fat left in place; several sprigs of fresh **thyme**, leaves only or 1 tsp dried thyme; 5–6 **sage leaves**, finely chopped or 1 tsp dried sage; optional – 1 tsp dried or fresh **savory**; 1½ tsp **coarse salt**; 2 tbsp **olive oil**; 2 tbsp **red wine vinegar**; 1 glass – 200ml – **red wine**, preferably Minervois; 1 bunch **watercress**, washed and dried; **salt, pepper**.*

Start preparing the pork a few hours in advance or even the day before if possible. Pound the herbs together with the salt and pepper in a mortar.

Carefully make diagonal slashes in the pork fat, cutting almost down to the flesh. Rub the fragrant herb mixture into the cuts and all over the meat and leave in a cool place to absorb the flavours for as long as possible, or in the fridge overnight.

Heat the oven to 200°C. Heat the olive oil in a casserole that will just fit the meat. Brown the pork, turning it over until it is golden on all sides. Add the vinegar, let it bubble once and then add the red wine. Cover and transfer to the oven for 35 minutes to an hour, according to how thick the piece of meat is. Turn the meat over 2–3 times while it cooks, and add a little water to the casserole if the juices are drying out.

When it is done, transfer it to a plate and allow it to rest, covered with foil, for 10 minutes. Boil the juices until they are slightly syrupy, shaking the pan to emulsify them. Carve the pork, which should be very juicy and tender, and serve with the pan juices and with watercress. (Serves 4.)

Roast Loin of Pork with Fennel
Longe de porc au fenouil

In August, with wild fennel plants turning the verges yellow with their flowers, it is hard to resist using fennel in everything. The warm aniseed flavour of the stalks and seeds partners pork particularly well. You can use wild fennel freshly picked or dried, but fresh is best for this recipe. The Pernod picks up and emphasizes the flavour. Sweet onions, like the ones from Citou or Lézignan-la-Cèbe, are the best for this dish. The cooking time will depend on the thickness of the loin.

*1kg **loin of pork**, skinned, boned and rolled; 60g **fresh fennel fronds** and pieces of **fennel bulb**, washed and finely chopped; ½ tsp **fennel seeds**, pounded; 2 cloves **garlic**, mashed; 4 tbsp **olive oil**; 350ml **white wine**; 1 tbsp **Pernod** (optional); 6 **sweet onions** (Citou onions are available in late summer) peeled and cut in half lengthwise, leaving the base intact; 150ml **chicken stock; salt, pepper**.*

Mix together the chopped fresh fennel (the bulb comes from the greengrocer, and is sometimes called Florence fennel), pounded fennel seeds and mashed garlic.

Score the pork fat in diagonal slashes both ways, like a ham, using a sharp knife and cutting almost, but not quite through to the meat. Push the chopped fennel and garlic mixture into the slashes as far as you can with your finger. Roll the whole joint in half the olive oil and then press the remaining fennel into the fat. Place in a small casserole, pour half the wine and the Pernod round it, without disturbing the fennel on top of the pork. Cover and place in the refrigerator for a few hours or overnight.

Heat the oven to 220°C. Drain the meat and place it in an oval gratin dish or oven dish. Season with salt and pepper and cook for 10 minutes, then turn down the heat to 150°C and add the marinade. Cook, uncovered, for 30–40 minutes, turning the joint and basting it once or twice. Give a thicker loin up to 1 hour.

In a casserole, brown the onions lightly all over in 2 tablespoons of olive oil, turning them carefully so they remain intact. Pour in the remaining white wine and the stock and season with salt and pepper. Cover and cook, turning, over a low heat for 30 minutes, until meltingly tender.

Let the fennel-infused pork rest for 10 minutes, then carve into thickish slices and serve with the onions. (Serves 6.)

Ragoût of Pork Ribs and Turnips
Le ragoût traditionnel de coustillous et navets

This is real cold weather, mountain food which, unlike most stews, is best freshly made, as the turnips taste better when cooked just before eating. It uses humble inexpensive ingredients to make a dish of great character. In Languedoc there are long black turnips – the best being those from Pardailhan (see page 67) – but round, white turnips are splendid cooked in this way too.

> *800g thick, meaty **pork ribs** cut into short pieces; 500g **turnips**, preferably from Pardailhan; 1 tbsp **goose** or **duck fat** (or **olive oil**); 2 tbsp **olive oil**; 2 fat cloves **garlic**, peeled; pinch **sugar**; 100ml **fresh tomato sauce** (see page 98); 1 stick **celery**, chopped; 1 **bay leaf**; 1 clove; 100ml **water** or **chicken stock**; a few sprigs **flat parsley**; **salt**, **pepper**.*

Peel the turnips and cut them lengthwise into 'chips' about 2 cm thick. Heat the goose fat and oil in a casserole and brown the pieces of pork all over, a few at a time. Remove them to a plate, turn the heat down and fry the turnip chips in the same oil, together with the garlic cloves, turning them frequently over a gentle heat until they are lightly browned, after about 10 minutes. Add a pinch of sugar and cook a few minutes more.

Add the tomato sauce, celery, bay leaf, clove and chicken stock. Put back the pieces of pork and season well. Bring to a simmer and cook gently for 40 minutes, turning the pieces of pork from time to time. Sprinkle with chopped parsley before serving. (Serves 4–6.)

Stuffed Cabbage Leaves
Paquets de chou à la catalane

Traditionally, stuffed cabbage is a simple dish, but a complex recipe from that era of opulent dining, the Belle Époque, set out in *La Cuisine française. L'art du bienmanger* by Edmond Richardin (a work extolling the glories of the French provinces, first published in 1903), boasts a stuffing that includes minced pork chops, a blanched sheep's brain or two, a couple of *oeufs mollets*, a few leaves of lettuce and grated Gruyère cheese. He also recommends cabbage stuffed with chestnuts, sausages and larks, and served with a sauce of bone marrow and nutmeg.

This more homely recipe is a fine, comforting dish.

*1 **green curly cabbage** (Savoy is recommended)*

For the sauce:
*1 **onion**, finely chopped; 2 tbsp **olive oil**; 120ml **white wine**; 4 good **tomatoes**, skinned, deseeded and chopped, or 1 x 400g tin of tomatoes; ½ tsp **thyme**; 2 tbsp stoned **black olives**, chopped; 1 whole **chilli**; **salt, pepper**.*

For the stuffing:
*250g good **sausage meat**, crumbled; 2 tbsp **olive oil**; 1 good slice **country bread**; 2 **eggs**; 2 tbsp **pine nuts**, toasted; 2 cloves **garlic**; 2 tbsp chopped **parsley**; **salt**, plenty of freshly ground **black pepper**.*

Remove any damaged or excessively coarse leaves from the cabbage. Carefully break off fourteen outer leaves. Blanch them in a large pan of salted water for 4 minutes. Drain in a colander.

Make a tomato sauce. Soften the onion in 1 tablespoon of the olive oil, add the white wine, let it bubble, then add chopped tomatoes, thyme, black olives, chilli (which you leave whole for later retrieval) and seasoning. Cook to a fairly liquid sauce. Season well.

To make the stuffing, heat 1 tablespoon olive oil in a frying-pan and sauter the sausage meat until it starts to brown, then let it cool. Soak the bread in a little water, squeeze dry and crumble into a bowl, Mix thoroughly with the sausage meat, eggs, pine nuts, garlic and parsley. Season with salt and plenty of pepper.

Pat the blanched cabbage leaves dry, trim off part of the central rib, without cutting through the leaf, and place a heaped tablespoon of stuffing in the middle of each one. Use more for larger leaves, less for smaller. Roll them up into parcels – with the thicker part of the stalk towards you. First roll half way, until the stalk end is tucked under the stuffing, fold the sides in, then finish by rolling it up tightly into a cylindrical parcel. Give it a little squeeze.

Put the parcels in a shallow pan, packed in side by side, sprinkle with the remaining olive oil and spoon on the sauce, pushing it down between the parcels. Cover and simmer for 1 hour 15 minutes. Remove the chilli. These reheat very well, just add a little stock or water to the sauce. (Serves 4–6.)

Cabbage Stuffed with Sausage and Chard
Chou à la catalane

Winter cabbages in the Haut-Languedoc are curly giants standing in bare earth, flattened and knobbly, bred to resist the rigours of the Montagne Noire and considered at their best after a hard season (it can fall below –20°C). As Joseph Delteil says in his book about the simple cooking of our ancestors, 'There is only one cabbage, the curly kind that has survived the winter frost; throw the rest to the cows.'

These old-timer cabbages are solid, and have to be blanched for a while before they are cooked; a younger cabbage takes much less cooking. As sausage is traditionally made in winter, cabbage stuffed with sausage meat is a good cold weather combination, and a surprisingly fine one.

1 green curly cabbage, Savoy is ideal; 200g Swiss chard; 1 tbsp lard, pork dripping or olive oil; ½ onion, finely chopped; 1 slice (25g) country bread; 300g pure pork sausage meat, crumbled; 1 egg; 1 clove garlic, finely chopped; 3–4 sprigs thyme or 1 tsp dried thyme; 600ml chicken stock; a quantity of tomato sauce (see page 98); salt, pepper.

Heat the oven to 200°C. Remove a couple of the outer leaves from the cabbage and blanch these, and the cabbage itself, in boiling salted water for 10 minutes. Lift out and drain everything well, leaving the cabbage upside down in a colander to cool.

To make the stuffing, blanch the chard for 5 minutes in fresh boiling salted water. Drain well, chop coarsely and drain again. Heat half the lard or olive oil and fry the chopped onion over a gentle heat, without browning. Soak the bread in a little water, squeeze it dry and crumble it into a bowl with the sausage meat. Add the onion, egg, garlic and thyme and season well. Add the chard and mix it in.

Grease the bottom of a casserole with pork fat or lard and line with the loose outer cabbage leaves. Unfold the cabbage, carefully opening the leaves one at a time and bending them back till they crack, until you have a heart about the size of a small fist. Cut out this heart and replace with a similarly sized ball of sausage meat. Start to refold the leaves, placing a spoonful of the stuffing inside each leaf, and flattening it down, before you fold the leaf up and pat it back into place. Continue until all the leaves are stuffed and folded back.

If stuffing is left over, it is tempting to force it into the cabbage; it is better to make a patty out of it, fry it up and serve it on the side.

Tie string around the cabbage like a parcel, to hold it together. Place a couple of long folded strips of foil or greaseproof paper in a cross inside the casserole, with their ends hanging over the sides of the pan. If you put the cabbage on top of the cross, you will find these bands will help in lifting it out once it is cooked. Put the loose large leaves in first, topped by the tied-up cabbage. Add the chicken stock, cover the pan and simmer for 1 hour 20 minutes.

When it is ready, lift out the cabbage carefully, by holding the strips of foil (easier with two people), and transfer it to a dish. Remove the string and serve sliced into wedges, like a cake, sprinkled with the cooking juices. Put hot tomato sauce in a bowl, to hand round. If the cooking liquid is too thin, reduce it by boiling once the cabbage has been taken out. (Serves 4–6.)

Herb Marinade for Barbecues

My simplified, everyday version of a splendid recipe given by Paula Wolfert in her book *The Cooking of South West France*. It can be used for barbecued lamb chops, pork chops or spare ribs.

> ½ tsp **sea salt**; ½ tsp ground **black pepper**; 1 **bay leaf**, crushed; 1 tsp **thyme leaves**, fresh or dried; 2–3 sprigs **fresh rosemary**, chopped; 6 **mint leaves**, chopped; 4 **sage leaves**, chopped; 2 cloves **garlic**, coarsely mashed with a fork; 1 tbsp **olive oil**; **lemon** wedges

Put all the ingredients except the olive oil and lemon wedges into a mortar and grind them together. Mix in the olive oil and rub whatever meat you are going to cook on both sides with this mixture.

Let the meat sit in the marinade for an hour or two or overnight.

Barbecue in the normal way, but without added fat or oil, turning with tongs over a moderate heat, it is important not to overcook the meat, it must be juicy.

Serve with a slice of lemon, a green salad, perhaps potatoes and some good bread to mop up the juices. (Enough for 2 servings.)

Cassoulet – Le plat Gargantuesque

A dish worthy of Gargantua's monstrous appetite, cassoulet is a thundering dish and as such it should never be made or eaten in stormy weather. There seems to be some sort of sympathetic magic going on between beans and low atmospheric pressure, and they may turn on you. I made this mistake when we were eating a fine cassoulet in the gothic Hôtel de la Cité in the citadel of Carcassonne, and ever since that day I have always conjured a vision of gargoyles and heraldic flags, thunderclaps and purple lightning (as well as a quick weather check) whenever I start to think of making cassoulet. Keep it for cold weather, is my advice.

Some recipes for cassoulet suggest putting crumbs on the top and stirring them in several times, but many of the local recipes I have come across do not use breadcrumbs at all. They do suggest stirring the beans as many as seven times – seven being a mystical and significant number – which releases the starch from the beans, absorbs the fat and thickens up the juices, turning them suave and succulent. This effect is increased by the use of cheaper cuts of pork, which have a natural tendency to turn into a jelly.

In the Corbières they like to add a pig's ear or two and even a tail or two, a rather Spanish touch. Ideally the pork is from a nutty-tasting pig from the mountain forests of Haut-Languedoc or the Pyrenees, fed on acorns or hazelnuts. These pigs seem to run wild, making tracks through the woods, but are well looked after and fed a little something daily to keep them coming back to their owner.

The *confit* duck or goose should be, one butcher explained to me, drumsticks or wings; the thighs, which are more expensive, will dry out too quickly in the cooking.

It can be made with more meat than beans – two thirds meat to one third beans, when it is rich and succulent – or with more beans than meat, same proportions reversed, when it is cheap, comforting and rustic.

As far as vegetables are concerned, garlic is indispensable; use from half a clove to two cloves per person. If you want authenticity, it can be mashed up with pork fat. The best is the aromatic pink garlic from Lautrec, on sale at all the markets, which is known as the poor man's truffle. You can also add a little bit of tomato for colour, and a sweet onion or two and perhaps a carrot. The herbs – thyme, parsley and savory – can be bundled up inside a few leek leaves. Add a scattering of whole peppercorns and perhaps one or two cloves – nothing else is needed. Sundays, market days and fair days are cassoulet days.

Cassoulet de Toulouse

This version of cassoulet is based on a recipe by the *patron* of Restaurant Émile in Toulouse, on the Place Saint-George, right in the heart of the city. Émile is at ease with itself, has a warm and uninhibited feeling, an interior bordering on the flowery and a maître d' who is *'bien dans sa peau'* and loves his customers, his food and his work, showering all with jokes and encouragement. The customers themselves are businessmen in jackets, which they immediately take off, and smart, beautiful Toulouse businesswomen tucking into huge earthenware dishes of fish soup and cassoulet as they smile and raise their fine black eyebrows.

Rather timidly, I have left out the 80g of aged pork fat that is added in the original recipe, but it could be put in.

*1 **fresh sausage** weighing 250g–350g – ideally a French saucisse such as Toulouse or Morteau, or Polish kielbasa; 600g dried white **haricot beans** such as Soissons, cannellini or Spanish judion; 150g smoked **ventrèche** (rolled belly pork), **poitrine fumée**, or **pancetta** (streaky bacon) with rind, in a piece; 1 bouquet garni of **thyme, bay, savory** and **parsley**; 1 **carrot**; 1 **onion**; 1 **clove**; 4 cloves of **garlic**.*

To cook the pork:
*400g shoulder or ribs (échine or longe) free-range **pork**, cut in large pieces; 4 tbsp **goose** or **duck fat**; 1 **onion**, chopped; 1 **carrot** sliced; 1 tsp **tomato purée**; ½ **stock cube; salt, pepper**.*

*6 wings or 6 drumsticks of **confit of duck**; 50g **breadcrumbs**.*

Two days before you serve the cassoulet, soak the beans in cold water.

The day before, drain the beans, put them into a pan with plenty of cold water and bring to the boil, simmer for a couple of minutes then drain and start cooking them afresh in plenty of hot water.

Add the bacon or cured pork to the beans with the thyme, bay, parsley, a carrot and one onion stuck with a clove. Crush the garlic to a paste and add it to the pot, put on the lid and simmer slowly, add a little salt after 30 minutes and start testing the beans from time to time. Take them off when they are still firm to the bite, but no longer hard.

Meanwhile make a ragoût with the fresh pork. Heat 1 tablespoon of duck or goose fat and brown the pieces of meat. Remove them and throw in the chopped onion and sliced carrot. Let them soften a little, stirring, then add the tomato purée. Stir it in then put back the pork, add water almost to cover and add salt and pepper and half a stock cube. Turn down the heat and simmer slowly for 50 minutes.

Heat the oven to 150°C. Cook the sausage in the oven. Slice into chunks. Drain the beans, reserving their liquid. Remove the carrot and the herbs. Join the beans and sausage together with the pork. If necessary, add enough of the bean liquid to come almost to the top of the bean and pork mixture. Cook very gently for 1½ hours, covered. Stir the beans, and cook uncovered for a further hour, then stir again. You can add more liquid if necessary.

Half an hour before the end, brown the duck confit in a little of its own fat. When it is golden on both sides, place on top of the simmering cassoulet, sprinkle with breadcrumbs and cook for a further 30 minutes.

Serve with a green salad. (Serves 4–6.)

A Simple Paella without Fish
Riz au costellous

Paella has become one of the staple foods of Languedoc, served at every fête, bullfight, and on every Sunday market throughout the region.

Joseph Delteil, born in the Aude, surrrealist author and friend of Henry Miller, Georges Brassens and Charles Trenet, in his amusing and poetic book *La Cuisine Paléolithique*, lays out his rules for making paella, none of which we can hope to follow.

The three secrets of paella…
1. The fire.
2. Orange-tree wood.
3. The gesture: from time to time the cook, if she is from Valencia, passes her hand over the dish, in a circular gesture, and smells the air; as she smells it, she can tell if it is alright, or if it is sticking. If you haven't seen this gesture, you cannot imagine it – nor invent it, it is direct from nature.

Long queues form on Sunday mornings at Saint-Chinian market to buy the ready-cooked Languedoc version of paella, golden-red and dotted with black mussels and pieces of cuttlefish, steaming in vast black pans. It is said that the Catalan version is always cooked covered, whereas Valencian paella and rice dishes are cooked uncovered. I like this covered version, without seafood, which is a particularly toothsome way to cook Spanish rice. If you are afraid the rice will burn underneath, cook it covered in a preheated oven at 200°C, for 10 minutes, then turn off the oven and let it sit for a further 10 minutes to absorb the cooking liquid. The word *costellous* denotes various cuts of pork.

> *4 meaty **pork ribs** (costellous) each cut in 3 pieces; 6 **chicken thighs** and **drumsticks**; 150g **hot chorizo**, sliced; 4 tbsp **olive oil**; 2 **onions**, chopped; 2–3 cloves **garlic**, sliced; 4 large **tomatoes**, skinned, deseeded and chopped; 1 **red** and 1 **green pepper**, roasted, skinned and sliced (p. 187); ½ tsp **thyme**; 100g **Spanish rice** (bomba or Calasparra); 250ml **chicken stock** or water; pinch **saffron**; 1–2 tsp **harissa** or tomato purée; handful of **green beans**, cooked (optional); 12 **black olives** (optional); **salt, pepper**.*

Brown the pork, chicken and *chorizo*, a few pieces at a time, in olive oil in a wide sauté pan or paella pan with a lid. Remove them to a plate, turn down the heat and add the onions and garlic to the pan. Let them soften in the same oil and then add the tomatoes, peppers and thyme. Cook for a few minutes then add the rice, stir it in well and cook until it turns transparent.

Heat the stock. Add enough boiling hot stock to almost cover the rice, then add the saffron and harissa or tomato purée. Place the ribs, chicken and *chorizo* on top, pushing them down into the rice, season with salt and pepper and cover. Turn down the heat and simmer for 15 minutes without stirring. Add more stock if the rice dries out before it is tender.

You can add green beans and olives at the end. First cook the beans in boiling salted water then arrange them on top of the paella, with the black olives, for the last 5 minutes.

Turn off the heat and leave the rice to sit, covered, for 5 minutes to finish cooking. (Serves 4.)

Paella with Rabbit
Riz catalan

It is only further south in Valencia that they like to put snails in this paella; they do go very well with the rabbit; both provide food for free and have lived on much the same diet of aromatic plants out in the *garrigue*. Wild rabbits are sometimes called *lapins gariguettes*. I must admit that I prefer the taste and texture of farmed rabbit.

Penelope Casas, author of the excellent and comprehensive *The Foods and Wines of Spain*, adds mange-tout peapods to her Catalan rabbit paella, from which this recipe is adapted, or, as in the previous recipe, you could add green beans.

> *1 **rabbit**, farmed or wild, cut in 12 pieces; 3 boneless, fatty **pork chops**, weighing 500g with their fat; 250g large **boiling-type sausage** (**butifarra**) or black pudding; 250g **hot chorizo**; 4 tbsp **olive oil**; 1 **onion**, finely chopped; 4 cloves **garlic**, finely chopped; 100g **lardons**; 1 large ripe red **tomato**, skinned and cut into large dice; 1 tsp **tomato purée**, if tomatoes are too anaemic; 250g **Spanish rice** (bomba or Calasparra); 600–700ml **chicken stock**; 1 **red pepper**, grilled or roasted and skinned; 12 **black olives**; salt, pepper.*

Heat 2 tablespoons of olive oil in a very large pan, ideally a paella pan, but a large, deep frying-pan will do. Fry the pieces of rabbit to a golden brown. Meanwhile cut the pork chops into 4 or 5 pieces, and slice the sausage or black pudding and the *chorizo* rather thickly.

Remove the pieces of rabbit to a plate, add a little more oil and lightly brown the pork, remove the pieces and fry the sausages briefly, the black pudding only needs a few seconds.

Keep all the meat on one side, lower the heat and soften the onions and garlic together with the lardons for 10 minutes. Add the tomato and, if needed, tomato purée, season well and cook for 5 minutes.

Add the rice and stir to coat it well with the oil. Push the rabbit, pork, sausage or black pudding and *chorizo* into the rice and pour on the stock, which should almost, but not quite, cover the rice. Add salt if the stock was unsalted.

Cover the pan and cook for 15 minutes, over a low heat. Check after 10 minutes to see if there is still enough liquid. Arrange the strips of red pepper and olives on top and cook a further 5 minutes or until the rice is just tender. Remove from the heat and leave to sit for 5 minutes, before serving. (Serves 6.)

Rabbit in Red Wine with Chanterelles
Civet de lapin de forain aux girolles

*1 large wild or small domesticated **rabbit**, cut into pieces, keep the liver.*

For the marinade:
*1 bottle **red wine**; 2 tbsp **red wine vinegar**; 1 large **onion**, sliced; 1 **shallot**, sliced; 1 large clove **garlic**, sliced; 1 **lemon**, peeled and sliced; 15 **black peppercorns**; 4 **bay leaves**; 4 sprigs **thyme**; 2 sprigs **rosemary**.*

To cook the rabbit:
*2 **onions**, chopped; 1–2 tbsp **flour**; 1 cube **sugar**; 350ml **chicken stock**; 150g **chanterelles** or other small mushrooms; 1 clove **garlic**; 4 tbsp **olive oil**; 30g **butter**; **salt**, **pepper**.*

Marinate the rabbit in the red wine with all the other marinade ingredients for 3 or 4 hours.

Remove the pieces of rabbit to a colander and let them drain. Pat them dry with kitchen paper. Heat 2 tablespoons of olive oil in a wide casserole together with 20g of butter. When the butter starts to colour, fry the pieces of rabbit until they are a glossy, mahogany brown, then transfer them to a plate.

Turn down the heat a bit and brown the onions. Add a tablespoon or more of the flour, according to how thick you want the gravy – I do not like it too thick, and prefer to use less flour. Stir the flour together with the juices in the casserole until brown, then add a cupful of the marinade. Stir it well and then add the rest. Season with salt and pepper.

Add a cube of sugar and the stock, bring to simmering point, return the pieces of rabbit and simmer gently for 25–30 minutes for a tame rabbit, 1–1½ hours for a wild one, until the meat is tender. Turn the pieces of rabbit occasionally and add more liquid if needed.

Remove the pieces of rabbit to a deep dish. Cover with foil and keep warm. If necessary, reduce the sauce until it reaches a velvet consistency. Strain it and return it to the casserole.

Heat the remaining oil and butter in a frying-pan, together with the crushed clove of garlic. Fry the mushrooms briefly and add them, together with the pieces of rabbit, to the sauce. Fry the rabbit liver, slice it and add it to the casserole. Heat through and serve with baked potatoes and a green salad. (Serves 4.)

Civet of Venison
Civet de chevreuil

Originally a civet was thickened with the blood of the animal at the end of the cooking. Using a little flour instead does not spoil this rich and well-balanced stew.

If you buy venison from a good butcher, it will not be old and tough and will not need long marinating. In fact, if it is farmed venison, it does not really need marinating at all. I find you get a better flavour if you marinate for 3–4 hours rather than overnight.

*1.5kg of stewing **venison**, such as shoulder, cut in fairly large pieces.*

For the marinade:
*500ml **red wine**; 6 tbsp **muscat wine**; a few sprigs of **thyme**; 3 **bay leaves**; 1–2 long strips **orange peel**; 1 tbsp **juniper berries**, lightly crushed; 1 tsp **peppercorns**; 1 whole head of **garlic**, cut in half.*

For cooking the venison:
*2–3 tbsp **olive oil**; 1 **onion**, chopped; 150g **lardons**; 30g **flour**; 2 **red chillies**; 500ml **chicken stock**; **salt**, **pepper**.*

Put all the marinade ingredients in a bowl with the venison. Marinate for 3–4 hours, then drain in a colander, keeping the marinade on one side, and dry the meat a bit.

Heat the oil in a casserole and brown the pieces of meat on all sides, in batches. Transfer them to a dish.

Put the onions and lardons in the same oil and allow to brown for about 15 minutes. Stir in the flour and let it fry for a few minutes, stirring. Strain in the marinade. Add the orange peel and garlic. Stir to make a smooth sauce, throw in the chillies and add the meat. Add enough stock to almost cover the meat. Season with salt and pepper, checking the salt first as the lardons are salty, and simmer gently for 2 hours. The civet can be allowed to mature overnight and reheated the next day.

There should be plenty of juicy gravy; venison can be dry and needs this to complement it, but if you decide the braising liquid is too thin, strain it into a saucepan and simmer it to reduce it. Then return the venison and heat it through. (Serves 6.)

Roast Venison with Chestnuts and Red Wine
Rôti de biche du réveillon

Bilberry jam or blueberries are sometimes added to this dish from the Cévennes, which is often served at Christmas.

> *1.2kg **venison**, rolled ready for roasting; 600g **potatoes**; 2 tbsp **olive oil**; 100g large lardons cut from a piece of smoked **poitrine fumée** or **pancetta**; 200ml **red wine**; 250g vacuum-packed **chestnuts**; 2 tsp **sugar**; 1 tsp **mustard**; 25g **butter**, cut into cubes; **salt**, **pepper**.*

Remove the venison from the fridge and let it reach room temperature – keep any juices that may run out. Heat the oven to 250°C. Wash the potatoes and slice them into rounds.

Heat half the olive oil in a heavy pan and fry the lardons. Remove them and, in the oil and bacon fat, brown the venison all over. Remove the meat and deglaze the frying-pan with the red wine. Keep it on one side for making the sauce.

Put the venison in a medium-sized roasting tin and pour the remaining olive oil over it. Put the potatoes and chestnuts all round it and sprinkle them with olive oil. Season and roast for 15 minutes. Turn down the heat to 220°C, add the lardons and cook for a further 30 minutes, turning it after 15 minutes and sprinkling it with a little water. Remove it and the garnish to a warm dish and cover with foil.

Add the red wine in the frying-pan to the roasting pan; let it bubble, then stir in the sugar and the mustard, scraping the juices from the bottom of the tin. Season and simmer the liquid until the wine tastes mellow. Away from the heat whisk in the butter, cut into cubes, to make a smooth, silky sauce.

Serve the venison sliced, with its sauce and the roasted chestnuts, lardons and potatoes. (Serves 4–6.)

Saupiquet Sauce for Game
Sauce saupiquet

The first time I tasted *saupiquet* was in a little restaurant in the hills near Saint-Chinian. A winding track took us to a tiny hamlet, beneath which a perilously steep car park had been hacked out of the hillside. That winter's day it was ankle deep in mud, which was causing a lot of trouble to drivers and people in smart shoes, but local couples and families were picking their way eagerly up to the pink house where dinner was waiting.

The restaurant specializes in game and poultry cooked on a spit in front of a fire of vine stumps. We ordered rabbit, and with it came roasted Mediterranean vegetables and a bowl of *saupiquet*, a warm, unctuous emulsion made with pounded rabbit livers and garlic, vinegar and olive oil, plus some of the juices that dripped from the roasting rabbits. It was delicious and just what was needed with the meat.

In the past this dish was made with raw minced garlic and liver mixed with the hot juices in the dripping tray under the spit. For a rabbit, hare, wild boar fillet or venison fillet roasted in the oven, it can be made with cooked garlic and chicken or duck livers, pounded or whizzed together, and then mounted with vinegar and olive oil.

You can cook the garlic by boiling it for 10–15 minutes or, if you have an open fire, you can roast it *en chemise* – in its shirt – which works beautifully with fresh, new garlic. Roast it according to the recipe on page 100 or simply put a whole, plump head of garlic – still in one piece – on a heated grill over the embers. Turn from time to time and cook for about 15 minutes. Peel the charred skin off and rinse off any black bits. You can wrap it in foil if you prefer a less char-grilled, smoky taste.

> 2 *chicken* or *rabbit livers*; 1 *whole head of* **garlic**, *boiled or roasted*; 1 *tbsp* **white wine vinegar**; 4 *tbsp* **olive oil**; *salt,* **pepper**.

While the piece of game is roasting, colour the livers lightly in a tablespoon of olive oil for about 3 minutes on each side. Remove them and either pound them with the garlic, using a pestle and mortar, or put them in the food processor. When you have a rough paste, gradually add the vinegar and then the olive oil, a little at a time, to make an emulsion. Season with salt and plenty of pepper and keep hot. Mix with the bubbling-hot juices from the roasting tin

Chapter Eight

Vegetables, Pulses and Wild Foods

Confit Potato Cake
Crique

This is an everyday sort of dish, for an easy-going lunch to be eaten with a garlicky green salad, or as something to set off a roast chicken or grilled sausage. It can be made savoury with fried onions, or aromatic with a *persillade* of chopped garlic and parsley, while in the Aveyron, in northern Languedoc, the potatoes may be mixed with grated cheese – Laguiole or Cantal.

The potato cake, cooked from raw, particularly with duck fat or lard, becomes succulent, fondant and almost sticky – like a confit of potatoes, which in a way it is.

> *500g **potatoes**, peeled; 2–3 tbsp **lard** or **duck fat** or a mixture of olive oil and duck fat; 1 large **onion**, sliced; **salt**, **pepper**.*

Melt the fat in a medium (25 cm) frying-pan and fry the onions gently until they are soft and golden.

While they are cooking, grate the potatoes – this is easily done on the coarse side of a cheese grater, but the coarse grater blade of a food processor can be used.

Gently squeeze some of the water out of the potatoes and stir them into the onions. Season lightly. Press down gently with a wooden spatula to form a sort of cake, and cook over a medium heat until golden brown and crisp underneath.

Loosen the cake and turn it out onto a plate. Return it to the pan with the cooked side uppermost, like a Spanish omelette. Season again and return to the heat until it is cooked through. (Serves 4–6.)

La truffade

Another popular rustic cheese and potato dish from the north of the Haut-Languedoc, is *truffade*. It is not so called because it once contained truffles, but after *truffas*, the old Occitan word for potatoes. You can make it with or without bacon, and with or without *crème fraîche*. The cheese used is a young *tomme* or *tome*, which is soft, white and melting. If you cannot find it, try using a young Wensleydale cheese.

This dish should all be eaten in one sitting, as it does not reheat particularly well.

*500g **potatoes**, peeled; 50g **lardons**; 2 tbsp **lard**, duck fat or olive oil (lard is the most authentic); 200g **fresh white cheese**, preferably tomme or tome, cut into thin slices and then into strips; 4 tbsp **crème fraîche**; **salt, pepper**.*

Slice the potatoes into thin rounds.

Sauter the lardons in a large dry frying-pan until their fat runs out. Remove and keep them hot. Add the lard, duck fat or olive oil to the pan and heat. Add the potatoes, season them and let them cook over a medium heat, turning them over regularly with a spatula for about 20 minutes.

Add the lardons. When the potatoes are just tender, turn up the heat a little and add the strips of cheese and let them melt on top of the potatoes; cover with a lid to help the cheese melt evenly. Add four tablespoons of *crème fraîche* and heat through.

Serve with a green salad, or with *boudin noir*. (Serves 4–6. It is very rich.)

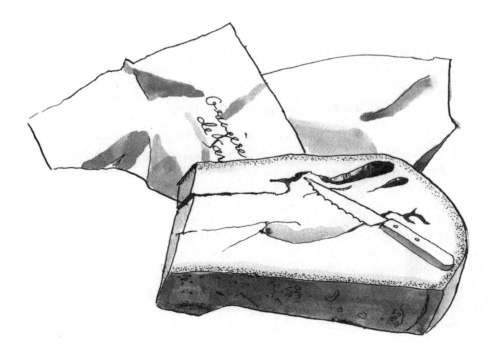

Doormat Potatoes with Garlic
Pommes paillasson à l'ail

Paillasson means doormat or strawmat, and the grated potatoes look like a golden mat when they are crisped on the outside to a golden brown. You can use goose fat for this dish, which makes the doormat even more chewy and succulent.

> *750g **potatoes**, peeled; 3 cloves of **garlic**, finely chopped; 2 tbsp **olive oil** or goose fat; 1 tbsp **butter**; **salt, pepper**.*

Work quickly with the potatoes as they tend to turn brown once they are grated.

Grate the potatoes either with a grater or in the food processor; squeeze them with your hands to remove excess water if they seem at all wet. Mix them with the garlic and season with salt and pepper. Gently heat the oil and butter in a large frying-pan

Turn up the heat under the pan for a moment then put in the grated potato and garlic and press it down into a kind of thin straw mat.

Cook over a low heat for 10–15 minutes, making sure it does not stick or burn. Flip the mat over or turn like a tortilla, by using a large flat plate, and cook the second side for a further 10–15 minutes.

Cut it like a cake and serve with confit and green salad, dressed with olive or nut oil and lemon juice. (Serves 4.)

Potatoes Cooked in Goose Fat

> *1 kilo small smooth **potatoes**, well washed, but not peeled; **goose fat**; olive oil; 6 cloves of **garlic**, unpeeled; 3 sprigs fresh **rosemary**; 3–6 **bay leaves**; 1 tsp dried **thyme**; 3 cloves **garlic**, peeled and sliced; 3 tbsp chopped **parsley**; **salt, pepper**.*

Heat the oven to 200°C. Bring a large pan of salted water to the boil. Boil the potatoes until almost cooked but still firm. Drain and allow to cool a bit. Heat the goose fat and olive oil in a roasting tin, while you cut the potatoes in half lengthwise.

Put them into the hot fat with the whole cloves of garlic, the rosemary, bay leaves and thyme. Jumble the potatoes round in the fat until they are well-coated and roast until lightly browned, about 25–30 minutes, turning them occasionally.

Take them out of the oven and pour off some of the fat. You can set them aside at this point, ready to finish off when you want them.

Well before you want to serve the potatoes, turn up the oven to 250°C. Remove the bay leaves and rosemary and squeeze the garlic pulo out of its skins. Jumble the potatoes round to roughen and break them a bit, scatter with half the parsley and and roast until crunchy, turning them over once or twice. This will take about 15 minutes. Add back the garlic pulp and stir it in 5 minutes before the end of the cooking Do not let the garlic burn, this is crucial as it tastes bitter when over-browned. Scatter on the sliced, raw garlic and the rest of the parsley at the last moment and stir them in. (Serves 4–6.)

Potatoes with Ceps
Pommes de terre aux cèpes

I recently made this with firm young ceps from the Carcassonne Saturday market – they had come from the Lozère, where it had rained heavily, while in the south we were hazed in September sunlight. Although traditionally this dish is cooked for at least half an hour, the ceps are nuttier and more delicate if cooked rather more briefly.

> *250g firm young **ceps**; 500g **yellow-fleshed potatoes**, peeled; 2 tbsp **duck fat**; 1 tbsp **olive oil**; 4 cloves **garlic**, peeled and chopped; 3 tbsp **parsley**, chopped; **salt, pepper**.*

Pare the stems of the ceps and wipe the caps with a piece of damp kitchen paper to remove dirt. Cut into pieces about 1 cm thick and 3 cm across. Cut the potatoes into small chunks.

Heat the duck fat and oil in your largest frying-pan. When it is hot put in the potatoes and fry over a good heat, turning them until brown all over.

Add the ceps and fry for 3 minutes, turning them, then add the garlic and half the parsley. Season well and reduce the heat. Cover the pan and cook until the potatoes are just tender – about 10 minutes. Remove the lid, evaporate any moisture and sprinkle with the remaining parsley. Serve by itself with a green salad or with duck confit, steak or roast pork. (Serves 4.)

Gratin of Potatoes and Mushrooms
Estouffade de pommes de terre et champignons

When they are in season, you can use wild mushrooms for this rich dish, *cèpes* or *pleurottes* – ceps or oyster mushrooms (or morel would be even better) – in which case you will not need the dried cep powder which is there to add a more powerful flavour to the cultivated mushrooms.

> *300g **small button mushrooms**, thinly sliced; 750g **potatoes**, peeled and thinly sliced; 30g **butter**, softened to room temperature; 1 clove **garlic**, cut across; 250ml **crème fraîche**; small handful **dried ceps**, dried in the oven until crisp and ground to a powder; 50g **Gruyère cheese**, grated; **salt, pepper**.*

Heat the oven to 200°C. Liberally coat a gratin dish with half the butter, and rub with the cut surface of the clove of garlic.

Arrange half the potatoes over the bottom of the dish, season with salt and pepper and anoint with 2 tablespoons of cream.

Cover with the sliced mushrooms and sprinkle the powdered ceps over the top. Season with salt and plenty of pepper, coat with 2 more tablespoons of cream and cover with the remaining potatoes, laid on to overlap like the scales of a fish.

Season lightly, dot with the remaining butter and cover with foil. Cook for 45 minutes.

Remove the foil and bake a further 30 minutes. Turn up the heat to 220°C, coat the potatoes with the remaining cream and scatter the grated cheese over the top. Return to the oven for about 10–15 minutes, or until the top starts to fleck with golden patches. (Serves 6.)

Marinated Mushrooms with Raisins
Champignons à la grecque

The chosen local mushrooms for this dish are *Lactarius sanguifluus,* a Catalan favourite known locally as *rovello,* or *lactaire vineux* or *lactaire sanguin le vineux* to give it its full title – milk caps of a reddish bronze colour – and *Lactarius deliciosus,* known as *roussillous, barigoules* or *catalans.*

Elsewhere, milk caps would be the right choice if you are a mushroom hunter. If not, portobello mushrooms work very well.

> *500g **mushrooms**, preferably milk caps – but chestnut or portobello mushrooms are good too, cut into fairly large pieces; 12 little **white onions**, root ends removed; 4 tbsp **olive oil**; 50g **raisins**, soaked in warm water for 30 minutes; 2 **tomatoes**, skinned, deseeded and chopped; 4 sprigs **thyme**; 30g **lardons**; juice of 1 **lemon**; 125ml **red wine**; 12 **peppercorns**; **salt**.*

Put the pickling onions in a bowl and pour boiling water over them. Leave for 2–3 minutes, then peel.

Heat 2 tablespoons of olive oil in a sauté pan and put in the small onions; cook them gently for about 15 minutes, until they are they are lightly browned.

Add the drained raisins, the chopped tomatoes, thyme sprigs, lardons and peppercorns. Cook gently until the liquid has evaporated, about 5 minutes.

Add the remaining olive oil and then the mushrooms. Stir them round a few times. Cook fairly briskly for 5 minutes, then add the wine and the lemon juice.

Season and cook over a low heat for 20 minutes, uncovered, remembering to stir them occasionally. Remove the twiggy parts of the thyme branches and allow to cool. Serve just warm or at room temperature; they make a refreshing first course. (Serves 4.)

Mushrooms, Mountain Style
Champignons à la façon de la montagne

You can make this with wild or cultivated mushrooms, but wild are
better, the best being ceps, which are plentiful on the markets after the
first summer thunderstorms in mid-August. This is typical Languedoc
food – simple, basic, easy to throw together and delicious.

> *1kg* **ceps***, chestnut mushrooms or a mixture of chestnut mushrooms and ceps,
> trimmed, cleaned, drained, and sliced (if using ceps, include the sliced stalks);
> 2–3 tbsp* **olive oil***; 3* **shallots***, chopped; 100g thick slices of* **jambon cru**
> *(Lacaune or Serrano ham) with its fat, or* **poitrine fumée** *(smoked streaky
> bacon in a piece), or* **pancetta** *– whichever you use, cut it into lardons; a little
> salt, as the bacon is salty,* **pepper***.*

Heat the olive oil in a large shallow pan, over a moderate heat and add
the shallots. Cook, stirring, until they are softened and transparent. Add
the pieces of ham, bacon or pancetta and let them just start to brown.
Add the mushrooms, fry for 5 minutes, then turn down the heat. Season
with plenty of pepper and a sparing amount of salt, cover the pan and
let the mushrooms release their juices over a low heat. Continue to
cook until the juices are absorbed again, but do not allow to dry out too
much.

   Serve, if possible, with an enormous sausage, and then get out your
walking boots. (Serves 4–6.)

Ceps with Chervil
Cèpes sautées

I learned this method from a friend who was a great mushroom hunter.
If there has been a lot of rain the mushrooms can throw off a lot of liquid
in the cooking. If you don't collect this liquid from the mushrooms, they
run the risk of stewing in their own juice rather than being sautéed.
The liquid can be reduced separately and added back at the end of the
cooking.

> *4* **ceps** *weighing about 200g each, or 800g of differently sized ceps, trimmed
> and cleaned; 3–4 tbsp* **olive oil***; 40g* **butter***; 4 cloves* **garlic***, chopped; handful
> chervil***, chopped (or use parsley or mint);* **salt***.*

Slice the ceps very carefully. Heat a tablespoon of the olive oil in a large frying-pan until it is really hot, but not smoking. Put in one quarter of the mushrooms and fry the slices, in batches, for a minute or two on each side – when the water in the mushrooms starts to surface, transfer them to a colander over a bowl. Continue until all the mushrooms are fried.

If your mushrooms are dry, do not bother straining over a colander. If wet, quite a lot of liquid will collect in the bowl. Return this liquid to the pan and let it evaporate to just a couple of spoonfuls, then put in the butter and when it starts to brown, fry the slices again, to a lovely gold colour, season them with salt and throw in the chopped garlic and chervil. Let it cook for a minute or two and serve the mushrooms straight out of the pan. (Serves 4.)

Preparing Chanterelles (called *girolles*)

Pick off any leaves or moss and trim the ends of the stems. If necessary, wash them very briefly – it's a pity, but they are spoiled if they have grit in them. Hold them under the tap in a colander, turn them over a few times – any with persistent dirt may need individual washing, but make it as brief as possible. Drain them first in a colander and then on kitchen paper, place more folded kitchen paper on top and and gently pat them dry.

Another method, told me by the market lady in Narbonne Halles, is quicker. Bring a pan of water to a boil, drop in the chanterelles, boil for 1 minute, drain in a colander, then spin them gently in the salad spinner.

To Cook Chanterelles

Heat some butter and olive oil, add the mushrooms and fry them briefly. They are best if cooked for no more than 4–5 minutes – if water comes out, pour it away. At the last moment, season and add chopped garlic and finely chopped flat parsley. Let the garlic cook a little, stirring to blend with the mushrooms.

Gratin of Artichoke Hearts
Gratin d'artichauts

Although they were enjoyed by the Romans, who sometimes ate them as dessert, it was from Italy, at about the time of the Italian wars at the end of the fifteenth century, that artichokes first took root in Languedoc. By the middle of the next century they were well established. The artichokes of the Midi are a totally different animal to the huge green Breton ones; enchanting little *violets*, eaten as small and tender buds, not even cooked, are sold in bunches of five, with their stalks and leaves. Artichokes at one time were thought to be an aphrodisiac – as the street cry boasts:

> *Artichauts, artichauts,*
> *C'est pour monsieur et pour madame,*
> *Pour réchauffer le corps et l'âme*
> *Et pour avoir le cul chaud.*

> Artichokes, artichokes,
> For ladies and gentlemen,
> To warm body and soul,
> And heat up your backside.

*10 or 15 **baby artichokes**; 5 tbsp **olive oil**; 2 slices (60g) **country bread**, not too fresh, crusts removed, cut in cubes; 4 tbsp chopped **parsley**; 4–6 cloves **garlic**, chopped; generous pinch **cayenne pepper**; juice ½ **lemon**; salt, plenty of freshly ground **black pepper**.*

Heat the oven to 220°C. Prepare a large bowl of water with half a lemon squeezed into it. Trim the artichokes by removing all but 3 cm of the stems and pulling off the outside green leaves. Pare or peel the stems and cut across the buds 3 cm above the base to remove the tough, spiny tops of the leaves. If they are baby, they will have no choke.

Slice them lengthwise, not too thinly, and sauter them on both sides, in a tablespoon of olive oil, until just tender, about 10 minutes. Lay the artichoke slices in layers over the bottom of a gratin dish.

Put the bread cubes in the processor or blender until you have fine breadcrumbs. Add the parsley, garlic, cayenne pepper and pinch of salt and pepper. Pulse for a moment, then add lemon juice and 4 tablespoons of olive oil and pulse again.

Spread the mixture over the artichokes and bake for 15–20 minutes. (Serves 4.)

Braised Artichokes
Artichauts à la barigoule

There is some controversy over the name of this dish – some people think it is named after a local mushroom, a milk cap called *barigoule*, which can be cooked in exactly the same way but, according to Occitan food expert Jacques Médecin, the word is a deformation of the Occitan word for wild thyme – *farigoule* or *farigoulette*. Either way, that earthy flavour is essential to the recipe. The thyme of the rocky *garrigue* is grey in colour, small leaved with ash-pink clouds of flowers in spring; it tastes of the earth. If you can't get wild thyme, use dried thyme.

*12 or 18 **small artichokes**; 4 tbsp **olive oil**; 2 small **onions**, finely chopped; 3–4 cloves **garlic**, peeled; 300ml **white wine**; 3–4 sprigs fresh **thyme** or ½ tsp dried thyme; 3 **bay leaves**; 3–4 **fennel stalks**, broken into 10 cm lengths; 1 tbsp **tomato purée**; 2 whole **red chillies**; salt, pepper.*

Prepare the artichokes as described at the beginning of the recipe above. Rub the cuts with half a lemon as you go. Next, cut them in half downwards and remove the spiny chokes in the middle with a teaspoon. Rub the cut surfaces of the artichoke halves with lemon and drop them into acidulated water to prevent them going brown. Cut them into quarters if they are large.

Heat the oil in a sauté pan over a medium heat and soften the onions for 10 minutes, without browning. Add the garlic and cook one or two more minutes, then add the artichoke halves, turning them a few times in the hot olive oil, and let them cook gently for 5 minutes, before adding the white wine. Let it boil up for a minute, then turn down the heat, add the herbs, tomato purée, chillies and a little seasoning, and simmer, covered, for 20–30 minutes, turning them from time to time. Test with the point of a knife to see if the artichokes are tender, if not continue to cook until they are.

Transfer to an earthenware dish (a small paella dish would be ideal) and, if whole, turn them all bottoms up. Scatter the fennel branches, cloves of garlic and chillies on top and then pour on the liquid. If there is too much or it seems very thin, boil to reduce it to a few tablespoons. These can now be kept in the refrigerator for 3–4 days.

Serve at room temperature. (Serves 4.)

Smothered Artichokes
Artichauts à l'étouffé

This is a Catalan recipe.

> 12–15 **young violet artichokes** (*these come in bunches with their leaves – usually bunches of five*); 2–3 tbsp **olive oil**; 30g **bacon in lardons**; 3 fat cloves **garlic**, *chopped finely*; small bunch **parsley**, *chopped*; **salt, pepper**.

Prepare the artichokes as in the recipes above. Heat a large pan of boiling salted water and blanch them for 2 minutes. Drain well.

Heat the olive oil in a wide sauté pan and add the artichokes. Season them with salt and pepper, cover the pan, turn down the heat and let them cook for 10–12 minutes, turning them from time to time.

When they are tender, remove the lid, throw in the lardons and cook, turning the mixture gently with a spatula and adding more olive oil if it seems dry, until the lardons are brown and cooked through. Add the garlic and parsley and cook for a few minutes more. Serve hot or warm. (Serves 4.)

Artichokes Greek Style
Petits artichauts à la grecque

The brave Phocaean Greeks from Ionia ventured across the Mediterranean in their sea-going galleys from the sixth century BC, founding
colonies at Marseille, on Corsica, and in Catalonia as they went. Parties
from Marseille continued to explore the French coast in the fifth century,
landing at the base of an extinct volcano, Mont Saint-Loup, on the river
Hérault. They were looking for sites to set up trading posts, and here
they founded Agde, built of the volcanic black basalt. One export of
the new settlement was slaves, another basalt mill stones, both quite
unpleasant cargoes. Agde is a handsome and historic old town (not the
same as modern Cap d'Agde, nearby, home of the finest nudist beaches
in France).

A whole new civilization came on these ships – the local tribes
(Iberians, Ligurians and Celts) began to find out about cultivating vines
and olives, money, irrigation, architecture, writing, new belief systems,
even hairstyles and footwear and, no doubt, food and cooking, since
the valleys of the Aude and the Hérault can boast the earliest traces of
Greek pots in the whole of the Midi.

*12 **purple artichokes**; 1 **lemon**; 150ml **olive oil**; 2 small **onions**, sliced;
sprinkle of **thyme leaves**; 1 level tbsp **tomato purée**; small pinch **sugar**; ½ tsp
black peppercorns; 2 tbsp **white wine**; juice of ½ **lemon**; 75g stoned **green
olives**, sliced; 75g stoned **black olives**, sliced; a small bunch **flat parsley**,
coarsely chopped; **salt**.*

Prepare the artichokes as explained in the previous recipes. Heat the
olive oil in a small sauté pan and soften the onions, with the thyme
leaves, for 10 minutes. Slice the artichokes about 1 cm thick, add to
the pan and sauter for 3–4 minutes. Add the tomato purée, sugar and
peppercorns, white wine, lemon juice and the olives. Season with a little
salt and cook, covered, for 10–15 minutes if the artichokes are young,
20–25 minutes if older. Sprinkle with coarsely chopped parsley. Serve
warm or cold. (Serves 4.)

French Beans with Garlic
Haricots verts à l'ail

I first had this sitting in my friend Suzanne's garden beneath an olive tree in La Livinière, an excellent wine-village in the Hérault. Cooked by Suzanne's god-daughter Anne-Liese, a stunning cook, the simple green beans, tasting of summer and of the delicate rose-coloured garlic of Lautrec, added freshness to the grilled duck breasts which accompanied them.

*500g fine **French beans**, topped and tailed; 150ml **crème fraîche**; 1 plump clove **garlic**, finely chopped; **salt**, **pepper**.*

Bring a large pan of salted water to the boil. Throw in the beans and let them cook until just tender, 8 minutes is just right for fine beans. Meanwhile simmer the garlic in the *crème fraîche* in a small non stick pan for about 5 minutes, until the garlic starts to smell fragrant.

When they are ready – I do not think they develop their flavour properly if they are eaten too crisp and raw – drain the beans thoroughly, refresh them under cold water if you want to serve them later and drain again. When you are ready to serve them, toss them in the cream and garlic mixture and heat them up in it. Season with pepper and add salt if necessary. Serve with roast or grilled meat or chicken – such as the *poulet au vinaigre* on page 195. (Serves 4.)

Broad Beans with Bacon
Fèves au lardons

Broad beans, as it is written, must be picked at dawn (some say on your knees); the broad bean does have something sacred about it, something to do with initiation, something almost sexual. It is the tender nickname by which the boys of my village named their young penis – *fève*.

  Between the first broad bean of May Day and the bean in a toga with its black ribbon, what a stepladder of flavours!

Joseph Delteil, author and poet.

*2kg **broad beans** in their pods, shelled; 2 tbsp **olive oil** or **goose** or **duck fat**; 1 **onion**, finely chopped; 125g **lardons** from poitrine fumée; **water** or **chicken stock**; **pepper**.*

Heat the olive oil or goose fat in a heavy-bottomed frying-pan over a gentle heat. Add the lardons and let them cook until the fat starts to run, then add the onions and let them soften, stirring them round, for 10 minutes.

Add the broad beans and barely cover with water or chicken stock. Simmer for 10 minutes until the beans are tender. Strain off the liquid and reduce it down in a small saucepan, this concentrates the flavours – watch out for salt from the lardons – and return the liquid to the beans. You will probably find the dish does not need more salt. (Serves 4–6.)

Beans with Anchovies
Haricots à l'anchoïade

*200g **haricot** or **butter beans**, soaked overnight; 1 **onion**, cut in quarters; 2 **bay leaves**; 2 cloves **garlic**, crushed with a fork; 10 **anchovy fillets**, cut in pieces; ½ tsp **chilli flakes** or **cayenne pepper**; 2 **egg yolks**; 200ml **olive oil**; 1 tbsp of **white wine vinegar**; 1 tbsp **sherry vinegar**; 2 tbsp chopped **flat parsley**; **salt, pepper**.*

Drain the soaked beans and put them in a pan of cold water, bring to the boil and then remove from the heat and drain. Put the beans in a pan of fresh cold water, together with the onion and bay leaves. Cook for 30–40 minutes until almost tender, then add salt and cook for a further 20–30 minutes, until completely so. Drain them and put them in a pottery bowl.

Mash the garlic and anchovy fillets finely with a fork and then pound to a paste in a pestle and mortar. Add the chilli flakes and egg yolks and incorporate them with the garlic and anchovy paste.

Gradually trickle in the oil, whisking it in little by little to make and emulsion. (If using a food processor add the oil a little at a time, pulsing to mix it in.)

Add the vinegar, taste for seasoning. Mix the anchovy dressing into the beans. Stir in the chopped parsley and serve slightly warm or at room temperature. (Serves 4–6.)

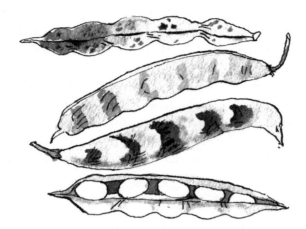

Beans with Tomato, Parsley and Garlic
Mongetes catalans

The name *mongetes* or *mojetes*, now meaning haricot bean, was once used for black-eyed (*Vigna*) beans, a rather coarse and mealy cowpea originating in Africa and, along with a type of broad bean, known in the Mediterranean ages before haricot beans arrived.

Later, the term came to mean beans of the *coco* (*borlotti*) or *Soissons* type – *Soissons* are large flat beans, like small butter beans, but you can also use top quality haricots. Spanish are good.

> *250g Soissons, Tarbais or other large **white beans** similar to butter beans, or good sized haricot beans, soaked for 24 hours; 1 stick **celery**, sliced into crescents; 1 **onion**, finely chopped; large bunch of aromatic herbs – such as **savory**, **thyme** and **flat parsley**, tied with string; 3 tbsp **olive oil**, plus extra for trickling on at the end; 4 **tomatoes**, peeled, seeds removed and chopped; 1–2 small **red chillies**, deseeded and chopped; 3 cloves **garlic**, peeled and coarsely chopped; 4 tbsp home-made **tomato sauce** or passata; 2 tsp **tomato purée**; pinch of **sugar**; 3 tbsp chopped **parsley**; **salt, pepper**.*

When the beans have been soaked and have swollen up completely, put them in a saucepan of cold water, bring to the boil, discard the water and start again with fresh cold water. Add the celery, onion and the large bunch of herbs and bring to the boil. Do not add salt at this point.

Simmer for 1–2 hours until the beans are nearly tender. Add salt and cook on until they are tender and almost floury in texture. Remove from the heat. Take out the bunch of herbs.

In a small sauté pan heat the olive oil and add the tomatoes, chillies and garlic. Season with salt and pepper and simmer until all the juice has cooked right down to a jam-like consistency. Add the passata or tomato sauce, tomato purée and sugar.

Reheat the beans in their liquid, drain them and stir in the *sofregit* – (the tomato mixture) and parsley, trickle a little olive oil over them and serve hot or warm. (Serves 4–6.)

Chichoumeye

On the markets *chichoumeye*, finely cut aubergines, onions and peppers, held together with tomatoes, is dished out with the rôtisserie chickens – the juice from the chickens drops into the vegetables, which smell and taste like heaven. You can add diced courgettes to the mixture. Customarily eaten with roast or sautéed chicken (such as *Poulet à la Barthelasse* on page 192), *chichoumeye* is also good with eggs, an omelette or *tortilla*, and with any grilled fish. In the Hérault it is used fill a tart, with Gruyère cheese scattered on top in a thick layer. When it is baked the cheese melts into the base – one of Languedoc's answers to pizza, the other is *coca de recapte* (page 295).

> 2 **aubergines** (350g), *peeled and cut into small dice (about 1 cm); 1 large* **red onion**, *finely chopped; 6–7 tbsp* **olive oil**; *300g ripe, red* **tomatoes**, *skinned, deseeded and finely diced; 1* **red pepper**, *grilled, skinned and cut in small dice;* **salt, freshly ground pepper.**

Put the diced aubergines in a colander and sprinkle with fine salt, tossing them to distribute it evenly. Allow to sweat and drain for 20–30 minutes, rinse and dry well in a tea towel.

Heat 4 tablespoons oil in a heavy casserole and put in the diced aubergine. Toss them so that all sides are lightly browned, and then turn down the heat a little. When the aubergine has softened, add the onions and one more tablespoon of oil if it is needed, season with salt and pepper and allow to cook for 10 minutes, turning and lifting the vegetables without breaking the aubergines. Add tomatoes and peppers and more oil if necessary. Season with black pepper and simmer gently until just cooked through. *Chichoumeye* can be served hot or cold. (Serves 4–6.)

Grilled Vegetables
Escalivada

I love this Catalan dish best when the vegetables have been grilled over the fire, which is the atavistic way of getting the perfect, mellow, smoky flavour. But, failing that, they can be cooked under a grill; in which case, avoid undercooked aubergines, which are a bit like eating tree bark, by frying them first. This version ensures that everything is cooked and harmonious.

> 2 **aubergines** (500g); 4 small **green** (or 2 **green** and 2 **red**) **peppers**, seeded and cut into strips; 2 large **tomatoes**, skinned and chopped; 3–4 tbsp **olive oil**; 1 tsp **sugar**; **salt, pepper**.

Cut the each of the aubergines lengthwise into 8 wedges, sprinkle them with fine salt and leave in a colander to drain for 40 minutes. Rinse and pat dry with kitchen paper. Coat them all over with 1–2 tablespoons of olive oil. Put them in a roasting tin, together with the peppers coated with oil, insides up, and tomatoes seasoned with a little salt and a pinch of sugar and a sprinkling of olive oil. Put them under a hot grill and let them cook, turning them once. They are ready when the aubergines are tender and very brown and the peppers are black and blistered. (Serves 4.)

Ratatouille with Olives
Ratatouille aux olives

This version of ratatouille is from the Hérault. It has no courgettes, replacing them with celery. This changes the character, making it fresh and crunchy instead of mushy. By also adding black olives, it has a strength of flavour it sometimes lacks. If you skip the salting of the aubergines, which some cooks do, it adds a peppery bite.

> 2 **aubergines**; 2 **onions**, chopped; 3 cloves **garlic**, chopped; 3 **long green peppers**, cut into strips; 6 tbsp **olive oil**; 1 small head of **celery**, sliced into crescents; 2 large **tomatoes**, skinned and cut in pieces; 60g stoned **black olives**; 3–4 sprigs of **thyme**; 2 **bay leaves**; 2 pinches of **sugar**; **flour**; small bunch **flat parsley**, coarsely chopped; **salt, pepper**.

Cut the aubergines in quarters lengthwise and then into chunks. Salt them as described for *chichoumeye*. Soften the onions, garlic and peppers in 2 tablespoons of the olive oil over a gentle heat for 5–10 minutes, then add the celery and cook 5 minutes more. Add the tomatoes, olives and herbs, and two pinches of sugar, season lightly (the olives are salty) and cook until the liquid from the tomatoes is mostly evaporated.

Season the flour with a little salt and plenty of black pepper. Flour the pieces of aubergine and then fry them in hot oil until they are brown on all sides and tender when tested with a knife. Tip the pan and let some of the oil run out of the aubergines, then transfer them to a pottery plate and spoon the pepper mixture over the top. Sprinkle with chopped parsley and serve hot or cold. (Serves 4.)

Aubergines with Tomatoes, Anchovies and Black Olives
Aubergines à la méridionale

Because of their closeness to Italy and their connections with the Middle East, Languedoc and Provence were the first areas of France to cultivate aubergines, and to associate them with garlic, herbs and olive oil – and, when they arrived, happily, with tomatoes, *pommes d'amour*.

> *2 large **aubergines** (500g); 4 tbsp of more **olive oil**; 2 large **onions**, chopped; 4 cloves **garlic**, sliced; 3 cloves; 3 **bay leaves**; 2 tbsp chopped **thyme** and **marjoram**; 100ml **chicken stock**; 300g **tomatoes**, skinned, deseeded and chopped; pinch of **sugar**; 1–2 tbsp stoned **black olives**; 8 **anchovy fillets**; **salt, pepper**.*

Heat the oven to 180°C. Peel the aubergines with a potato peeler. Slice them into rounds 2 cm thick. Put them in a colander and toss well with fine salt. Leave them for 30 minutes, rinse quickly and pat dry with a tea towel until very dry.

Heat 2 tablespoons of olive oil in a wide casserole and soften the onions, sprinkled with salt, for 10 minutes, stirring from time to time. Add the garlic and continue to cook for 10 more minutes. These should not be browned. Remove the garlic and onions to a dish.

Put the sliced aubergines in the same pan and let them cook for a while, adding most of the remaining olive oil, a little at a time. Turn them over and over so that they soften and wilt, and continue until they are all translucent and tender. Add back the onions and garlic, plus cloves, chopped herbs and stock, and season with a pinch of salt. Cook for 20 minutes over a low heat; try not to break up the aubergines.

Meanwhile put the tomatoes in a smallish pan, season with salt and pepper and a pinch of sugar and simmer gently until they reach a thick, syrupy consistency. Place the aubergines in a dish, put the tomatoes over them, arrange the olives and anchovies on the very top, trickle with olive oil and bake for 15–20 minutes. Serve hot or cold. (Serves 4–6.)

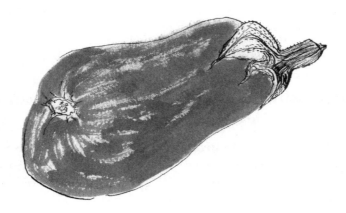

Gratin of Aubergines
Aubergines en gratin

Aubergines were at one time regarded with both suspicion and super-stition. The *aubergine de Narbonne*, also known as the *violet longue*, has several unflattering names in the vernacular – *pomme furieuse*, raging apple, *poule pondeuse*, laying hen and, worst of all, *vit de l'âne*, donkey's pizzle.

This last name may hint at a long-held belief that eating aubergines made men feel more attractive to women, even though, in the early seventeenth century, these sombre vegetables were also thought to bring on headaches, sadness and melancholy.

This unexpected and extremely delicious dish is similar to Colman Andrews' aubergine flan, in his book *Catalan Cuisine*. In the Aude they serve it with melted cheese on top and sometimes add chopped ham to the aubergine purée, while the Catalan version requires no cheese but calls for a red sauce (try the beautiful sauce for *calçots* on page 113) which adds a Goyaesque dab of hot colour to the pale dusky hues.

3 large aubergines (700g); 2 tsp flour; 250ml crème fraîche; 3 eggs; 50g grated cheese; salt, plenty of freshly ground black pepper.

This is easily made in a food processor. Heat the oven to 180°C. Stick a fork into the aubergines a few times to prevent them bursting and bake them for 40–50 minutes, depending on their size. They must be very soft when pierced with a knife. Place in a plastic bag to cool. Skin, chop the flesh and leave it in a colander for 20 minutes to drain, if it is very juicy.

Pulse the chopped aubergine in the processor with the flour, cream and the eggs, and a decent seasoning of salt and pepper, until smooth.

Transfer to a buttered gratin dish, sprinkle with grated cheese and bake for 25–30 minutes until just set and starting to brown. (Serves 4.)

Red Peppers with Tomatoes
Poivrons à la tomate

Cooked in this way the peppers transform themselves and become mellow and sweet, losing any hint of harsh or coarse flavours. This fundamental Languedoc dish is useful in so many ways – it can be served hot to accompany roast lamb or grilled or roasted sea-bass or any other fish, or cold with cold chicken, or as a starter with slices of *jambon cru*. It also makes a good light lunch when served hot with fried slices of *chorizo* or black pudding, or with fried eggs.

4 red or red and yellow peppers; 4 tbsp olive oil; 2 onions, chopped; 4 cloves garlic, peeled and sliced; 1 bay leaf; 700g tomatoes, skinned and de-seeded; 6–8 leaves of basil, cut into strips; salt, pepper.

Heat the oven to 220°C. Roast the peppers for 15 minutes or until the skins bubble and blister, turning black in places. Remove carefully (hot juices can spill out from inside the vegetable) and put in a plastic bag or a folded cloth to steam. When cool, skin and remove the cores and seeds. Cut into strips.

Heat the olive oil and sweat the onions gently with a pinch of salt until tender and transparent. The onions should be almost caramelized but not burnt. Add the garlic and the bay leaf and cook a few minutes more. Add the peppers and tomatoes, season and cook, stirring, for 20–25 minutes. Scatter with the strips of basil. (Serves 4–6.)

Stuffed Tomatoes
Tomates farçies

'Ripe tomatoes – you are the joy of the world and the volupté of the guts. Your bittersweet flesh is as nourishing as the breast and as pink as a lady's vulva.' So says Joseph Delteil about his favourite vegetable.

Stuffed tomatoes, often side by side with half a baked potato in its skin, sprinkled with salt and pepper and olive oil and browned in the oven, may be a cliché, but taste wonderful and are an essential accompaniment to roast or grilled meat.

*4 large **tomatoes**; 4 slices good **bread**, grated or torn into small pieces; 120ml **milk**; 2 fat cloves **garlic**, finely chopped; 8 sprigs **flat parsley**, finely chopped; 8 stoned **black olives**, chopped or 1 tbsp **black olive tapenade**; 1 tsp dried or fresh **thyme** leaves; 100–120ml **olive oil**; **salt**, freshly ground **black pepper**.*

Heat the oven to 200°C. Cut the tomatoes in half across the middle, through their equator. Remove the seeds and cut out the internal ribs, taking care not to cut through the shell.

Soak the bread in milk until the liquid is completely absorbed. Mix into it the garlic, parsley, olives or tapenade and thyme. Add half the olive oil and season with a little salt (the olives are salty), and plenty of black pepper. Stuff this mixture into the tomatoes, packing it down gently, and place them side by side in an oiled roasting tin or gratin dish.

Sprinkle the remaining oil on top and bake for about 30 minutes, until the tomatoes are completely soft and the stuffing is brown and crisp on the surface. If the stuffing dries out during cooking, moisten with a little extra olive oil. (Serves 4.)

Gratin of Courgettes
Courgettes en cazuela

Puffy and golden, this appetizing and smooth-textured way of cooking courgettes is good enough to be eaten stand-alone or would be an ideal accompaniment to roast or grilled meat, particularly lamb; in restaurants, such gratins are often cut into squares and served individually but I favour putting the whole dish on the table, to share.

In the Roussillon this would be cooked and presented in an auburn-coloured, round and shallow terracotta dish called a *cazuela*, glazed on the inside. These are made in le Bisbal in Catalonia and often appear on Languedoc markets, costing about 2–3 euros each; they are good in the oven, and even on the top of the stove, provided you use a heat diffuser. To prepare a new one for use, see page 86.

> *1 kilo large* **courgettes**; *4 tbsp* **olive oil**; *1 medium* **onion**, *chopped; 4 cloves* **garlic**, *chopped; 3* **eggs**, *yolks separated from whites; 200ml* **béchamel sauce**; *50g grated* **Gruyère cheese**; **salt, pepper**.

Grate the courgettes and sprinkle them with ½ teaspoon fine salt. Mix it in well and leave in a bowl for 20 minutes. Sweat the onion in half the oil for 15 minutes without browning. Add the garlic and continue for a few minutes. Make a béchamel with a tablespoonful of butter and flour and 200ml milk.

Pick up handfuls of the grated courgettes and squeeze out as much of the moisture as you can with your hands or force the moisture out by wringing the courgettes in a tea towel.

Add the remaining oil to the onion and when it is fairly hot, add the courgettes and cook them, stirring from time to time, over a low heat for 20 minutes, until they are tender. Add more oil as necessary and season well with a little salt and plenty of pepper. Allow to cool.

Heat oven to 160°C. Lightly oil the *cazuela* or gratin dish. Whisk the egg white to a soft foam. Stir the béchamel sauce and then the egg yolks one by one into the courgette mixture. Fold in the whites lightly and transfer the mixture to the prepared dish. Scatter the top with the grated cheese. Put the dish in the oven for 30 minutes or until puffy and golden. Serve at once. (Serves 4.)

A variation of this recipe uses Parmesan as well as Gruyère, less garlic and a little nutmeg. Instead of the béchamel, the custard is made with single cream and 3 whole eggs. Cook it in a gratin dish in a *bain marie*.

Courgette Pancakes
Paillassons de courgettes

*350g fresh **courgettes**; 4 tbsp **sunflower oil** for frying; 1 **small onion**, finely chopped; 2 large **eggs**; 2 tbsp **flour**; **salt**, **pepper**.*

Grate the courgettes on the coarse side of a grater. Salt generously and put them in a colander to drain for 20 minutes. Rinse thoroughly and put into a tea towel; squeeze out all the water by twisting the tea towel.

Soften the onion in one tablespoon of oil for about 10 minutes, stirring them around until they are tender but not brown. Let them cool and add them to the courgettes.

Beat the eggs in a bowl and then shake the flour onto the eggs through a sieve, whisking all the time with your other hand. When all the flour is mixed in, give it a good beating to get rid of any lumps. Season with pepper but do not add salt just yet.

When you are almost ready to serve the *paillassons*, stir the courgettes and onions into the batter. Heat the remaining oil in a large pan. Season the mixture with salt and drop large spoonfuls into the hot pan, flattening them lightly with the back of the spoon. Cook them in batches of two or three, depending on the size.

Fry for 4–5 minutes over a medium heat, turn them and fry a further 5 minutes. Do not let them get too brown, they should be golden.

Dry them on kitchen paper and serve hot with grilled lamb cutlets, *gambas à la plancha* or on their own with a green salad. (Serves 4.)

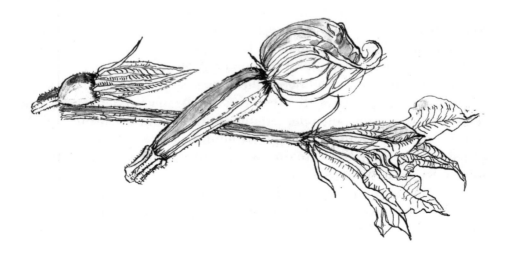

Grilled *calçots*

Cultivating *calçots* is an art in itself, and involves planting fully developed sweet white onions in well-mulched trenches, 8 inches deep, in late summer. As they grow, they must be earthed up like potatoes. By February or March, they are 2 feet long, and when they are dug up, each onion has between 6 and 16 fat shoots, looking like stumpy leeks.

These should be washed, trimmed of roots and leaf tops and thrown straight on the barbecue grill, without oil, and turned with tongs until cooked through. Serve in newspaper or a curved, terracotta roof tile. Peel off the charred outer skin, dip into romesco sauce or calçot sauce (pages 98 and 113) and enjoy.

Allow plenty of calçots. Small leeks can be substituted, but can be stringier and harder to swallow.

To cook indoors: heat the grill – this can be a ridged grill pan or an overhead grill. Grill on all sides until tender and lightly browned.

Cabbage with Potatoes and Bacon
Chou braisé

*1 large green **spring cabbage**, or half a **Savoy cabbage**; 8 **new potatoes**, boiled until just tender; 1 tbsp **olive oil**; 1 tbsp **duck fat** or 2 tbsp pork dripping; 200g **lardons**, preferably smoked; 100ml **chicken stock**; **salt, pepper**.*

Cut the cabbage into quarters and remove the thick part of the central stalk. Slice the leaves into strips and cut these across in half, to make them easier to eat. Wash and drain the strips.

Bring a pan of salted water to the boil, drop in the cabbage and boil for 3 minutes for a spring cabbage, 5 minutes for Savoy. Drain well to remove as much water as possible. Dice the potatoes.

Heat the oil and duck fat or the dripping in a heavy sauté pan and fry the lardons for 2–3 minutes, until lightly browned. Add the diced potatoes and brown them all over, turning them regularly. Lastly add the cabbage and the stock, season with pepper and not much salt, and cook, turning the vegetables lightly, until the stock has evaporated. Make sure it does not catch on the bottom of the pan.

This is splendid with grilled fresh *saucisses* or on its own. (Serves 4–6.)

Sweet and Salty Turnips
Navets salés et sucrés

The best turnips are the wonderful black skinned, long turnips from Pardailhan with their firm white flesh (page 67), but ordinary turnips work well cooked like this.

Cut 2 or 3 peeled turnips like *pommes frites*. Heat 6 tablespoons of goose fat or olive oil in a pan and fry the 'chips' in two batches to brown them lightly over a gentle heat, turning them often. When they start to get brown, pour off most of the fat, turn down the heat, return all the turnips to the pan, season with sea salt crystals and cover the pan. Cook gently for 10 minutes or until tender and then remove the lid, sprinkle with one teaspoon of sugar or honey. Cook until caramelized, turning them frequently. Remove them from the pan when they look as if they might burn. (Serves 2–4.)

Braised Fennel
Fenouil confit

These melting, delectable slivers of fennel are served with *chorizo* and rice in the Portanel restaurant in Bages as an accompaniment to wild sea bass.

*2 large heads (800 g) **bulb fennel**; 2 tbsp **olive oil**; 150ml **chicken stock**; pinch of **thyme**; **salt**, **pepper**.*

Trim the roots off the fennel, taking only a thin slice, as the core will hold the pieces of fennel together in the pan. Cut the bulbs downwards into quarters. Halve the quarters carefully through the core, so that the pieces do not fall apart.

Heat the olive oil in a sauté pan over a gentle heat, and sauter the fennel for 10–15 minutes, turning the pieces carefully.

Add the stock, season lightly, add the thyme and cover the pan. Simmer for 10 minutes covered, until the fennel is just soft, then remove the lid and continue until the stock has evaporated – you will hear it start to sizzle – and the fennel is glazed and melting. Stop when it starts to brown. (Serves 4.)

Gratin of Chard Stalks
Gratin de côtes de blettes

*500g **chard stalks**, white part only, cut into batons 5 cm long; 1 litre **stock** made with chicken stock cube; 2 **bay leaves**; 2 cloves **garlic**; 30g **butter**; 30g **plain flour**; 200ml **milk**; 6 **anchovies**, chopped coarsely; 50g **Cantal** or **Gruyère cheese**, grated; **salt**, pepper.*

Heat the oven to 200°C. Bring the stock, which should not be too salty, to the boil in a medium-sized pan and throw in the chard stalks, bay leaves and garlic. Cook for 15 minutes and drain over a bowl to catch the stock.

Make a béchamel sauce; melt the butter in a small pan, then add the flour, over a low heat. Let it cook for a minute or two without browning, and add the milk gradually, stirring until it is smooth after each addition. Add 250ml of the chard stock in the same way; when you have a smooth sauce, add the anchovies.

Retrieve the cloves of garlic and chop them finely, then add chard stalks and garlic to the béchamel sauce, cook for 3–4 minutes and transfer to a *cazuela* or an oval gratin dish. Sprinkle with cheese and bake for 25–30 minutes until the top is browned and bubbling. (Serves 4.)

Chapter Nine

Desserts, Preserves and Baking

Fig Tart
Tarte aux figues

In Languedoc most varieties of figs have two crops, the early ones are prettily named *figues-fleurs* and come in June or early July; the later crop, *figues d'automne*, come in late August, September and October. A beautiful, well-flavoured, juicy purple fig with a long season, very popular in the south-west, is *Verdane* or *Précoce Rond de Bordeaux*, bearing little dark-violet, round fruits throughout late summer and autumn.

*500g **figs**, preferably purple; 75g **sugar**; juice of half an **orange**; 1 tbsp **honey**; 1 **star anise**.*

For the pastry:
*175g **plain flour**; 40g **lard**, cut in pieces; 40g **butter**, cut in pieces; pinch of **salt**; 3 tbsp **cold water**, plus a few tsp to make the pastry.*

You can, of course, use ready-made pastry if you would rather. Otherwise, put the flour in a bowl with a pinch of salt and add the fat, rubbing it in with the tips of your fingers until you have a mixture with the texture of coarse breadcrumbs. Add 3 tablespoons of cold water, stirring it lightly into the mixture with a fork after each spoonful, until the pastry holds together, It may need a couple of teaspoons more.

Form a ball, but keep a light touch. Wrap it and let it rest in the fridge or a cool place for half an hour, or until you need it.

To cook the figs, cut them into quarters and put them in a pan with the sugar, orange juice, honey and star anise. Bring to the boil and cook for 10 minutes, stirring twice.

Remove the figs to a plate. Boil the remaining pink juices in a small pan until starting to turn syrupy. Allow to cool.

Heat the oven to 180°C. Line a buttered tart tin with the pastry, fill with baking paper and dried beans to keep the shape of the pastry, and bake for 20 minutes. Remove the beans and paper and cook for 15 minutes longer.

Let it cool a bit and then arrange the figs in concentric circles on the pastry base. Pour the fig juice over the figs and bake in the oven for 15 to 20 minutes, checking to see that it is not getting too brown. Serve the tart cool, with cream. (Serves 4.)

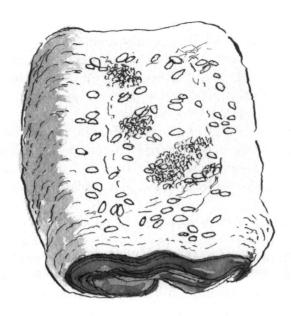

La Narbonnaise

Tart of Spiced Apples or Pears
Croustade narbonnaise

*1kg **apples** or **pears**; squeeze of **lemon**; 250ml **red wine**; 2 tsp **vanilla sugar** or ½ **vanilla pod**, split; 150g **sugar**; 3 sprigs **rosemary**; ½ tsp **cinnamon**, or more according to taste; 4 tbsp **ground almonds**; bought **flaky pastry**; 1 **egg yolk**, beaten.*

To decorate:
***flaked almonds, pine nuts** and **sugar nibs** (make them by breaking up 2 or 3 sugar lumps into little pieces).*

Peel, core and quarter the apples or pears and cut the quarters into thin slices. Put them into a bowl and squeeze a little lemon over the slices as you go along to prevent them from browning. Drain well, put the apples back into the bowl, pour on the red wine and add the sugar and vanilla sugar, rosemary, and cinnamon. Coat them well and let them macerate in the mixture for an hour or two.

Cook the fruit slowly in these juices, turning the pieces occasionally, until the liquid has been absorbed and thickened and taking care not to let it catch towards the end of the cooking. It should have an almost jam-like consistency. Allow to cool thoroughly.

Heat the oven to 200°C. Roll out the pastry into a rectangle so that you can line a tin with plenty of overhang on the two long sides. Prick the pastry with a fork. Sprinkle the ground almonds into the bottom in an even layer. Arrange the fruit on top.

Brush the hanging wings of pastry with milk, then bring the two long edges together, folding them inwards to overlap in the centre, making a sort of roll. Press the edges together. Turn the roll over at this point so that the join is on the underside and place this roll on an oiled baking tray.

Brush the surface with beaten egg or milk and, if using egg, either mark the top with diamond shapes with the back of a knife or scatter the top with almonds, pine nuts and sugar nibs. Once the tart or roll is in the oven, turn down the heat to 180°C. Bake for 40 minutes, covering the top lightly with aluminium foil when it starts to brown. Serve with cream.

You can make this with quinces, which can be bought from Iranian shops in winter, and which give a most elegant twist. They take much longer to cook than apples. Cook them covered until they are tender and then let the liquid evaporate. (Serves 6.)

Orange and Almond Tart
Croustade languedocienne or *Galette occitane*

If you buy this *croustade* in a pastry shop, it will be decorated in pastry or icing sugar with the beautiful Occitan cross or cross of Toulouse. The history of this emblem is much disputed. Whether it came from the eleventh-century Counts of Venasque in Provence, whose land passed to the Counts of Toulouse in Languedoc, or from the Cathars, or from the crusades and the Jerusalem cross, or from the Visigoths for whom it represented the twelve signs of the zodiac, or the Zoroastrian sun worshippers for whom it represented the sun – or whether it always belonged to the Counts of Toulouse who were given it by an angel after winning a battle at Bayonne – this heraldic cross is the symbol of the Languedoc-Roussillon (it is used on AOC Languedoc wine labels) and of the Occitan language.

On flags and shields, it appears in golden yellow on a red ground, and when there are marches demanding the restoration of the Occitan language, the banners too are in red and gold.

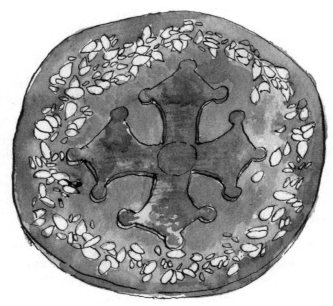

La Galette Occitane

*450g bought or home-made **puff pastry**; 125g **ground almonds**; 125g **demerera sugar**; zest ½ **lemon**, finely grated; zest 1 **orange**, finely grated; ½ tsp **orange flower water**; 1 tbsp **lemon juice**; 1 **egg**, beaten with a few drops of milk, for brushing; 2 tbsp **pine nuts**; 2 tbsp **flaked almonds**.*

Heat the oven to 180°C.

Divide the pastry into two and roll out two equal circles about 4 mm thick.

Put the ground almonds, sugar, lemon and orange peel, orange flower water and a squeeze of lemon juice, in a bowl. Mix everything together well with your finger tips.

Spread the mixture all over the middle of one of the pastry discs, leaving a margin of 2 cm or a bit more. Brush the margin with milk and place the second pastry disc over the top. Press the edges together and trim them, if necessary, so that they match. Brush the top with the egg wash and scatter with pine nuts and flaked almonds.

Place the tart on an oiled tray and bake for 30 minutes until golden. The almond mixture will have melted to give a delicately flavoured filling with the texture of thick honey. (Serves 4–6.)

Chocolate Tart
Tarte au chocolat

I first made this tart when I had friends staying and, as I was busy, I misread the original recipe and put in twice as much chocolate.

I used bought butter puff pastry (which the French stock in every supermarket and which is generally better-tasting than puff pastries available in Britain) and made it big – it was completely amazing and the best chocolate dessert I have had. You have to be bold, but it is definitely worth it.

*375g **dark cooking chocolate** such as Menier; 75g **butter** – I use unsalted; 3 **large eggs**; 35g **caster sugar**; 250g **butter puff pastry**.*

Heat the oven to 200°C. Place a round of baking paper in a shallow 38 cm tart tin and line it with thinly rolled puff pastry. Put in a sheet of baking paper and some baking beans. Bake blind for 20 minutes, check to see that it is baking evenly and turn it round if necessary. Bake 10 minutes more – it will only have 10 minutes more in the oven, so it needs to be fairly well cooked.

Turn down the oven to 150°C. Meanwhile, melt the chocolate in a large bowl over a pan of hot water on a low heat. Melt the butter and allow to cool. Whisk the eggs and sugar together with an electric whisk until pale and very frothy.

Remove the bowl of melted chocolate from the heat and stir in the butter a trickle at a time until it is all incorporated.

Give the egg and sugar mixture a final whisk. Fold it into the chocolate, a spoonful at a time. Spoon the mixture into the tart base, spread it to the edges and bake for 10 minutes. Allow to cool and serve with a dollop of *crème fraîche*. It can be served tepid. (Serves 6–8.)

Chestnut Tart
Tarte aux châtaignes

After various tests with *purée de marrons* in a tin (dull and dry), *crème de marrons* either in a tin or in tubes (light and sweet), fresh chestnuts (very fiddly) and vacuum-packed chestnuts, I much prefer the fine, sweet *crème de marrons* for making desserts.

> **shortcrust pastry** *(see page 280)*; 200g **crème de marrons** *(from a tin or 3 tubes)*; 200g **crème fraîche**; 2 **eggs** plus 1 **yolk**; 1 small **orange** – rind and juice; ½ tsp ground **cinnamon**; **icing sugar**.

Heat the oven to 200°C. Butter a 20 cm tart tin, and line with pastry. Put in a sheet of baking paper and some beans. Bake the tart shell blind for 20 minutes, remove the baking beans and cook for a further 10 minutes at 180°C.

Mix together the cream and chestnut purée, then add the eggs and egg yolk. Grate the rind and squeeze the juice of the orange and mix them in thoroughly with the cinnamon. Pour the mixture into the tart shell and bake for 40–50 minutes, until a knife stuck into the filling comes out clean.

Allow to cool and sprinkle the top with icing sugar. (Serves 4.)

Apple Tart with Chestnut Jam
Tarte aux pommes à la confiture de châtaignes

When apples are ripening on the trees in early autumn, this is a quick and easy tart. Golden Delicious apples taste quite good in this recipe, or use a Cox's Orange Pippin.

If chestnut jam, *confiture de châtaignes*, is not available, there is a good alternative in the *crème de marrons* mentioned in the previous recipe; it can be spread and tastes delicious. This tart is sometimes flavoured with finely grated orange peel which adds an interesting extra freshness.

> *300g **shortcrust pastry**; 4–5 **apples** (500g); 200g **chestnut jam** or 100g (1½ tubes) **crème de marrons**; 2 dessertspoons **rum**; 1 tbsp **crème fraîche**; **sugar**.*

Heat the oven to 200°C. Line a 20 cm greased tart tin with the pastry and prick the base with a fork. Line with baking paper and beans, and bake for 20 minutes.Remove the beans and paper, lower the heat to 180°C and cook a further 10 minutes. Allow to cool.

Peel, core, quarter, then thinly slice the apples. Keep in acidulated water until ready to use so that they don't brown.

Mix the chestnut jam or purée with the rum and cream. Spread the mixture over the base of the tart, and then cover with the sliced apples. Sprinkle with sugar. Bake for a further 35 minutes. Serve with liberal dollops of *crème fraîche*. (Serves 4.)

Chestnut Pancakes with Rum
Crêpes à la cévenole

With a handful or two of chestnut flour mixed with plain flour, these pancakes are a warm brown and the flavour is warm and nutty too. They are delicious, but not as light as pancakes made wholly with white flour, so try to make them small and dainty.

For the pancakes:
50g plain flour, 50g chestnut flour (or 100g plain flour); pinch salt; 4 tsp caster sugar; 2 eggs; 4–6 tbsp milk; 4 tbsp orange flower water (or water); 50g butter.

For the filling:
2 tubes crème de marrons; 2–3 tbsp rum; 4 marrons glacés, thinly sliced.

Make the batter in the usual way. Put the flour(s) in a bowl, mix in the salt and 2 teaspoons of sugar, break in the eggs, slowly whisk in the milk and orange flower water and mix everything together; only add enough liquid to give it a creamy consistency, it should form a ribbon when poured from a spoon. Allow to stand for an hour.

Meanwhile mix the chestnut purée with a tablespoon of the rum and the sliced *marrons glacés*.

Make the pancakes in the usual way. Melt a little butter in a frying pan, heat it until just starting to brown, then pour in half a ladle of batter and swirl it round to cover the bottom of the pan. When it is lightly browned and set, turn it over by flipping it or with a spatula, and cook the other side.

As they are finished, spread each pancake with the chestnut mixture, roll and place them side by side on a hot dish. Sprinkle with the remaining sugar.

Heat the rum not used in the filling, set it on fire and pour it flaming over the pancakes, leaning back to protect your eyelashes. It is best to do this at the table so the guests can watch the blue flames.

Serve with *crème fraîche*. (Serves 4.)

Pumpkin Tart
Tarte au potiron

Pumpkin is very much a staple vegetable all through the winter – the local pumpkins, blue, orange or mottled green, keep well and can be huge. This sweet recipe is from the Aveyron.

*400g **shortcrust** or **flaky pastry**, bought is fine; 900g **pumpkin**, flesh cut into chunks of about 5 cm; 100g **caster sugar**; 4 **eggs**; 1 **orange**, juice and grated zest; 250ml **milk**; pinch **salt**.*

Heat the oven to 200°C. Line a 22 cm greased tart tin with the pastry and prick the base with a fork. Line with foil and beans, and bake for 30 minutes. Remove the beans and turn down the heat to 180°C. Cook for a further 15 minutes. Allow to cool.

Cook the pumpkin flesh for 15 minutes in a little boiling water. Purée in a food processor. Give it quite a few minutes as the flesh can be fibrous. If you prefer a *moulin à légumes*, using the medium blade will remove the fibres.

Put the pumpkin mush in a saucepan with the milk, grated orange peel and orange juice. Reduce over a gentle heat for about 10–15 minutes, stirring frequently, until you have a soft, thickish purée. Beat the eggs in a bowl with the sugar and salt. Stir in the pumpkin purée.

Turn the oven back up to 200°C. Transfer the mixture to the pastry case and bake for 30 minutes or until the filling is just firm to the touch. (Serves 6.)

Cherry Clafoutis
Clafoutis aux cérises

The cherries of Céret, in the Pyrenees close to the border with Spain, are the earliest in France. The mountain village celebrates their arrival in early May with a festival, when the streets are mounded with cherries for sale. With its shady streets and cafés, it was a favourite with Picasso and many other twentieth-century artists. Picasso brought his friend Braque here not long before the First World War. They amused each other by dressing as musicians, which gave them a subject for extraordinary work. The drawings and paintings of café life (glasses, coffee cups, Gitanes) and of themselves with corked-on moustaches and guitars, gave birth to Cubism.

There are plenty of cherry products on sale in the village – jams and wonderful liqueurs and chocolates. This refreshing clafoutis is a fine way to use their exceptionally juicy fruit.

> *50g **plain flour**; pinch **salt**; 65g **granulated sugar**; 1 level tsp **baking powder**;*
> *1 **vanilla pod**; 2 **eggs**; 350ml **milk**; 1 tbsp **olive oil**; 500g **cherries**, stoned if*
> *you have a cherry-stoner, otherwise whole.*

Heat the oven to 175°C. Oil a 22 cm ceramic flan dish or shallow cake tin. Put the flour, salt and sugar and baking powder in a bowl. Split the vanilla pod and scrape out the seeds into the flour and sugar mixture. Mix everything together with your fingertips.

Beat the eggs and add them to the mixture, whisking them in to make a smooth batter. Whisk in the milk and olive oil. Stir the cherries into the mixture and transfer it to the flan dish, distributing the cherries evenly. Bake for 30 minutes until just set. Serve warm with cream. (Serves 6.)

Chocolate Pots with Chestnut Cream
Moelleux au chocolat et crème de marrons

An incredibly easy dessert.

*200g **dark chocolate**; 150ml **milk**; 100ml **double cream**; 75g **crème de marrons**, 1 tube.*

Melt the chocolate in a saucepan with the milk. Away from the heat, stir slowly and carefully until smooth. Allow to cool to lukewarm. Whip the cream until it is a soft snow, then mix in the chocolate.

Divide half the mixture between 6 little pots. Place a teaspoon of chestnut purée in each. Cover with the remaining chocolate and place in the refrigerator to firm. Serve with cream. (Serves 6.)

Raspberry Meringues

The basic meringue recipe I have used here is not French but comes from chef and food writer Alastair Hendy, with whom I have worked in the past, and whose instructions are bomb-proof. The idea comes from the gigantic meringues I see in all the local bakeries and pâtisseries, of which there are many; our village, Saint-Chinian, has three.

I had seen raspberry and poppy seed meringues in one bakery, and I tried adding poppy seeds to this sumptuous recipe, but nobody liked them.

*100g **raspberries**; 30g **sugar**; 4 **egg whites**; 120g **caster sugar**; 110g **icing sugar**, sieved; 1 tsp **cornflour**; 1 tsp **white wine vinegar**.*

Cook the raspberries and sugar for about 15 minutes until starting to go jam-like. Allow to cool and then mash them up with a wooden spoon. Heat the oven to 125°C.

Beat the egg whites with an electric whisk until forming soft peaks on the end of the whisk when it is turned upwards. Gradually add the caster sugar and whisk until very firm. Add the icing sugar, cornflour and vinegar and beat for a further 4 minutes. Fold in the the raspberries.

Line a baking sheet with baking paper, using little dabs of meringue to glue it in place. Spoon out the meringue onto the baking sheet, making 6 large or 12 small meringues. Bake for 1¼–1½ hours, until firm, then turn off the heat and leave to cool in the oven.

Glazed Figs in Muscat
Figues au muscat

Fig trees grow in every hedgerow and wall in Languedoc, seeding themselves promiscuously; some wild figs are deliciously juicy, eaten straight from the tree, others, like the proverbial barren fig tree, dry and shrivelled.

Although they are officially described as either *figues violettes* or *figues blanches*, they come in a huge number of varieties and can be deep purple, brown, blue, emerald green or golden; tiny and sweet or huge and luscious. Once there were commercial fig orchards, now people grow them in their vegetable gardens or close to their house, and the world enjoys free figs.

This recipe was given to me by fig-lover and restaurant critic Fay Maschler.

> *500ml **muscat wine; cinnamon stick; 4 cloves;** seeds from 3–4 **cardamom pods;** knob of **green ginger**, peeled, cut into slices; 2 tbsp **caster sugar;** 12 ripe figs.*

Heat up the wine with the rest of the ingredients minus the figs. When it comes to a simmer cut a cross in the top of each fig – cutting down about one third of the depth of the fruit – and place them in the hot wine. Cook gently for about 3–4 minutes. If necessary, do the poaching in batches. Remove with a slotted spoon, drain, and arrange in a bowl with the cut sides uppermost. Fish out the spices if you want it delicately spiced. Add the sugar and reduce the wine to a cupful of glaze and strain over the figs. Leave to cool. Very nice served with vanilla ice-cream. (Serves 4.)

Fig Jam
Confiture de figues, recette familiale

Apparently, the very best figs for jam-making are called Boutane. They are particularly sweet, so much so that in the Aude they are sometimes used in other jams to replace the sugar. This simple recipe is from *Le Figuier* by Jacques Vidaud.

> *1kg **Boutane or other figs**; 500g **sugar**; juice and pared rind of 1 **lemon**.*

Cut the figs in half and cover them with sugar. Add the rind and juice of a lemon, and leave to macerate overnight.

The next day, remove the lemon rind, and put the figs, with their juices, in a pan and boil for an hour or until setting point is reached.

Sieve the figs through a food mill, and cook for a further 30 minutes. Fill sterilized pots while the jam is still hot. (Enough for 2–3 pots.)

Spiced Pickled Figs
Figues épicées au vinaigre

Pickled figs, aromatic with spices, are excellent with cold pheasant, duck or goose, cold ham and with cheese.

> *350g **granulated sugar**; 200ml **red wine vinegar**; 120ml **water**; 3 **cloves**; 2 sticks **cinnamon**; 3 crushed **cardamom pods**; pinch **salt**; 700g **black figs**, not too ripe, washed and dried.*

Combine all the ingredients, except the figs, in a saucepan and bring to the boil. Boil until the smell of vinegar has lessened, about 15 minutes.

Place the figs in two 750 ml jars with airtight lids. Pour over the pickle liquid and allow to cool before closing the jars.

Keep a month before opening. (Makes 2 x 750 ml jars.)

Fig Chutney
Chutney à la figue

This chutney is easily made in Languedoc where, in September, there are figs of every hue dropping off trees everywhere. Go to Collioure and watch the crowds treading on carpets of fruit from the enormous trees on the promontary. They make an excellent chutney when combined with pumpkin.

*2 tbsp **olive oil**; 1 **onion**, chopped; ½ tsp **cayenne pepper**; ½ tsp ground **turmeric**; 1 tsp ground **coriander**; 1 tsp ground **cinnamon**; ½ tsp ground **cumin**; 500g **figs**, cut in pieces; 350g **pumpkin**, flesh cut into small cubes; 250g **brown sugar**; 250ml **white wine vinegar**; 1 **red chilli**, whole; **salt**.*

Heat the olive oil gently in a stainless steel pan and soften the onions for 10 minutes without letting them brown. Add the spices and heat them up to temper them. When they have cooked for 2–3 minutes, add the fig and pumpkin and stir thoroughly to permeate them with the flavours of the spices and onions.

Add the brown sugar, vinegar and whole chilli. Season and allow to simmer over a gentle heat for as long as it takes, stirring from time to time – probably at least an hour. The liquid will slowly evaporate. When you have a nice thick mixture, remove from the heat and transfer to sterilized jars. Keep for a month if possible!

Peach Chutney
Chutney de pêches et tomates

Since peaches and tomatoes are in such abundance in August, this is
when to make this golden, spiced chutney which goes so well with cold
roast duck or chicken.

> *1kg* **tomatoes**, *skinned and deseeded, keep skins and seeds in a bowl; 2*
> **peaches**, *preferably a bit under-ripe, blanched for 3 minutes and skinned;*
> *2* **onions**, *finely chopped; 175ml* **white wine vinegar**; *50g* **soft pale brown**
> **sugar**; *1 tbsp* **olive oil**; *1 heaped tsp* **coriander seed**; *1 heaped tsp* **mustard**
> **seed**; *pinch ground* **cumin**; *2–3* **bird chillies** *(pébrines); 2 cm piece of* **green**
> **ginger**, *peeled and grated; 1 tsp* **salt**.

Slice the peaches off their stones. Cut the tomatoes and peaches into 5
mm dice. Strain the juice from the tomato seeds and skins and reserve.

Combine the tomatoes and peaches and the strained tomato juice in
a large, reliable, heavy-bottomed pan. Add all the other ingredients.
Bring to the boil, lower the heat and simmer for about 1½–2 hours or
until thick. Transfer to clean warm jars.

Keep for a month or so before eating. (For 2 x 250g pots.)

Olive Chutney
Chutney olive

I came across *Chutney Olive* in Narbonne, in a small grocer's shop near the
twelfth-century archbishop's palace, where the aristocratic memoirist
Lucie de la Tour du Pin – whose autobiography tells us so much about
life during the revolutionary era and its imperial aftermath – used to
stay as a young girl with her uncle the Archbishop and her grandmother.
She describes eating a blue jelly (which may perhaps have been this
conserve, or at least a version of it) at one of the banquets there. Try it
with cheese or game – cold pheasant or venison – or with pork pie.

> *250g* **onions**, *finely chopped; ½ tsp* **salt**; *250g stoned* **black and green olives**,
> *cut into pieces; 100g* **raisins**; *100g* **dates**, *chopped; ½ tsp ground* **ginger**; *½*
> *tsp* **cayenne pepper** *or* **hot pimentón**; *150g* **tomatoes**, *skinned, deseeded and*
> *chopped; 2–3 tbsp* **olive oil**; *600ml* **cider vinegar**; *300g* **brown sugar**.

Soften the onions, lightly sprinkled with salt, in the olive oil for 20 minutes. Add the olives, raisins, dates and spices and cook for 5–10 minutes, then add the tomatoes and the vinegar. Cook, stirring from time to time, over a low heat for 30 minutes then add the sugar and stir until it dissolves. Simmer until the chutney thickens, at least another 30 minutes, stirring often.

Spoon into sterilized jars and keep until needed – let it mature for at least a month if possible. (Enough for 3 x 250g pots.)

Coca de recapte

The Catalan *coca* (plural *coques*) is part of the great pizza and flatbread family of the Mediterranean. Its Catalan name, however, shares the same linguistic root as our 'cake' or German's '*kuchen*'. This version, *coca de recapte*, can be translated as '*coca* with everything,' according to the authority on Catalan cooking Colman Andrews, who gives another local name, *coca enramada*, which translates as 'garlanded' *coca*. A flatbread embedded with vegetables and sausage, it is made to be eaten on Sundays or at a *calçotada* – spring onion feast – and at other celebrations. It can have all sorts of ingredients added to it – cheese and olives, ham, anchovies, possibly tuna; slices of *chorizo* or *botifarra blanca*, sausage, pork loin or sardines are also popular. The smell when the *coca de recapte* comes out of the oven is enough to make one faint with hunger.

> *For the bread dough:*
> 500g **plain flour**; 1 tsp **fine salt**; 1 level tsp **dried** (instant) **yeast**; 2 tbsp **olive oil**; 300ml **lukewarm water**.

> *For the topping:*
> 2 **red** or **green peppers**; 1 **courgette** (150g), thinly sliced; 1 **onion**, thinly sliced; 1 large, ripe **tomato**, skinned, seeds removed and chopped; 3 tbsp **olive oil**; and optional – 20 slices of **chorizo**, **botifarra blanca** or sliced pure **pork sausage**.

Mix the flour, salt and yeast in a large bowl. Make a well in the centre and pour in the water and oil. Mix with your hands and form the dough into a ball. Flour a work-surface and place the ball on it. Knead it for up to 10 minutes and place in an oiled bowl. Cover with cling film and allow to rise in a warm place until doubled in size.

Grill, skin and slice the peppers, removing the cores and seeds. Heat

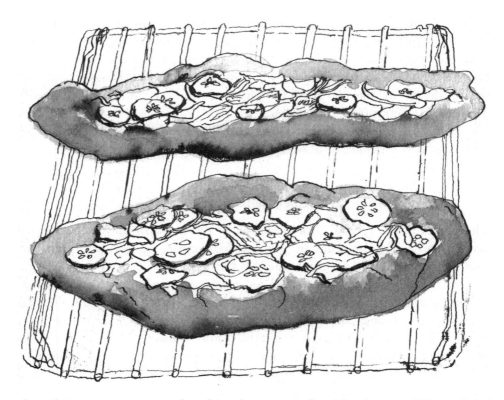

the oil in a sauté pan and soften the onions for 10 minutes. When they are tender and translucent add the courgettes and peppers and let them soften for 5 minutes, then add the tomatoes. Cook gently until any liquid has evaporated, the mixture should well-cooked and glistening. The mixture must be dryish, the vegetables whole and not overcooked. Allow to cool.

When the dough is ready, heat the oven to 220°C, divide the dough in half and shape each half into a ball on a floured worktop. Shake and pull and tease the balls into long, flat oval shapes, 35 x 15 cm is a good size, but *coques* can be up to 50 cm long. Place on oiled baking sheets.

Divide the vegetables and press lightly into the top of each bread, leaving a margin around the edge of at least 2cm. At this point add slices of sausage if you are using them, putting them on between the vegetables and pressing lightly.

Leave to prove in a warm place for 15–20 minutes, lightly covered with a cloth. When it has a slightly taut and puffy look, bake for 25–35 minutes, according to the thickness of the dough. Eat while still warm.

Spinach Beet *coca* with Pine Nuts and Raisins
Coca de pignons et de blette

This formidable flatbread, topped with toasted pine nuts to add a crunch to the soft spinach, features the irresistible Catalan combination of sweet and salty. To add some more salt, scatter fried lardons on top before baking or crumble white goat's cheese over the top before serving.

*Dough ingredients as in the previous recipe; 200g **chard** or **spinach beet** leaves, washed and shredded; 1 **onion**, finely sliced; 2 more tbsp **olive oil**; 2 tbsp **raisins** or sultanas; 1 tsp **dark brown sugar**; ½ tsp ground **cumin**; 2 tbsp **red wine vinegar**; 2 tbsp **pine nuts**; **salt**, freshly ground **pepper**.*

Make the dough as in the previous recipe and put it to rise. Meanwhile soften the onions gently in olive oil, with a pinch of salt, and after 10 minutes add the raisins. Cook for a further 5 minutes and add the brown sugar, cumin, vinegar and a little salt. Then stir in the shredded chard leaves and pine nuts and let them cook, covered, until just tender (chard is tougher than spinach beet). Allow to cool.

When the dough is ready, heat the oven to 220°C. Divide the dough into two, form it into 2 balls and work them gently into long oval shapes – don't roll or cut it, which will produce the wrong texture, but tease it out into long strips. Place the ovals, which should be 30 cm long or more (you can make them as large as the oven will allow) on oiled baking sheets or roasting tins. Top with the chard mixture, leaving a margin of 1cm, allow to prove for 15 minutes or until starting to puff a little and bake for 25–30 minutes. Eat while still warm. (Enough for a family-size *coca*, serving 6–8.)

Onion *coca*
Coca de ceba

*Dough ingredients as in the previous recipe; 2 **sweet onions**; 2–3 tbsp **olive oil**; 500g **melting cheese** such as raclette, tomme or Gruyère, thinly sliced; or 12 slices of **chorizo**; pinch **salt**.*

Slice the onions, not too fine, and soften them in the olive oil until they are tender and start to turn golden. Allow to cool. Make the long strips of dough as described in the first *coca* recipe. Cover them with pieces of cheese or slices of *chorizo* and then the cooked onions. Prove for 15 minutes and bake for 25–30 minutes, eat while still warm. (Makes 2.)

Walnut Bread
Pain au noix

The great baker Lionel Poilâne said that the perfumes of wheat and walnuts are a perfect marriage. This recipe is loosely based on his *pain au levain*. It is best made in winter when the walnuts are really fresh. The bread is a favoured accompaniment to cheeses such as Laguiole, Roquefort and of course goats' cheeses. The quantities are sufficient for 2 medium (600g) loaves.

To make the leaven starter (levain):
*35g **white bread flour**; a 7g packet – 2 level tsp – **dried instant yeast**; 100ml **water**.*

Mix the flour and yeast in a bowl then work in the water. Beat it to a smooth cream with a whisk. Cover the bowl and leave to rise in a moderately warm place (23–25°C). Let it ferment for 1½ hours.

To make the dough:
*580–600g **white bread flour**; 200g **spelt** or **rye flour**; 500ml **lukewarm water** – blood temperature; 1–1½ tsp **sea salt**; 200g **walnut halves** cut in pieces; 1–2 dessertspoons **olive oil**; **maize flour** or polenta for sprinkling.*

Dissolve the salt in the water. Put both the flours in a large bowl and mix them together thoroughly. Make a well in the centre and pour in the *levain*. Gradually add the water, mixing it in with one hand, making a sticky mixture. Keep 20g or so of white flour for sprinkling on the worktop a little at a time, when you knead the bread. Keep adding flour until you can just make a flattened sort of ball with the loose-feeling, stretchy dough. It should have a lively, springy feel to it. Knead for 10 minutes.

When the dough is smooth and silky, place it in an oiled bowl, roll it round in the oil and cover it with cling film. Leave in a warm place for 2–3 hours or in a cold place for 4–5 hours or overnight. If the latter, allow it to warm up again to room temperature and swell a bit more before proceeding – in either case it should rise to double its original size.

Heat the oven to 220°C – heat it up well ahead of time to achieve a good solid heat.

To shape the loaves, place the dough on a floured worktop and spread on a handful of chopped walnuts. Fold the dough over and spread again; keep doing this until all the walnuts are incorporated. Cut the dough in half and either make freehand loaves or loaves in tins.

To make freehand loaves, oval or round, draw the edges of the cut side of each piece of dough together and place on a baking sheet (that has been sprinkled with fine polenta) with this seam underneath, to give the top some tension. Cover with a cloth and a sheet of cling film and allow to rise in a nicely warmed place to almost double in size. Keep out of draughts. When the loaves have risen, slash the tops 3 times with a very sharp knife before placing in the preheated oven.

If you would rather make the bread in tins, oil two 600g loaf tins. Tuck the sides of each piece of dough underneath, tuck each end under also and drop the moulded dough into the tin, rounded side upwards. Cover with cling film as before and leave to prove for about an hour, or until the dough has risen almost to the top of the tins. Do not allow draughts. Place in the preheated oven.

A third alternative is to make *miches*. These are the round loaves, for example of *pain de campagne*, that are proved (upside down) in *bannetons*, round willow baskets lined with linen (available from Poilâne shops). You will also need large *cazuelas*, terracotta paella pans, to bake them in.

Divide the dough in two as before. Sprinkle the insides of two *bannetons* liberally with maize flour. Form nice balls of dough by tucking the sides underneath and place them, rounded side down, in the baskets. Cover loosely with a cloth and leave to rise until doubled in size.

When they are proved, grease two *cazuelas* with oil and heat them for 10 minutes in the preheated oven. Flour a bread board generously with maize flour, reverse one basket onto the board, sprinkle the top of the dough with maize flour and transfer, by sliding, into one of the pans, floured side up. Slash the top 4 times, 2 each way, with a razor-sharp knife. Place in the oven. Repeat with the second loaf.

Whatever the form of loaf, bake for up to 50–60 minutes. Tap the bottom of the loaf – if it sounds hollow it is done. Cool on racks.

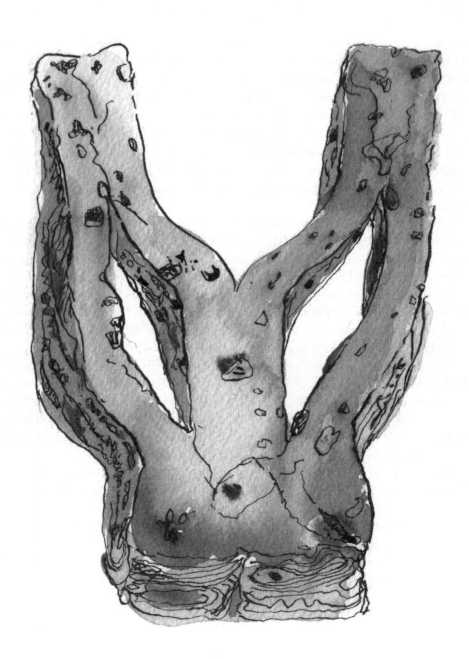

Savoury *fougasse*
Fougasse salée

The flatbread called *fougasse* in France, particularly in Provence where it often has the wheat-ear form pictured opposite, is also called *fogassa* in Catalonia and *focaccia* in Italy. The word in all these forms derives from the Latin *focus*, or hearth. It was originally baked on the sole or floor of the bread oven when it was being prepared for conventional loaves but was as yet too hot to bake them without burning the crusts.

*500g **strong bread flour**; 2 tsp (1 sachet) **instant yeast**; ½ tsp **salt**; up to 400ml lukewarm **water**; 2 tbsp **olive oil**; 20 small, stoned **black olives**, coarsely chopped; 8 **anchovy fillets**, coarsely chopped.*

Mix the yeast in a small bowl with 100g of the measured flour and then 150ml of the measured water. Allow to ferment for an hour in a warmish place.

Put the remaining flour in a bowl and stir in the salt, add the yeast mixture, olive oil and enough remaining water to make a malleable dough. Knead it on a lightly floured board for 10–15 minutes and place in an oiled bowl. Allow to rise, covered with cling film, for 2 or 3 hours or until doubled in size.

Heat the oven to 220°C. Oil one or two baking sheets. When the dough is well risen, return it to the worktop and cut it in two. Form into 2 balls, keeping one covered. Roll out the other into a long rectangle or oval, scatter it with some of the olives and anchovies, fold it over in half and repeat. Fold over again and roll for a third time to make a flat rectangle about 30–40 cm long. Slash it right through with 8 cm diagonal slashes in herringbone formation – one, two or three down each side and about 2.5 cm in from the edge. Pull the sides out to open the holes a bit. Transfer to an oiled baking sheet, brush with olive oil then make the second *fougasse* the same way. Allow to prove for 10 minutes or so and bake for 30–35 minutes. (Bake one after the other if the oven is small.) Cool on racks and eat the delicious bread while still warm. (This recipe makes 2 *fougasses*.)

Chestnut Flour Bread
Pain de campagne à la farine de châtaigne

This version of chestnut bread from Olargues keeps extremely well. I have sometimes taken the trouble to boil and peel 150g chestnuts and broken them into pieces to mix into the dough instead of hazelnuts, but it definitely results in a heavier loaf. This recipe is for one large loaf.

> *100g **chestnut flour**; 400g **white bread flour**; 1 tsp **instant yeast**; 1 scant tsp **salt**; 100g **hazelnuts**; 300ml **lukewarm water**; 1 tbsp **olive oil**.*

If you want, you can remove the skins from the hazelnuts by toasting them in a frying-pan and then rubbing them in a cloth, but what a fiddle. Chop them coarsely. Sieve the chestnut flour, breaking up the lumps with your fingers.

Blend the two kinds of flour with the yeast and the salt in a large bowl. Add most of the water and half the olive oil and mix into the flour until you have a workable dough – not too firm, it should be easy to knead on your table or worktop.

Flour the kneading surface lightly two or three times during the first few minutes of working, you should then obtain a dough that is silky and pliable. Knead for 10 minutes in all.

Clean your mixing bowl, pour in the rest of the olive oil and roll the ball of kneaded dough in it. Cover the bowl with cling film and allow the dough to rise for 3–4 hours at room temperature, or in the refrigerator overnight, until it doubles in volume. If you opt for the latter way of doing it, remove the bowl from the refrigerator and let it come back to room temperature before you start the next step.

This is to add the nuts, a handful at a time, folding the dough over them after each handful.

Heat the oven to 200°C. Form the dough into a round loaf and place it on a well-floured baking sheet. Cover and allow to rise once more, for up to a further 45 minutes. Slash the top quickly in three places with a sharp knife. Bake for 45–50 minutes. Test to see if it is done by knocking the bottom of the loaf. It should make a hollow sound. Cool on a rack.

Olive Soda Bread
Cake aux olives

I first saw these breads on a stall in the Narbonne market; some were made with green olives, some with black, and some had ham in them; they are basically soda bread, quick and easy to make and – with all that olive oil, and all those eggs – quite sumptuous, which cannot be said for most soda bread.

This recipe is based on one from Pierre and Hélène Vialla who farm at Combaillaux in the Hérault, not many kilometres north of Montpellier. It is enough for 2 loaves.

> *500g **white bread flour**; ½ tsp of **salt**; 20g **baking powder**; 4 **eggs**, beaten; 125ml **olive oil**; 125ml **water**; 150g **Gruyère cheese**, grated; 150g stoned **black olives**, coarsely cut into large pieces.*

Heat the oven to 220°C. Mix together the flour, a small amount of salt (the olives are salty), the baking powder and the beaten eggs. Add the olive oil and enough water to make a supple, kneadable dough. Knead until smooth.

Add the cheese and the olives a little at a time, working them in at each stage. Form the dough into 2 loaves.

Place the dough in oiled 500g loaf tins and leave to develop for 15–20 minutes. Bake for 35 minutes or more, until a skewer pushed into the middle comes out very clean. Allow to cool on a rack to room temperature before slicing.

Fritters
Bugnes

Bugnes are a cross between doughnuts and Spanish *churros*. We know them more readily as *beignets*, and the word is obviously closely related to the Spanish and Catalan *bunyols*. *Bugnes* are especially eaten at Eastertide. The most famous *bugnes* are perhaps those of Lyon when they are cooked for Mardi Gras. If you wanted to make *bunyols* in the Roussillon style, you can follow this recipe but add a teaspoonful of ground anise or aniseed. The *bunyols* should be formed into bracelets rather than left as cylinders. They are light and not at all greasy, so they lend themselves to dipping into melted chocolate.

> 250g **plain flour**; ½ sachet **dried** (instant) **yeast**; 50g **sugar**; pinch **salt**; zest of 1 **lemon**; 2 tbsp **lukewarm water**; 25g **butter**, very soft; 1½ **egg yolks**; 10ml **rum**; **vegetable oil** for frying; **sugar** for sprinkling.

Mix the flour with the yeast, sugar, salt, and grated lemon rind in a large bowl. Make a well in the flour and add the water, butter, egg yolks, and rum. Mix together and work into a ball of dough. Knead it for 5 minutes. Let it rise in the bowl, in a warm place, covering it with oiled cling film and a folded cloth.

When it has doubled in size, cut it into 12 pieces. (Weigh the dough and then divide it into half and then into half again. Cut each piece into three equal pieces.) Roll these pieces lightly between your hands, and then on a floured board, to make 12 snakes, 15 cm long. Let them rest for about 5 minutes.

Heat the oil until it is just starting to smoke, twist the *bugnes* to make a notional spiral and drop them, 5 or 6 at a time, into the oil. Turn them over once while they cook. When they are golden and puffed, remove them and drain any surplus oil on kitchen paper. Sprinkle generously with sugar. Eat while warm.

La Tielle Sétoise

Glossary

As I mentioned in the introduction, we know that the name Languedoc means 'the language that says *oc*' ('yes' in Occitan) as opposed to the northern 'language that says *oyi* or *oui*' or Languedoïl.

Officially, Occitan, which is not a form of French at all, and has a lot in common with Latin, was the language spoken by all those who live south of the line running from the Gironde in the west, eastwards through Limoges to Vichy and beyond. But when you look closer, you find, as did Abbé Henri Grégoire in 1764, that the language of Occitan turns out to be 'a muddle of incomprehensible dialects'.

Graham Robb, in his book *Discovering France*, devotes a chapter to investigating the subject and he emphasizes the importance of the report by Abbé Grégoire, which was called 'The Necessity and Means of Exterminating Patois and Universalizing the Use of the French Language'. He was an advocate of universal education and sent out a nation-wide questionnaire to find out exactly who did speak French.

It turned out that only 11 per cent of the country's population spoke French as we understand it. Although this changed over the next two centuries in the communes of northern France, the communes in the booming Languedoc of 1863 were still 90–100 per cent non-French speaking, with the exception of the area bordering the Rhône. They were the people who would not say *non*.

'Educated travellers were constantly amazed to find their French was useless', and that dialects changed faster than the landscape – the patois in one commune would be different to that in their neighbours', three kilometres along the track or just across the river.

In view of the fact that some two million people still speak Occitan and it can sometimes be heard in the village shop, it might seem a simple matter to give some currently used Occitan names for ingredients and to translate these into French and thence into English, or to find the object, say on a market stall, ask its name, see what it is, and to give its equivalent name in English. But even today, it can be difficult to pin down local names – for fish, for example – as they change from one town to another, and sometimes, although they may sound the same, they are spelled completely differently. But here are some of the dialect names currently in use (marked Occ for Occitan or Cat for Catalan with the occasional Prov for Provençal), and also some useful French (marked Fr) names.

AÏGO-SAU (Prov): literally water and salt soup, which can also contain garlic, white fish, thyme and a poached egg.

AÏGO BOULIDO (Prov): garlic soup.

BAJANAT (Occ): chestnut soup made with dried chestnuts.

BAR (Fr): sea bass, *loup de mer* (Fr), *llobarro* (Cat).

BAUDROIE (Fr): monkfish, also known as *rap* (Cat), and as *lotte* (Fr), very popular firm white, boneless fish, eaten when the size of a finger as well as when large, up to 25–30 kilos. The head makes a good stock.

BIJUT (Occ): you need courage to tackle the *violet*, a sea creature that looks like a sort of deformed potato. Eat, cut in half, alongside a plate of oysters and accompanied with shallot vinegar or a vinaigrette.

BIOU (Occ): pointed sea snail, *escargot de mer pointue* (Fr).

BRANDADE (Fr): purée of salt cod with olive oil, garlic, milk and sometimes potatoes. Nîmes is famous for its brandade.

BOUILLINADE (Occ): fish and potato stew.

BROCCIU: fresh Corsican sheep or goat's milk cheese made with whey, similar to *ricotta* or *fromage frais*.

BROUILLADE (Fr): scrambled eggs.

BROUSSE: a drained *fromage frais*, made with sheep or goat's milk, curdled with a natural rennet (or vinegar)and drained in a basket or similar, so it forms the shape of an upturned basket.

BULOT (Fr): whelk.

CABASSOL (Occ): sheep's head, also a dish made with sheeps' heads, stewed and served with mayonnaise, mustard and pickled mushrooms.

CAGARAUL (Occ): *petit gris* snail.

CAGARAULA (Occ): large snail.

CAGARAULETA (Occ): small snail.

CASTAGNADE (Fr): chestnuts, roasted over the fire in a *diable*, a large frying-pan with holes in it.

CAILLETTES (Fr): faggots of pork, often combined with Swiss chard.

CALAMAR, CALMAR (Fr): squid.

CARBASSOUS (Occ): little round courgettes, often served stuffed.

CARTHAGÈNE (Fr), CARTAGENA (Occ): an apéritif made with grape juice and grape alcohol, often made at home, it tastes similar to a fortified wine such as Pineau de Charente.

CHÂTAIGNONS (Fr): dried chestnuts.

CHIPIRON (Fr): tiny curled cuttlefish, *Sepia elegans* or *Sepiola rondeleti*, also called *sépioles* in French, also known as *supions*.

COCA (Occ): also known as *coque*, an oval flattish bread with a variety of toppings, often associated with saints' days and festivals.

COQUELET (Fr): baby chicken.

COUENNE (Fr): pork skin, this can be seasoned, rolled up and cooked like a confit in its own fat. It is used to give body to stews and braises and is also delicious to eat.

COURGE, CITROUILLE, POTIRON (Fr): pumpkin.

COUTEAU (Fr): razor clam, *ganivet* (Occ, Cat).

CRANQUE (Occ) or CRANC (Cat): male green crab, CRANQUETTE is the female. FAVOUILLE (Fr) is similar, as is CRABE ENRAGÉ (Fr), so called because it blushes red and attacks its enemy with its pincers when annoyed.

DAURADE (Fr): gilt-head bream, *orade* (Cat), *orada* (Sp), a delicious firm white-fleshed fish distinguished by the golden yellow and black markings on the head.

DOUCETTE (Fr): *salade mâche*, lamb's lettuce, cultivated or naturalized in the wild near old *hortes*, vegetable gardens.

ÉMISOLLE (Fr): small edible shark, smooth hound, also known as *petit requin*.

ENCORNET (Fr): squid, calamar.

ESCABECHE (Fr): fish fried and then marinated in vinegar (sherry vinegar is good for this), it keeps well and is eaten cold.

ESTOUFFADE (Fr), ESTOFADO (Cat): meat or game braised slowly in a little liquid.

ÉTRILLE (Fr): swimming crab, also known as *crabe espagnole*.

FAISSELLE DE BREBIS (Fr): a fresh curd cheese, similar to *fromage frais* but drained of its whey; also the name of the little pot with holes in the sides which is used to drain the cheese.

FARÇOUS, FARSOUS (Rouergue, Aveyron): *au maigre* (for fast days), it is a small green fritter or *beignet* made with flour, eggs, onions and a large quantity of *blette* (Swiss chard), parsley and chives; *au gras*, with meat, it is more like a patty or hamburger containing sausage meat, onion, garlic, bread, eggs and a large quantity of herbs and spinach. Popular in the Aveyron.

FARIGOULE, FRIGOULE (Fr): wild thyme which grows by the roadside and amongst the rocks of the *garrigue*. It has grey leaves and palest pink flowers and tastes strongly of the rocky terrain it clings to.

FIDEU (Cat): small vermicelli-like noodles, they are made into *fideuà*, a kind of noodle-based paella. *Fideo* in Spanish.

FOUGASSE (Fr): a type of bread cooked with sweet or salty ingredients (crystallized fruit, pine nuts, bacon, olives, pork scratchings, etc.) and sometimes with both sweet and salty flavours. The dough is slashed to form a palm-leaf shape.

FOULQUE (Fr): coot, *folca* in Occ, waterfowl of rivers, marshes and estuaries, an appreciated game bird with very dark flesh. Its cousin, the moorhen, is *poule d'eau* (*galinèla* in Occ).

FRICANDEAU (Fr): a faggot made of pork, pork liver and possibly *blette* (Swiss chard) wrapped in a piece of pig's caul and baked. It can be eaten like a pâté, with toasted *pain de campagne* and salad.

GALÈRE (Fr), GALERA (Sp): this crustacean has a strange appearance, with a fat body that sports mock eyes upon the tail, and a large head with feeble claws, a mantis shrimp, *squille* in Fr. It is used in making fish soup.

GARDIANE, GARDIANNE, GARDIANO (Occ): a long cooked stew of meat, usually beef but could be horse meat.

GOBIE (Fr): a small, ugly, rather charming rock fish, used in fish soup.

GRATTONS (Fr): the crisp grilled or roasted residue of pork fat that has been rendered. There are also goose and duck grattons. They are eaten as a snack or in salads, or baked into bread – *coca*, *fougasse* or a savoury brioche called *pompe*.

HORTES (Cat): usually at the edge of every village is an area of vegetable gardens going back many centuries, many of which are still cultivated assiduously. Equipped with wells, they contain fruit and olive trees, a seat, and a neatly rolled hose, plus perfectly kept rows of tomatoes, peppers, haricots verts, courgettes, melons and onions. The Occitan for garden is *òrt*; *òrta* is a large garden and *ortalet* is a small garden.

JOLS (Occ), JUELS (Fr): tiny sand-smelts, sold for deep-frying and served like whitebait. Another variety of sand smelts is known as *melet*.

LLISA (Cat): grey mullet.

MANOULS (Occ): a speciality of the Lozère, little parcels of sheep's stomach (*panse*) containing sheep's tripe and stomach, bacon and veal ruffle or mesentary (*fraise*), cooked overnight with vegetables, and eaten with potatoes – preferably for breakfast.

MORUE (Fr): salt cod.

MOURGETTES (Fr): little snails from the vineyards.

MOUSSERONS (Fr): fairy ring mushrooms, *Marasmus oreades.*

MUGE (Fr): grey mullet, see *llisa,* abundant in the salt lagoons.

PÉBRINE: bird pepper, a small and fiercely hot chilli.

POUFFRE (Sètoise), POFRE (Occ): octopus used in the famous *tielles* (see below).

POULPE (Fr): octopus.

POUTARGUE (Fr): salted, pressed mullet roe.

RÉGANEOUS (Occ): baby sea bass.

SALICORNE (Fr): samphire grows plentifully in the salt marshes of the Languedoc coast, it is eaten pickled in vinegar or blanched for seconds in boiling water, to accompany fish.

SPIGOL: the Spanish spice mixture often used in paellas as a substitute for highly priced saffron. It contains turmeric, paprika, mixed spice and about 3 per cent saffron.

TENILLES (Fr): tiny thumbnail-sized clams.

TIELLES: little round, individual pies made with olive oil pastry, filled with octopus cooked in a rich tomato and spice-flavoured sauce.

Bibliography

Andrews, Colman, *Catalan Cuisine, Europe's Last Great Culinary Secret* (Grub Street, 2002).

Baradez, Marie-Laure, *Recettes cévenoles et languedociennes de nos grands-mères* (Éditions Reflets de Terroir CPE, 2006).

——, *Recettes toulousaines de nos grands-mères* (Éditions Reflets de Terroir CPE, 2006).

Bertholle, Louise, *Secrets of the Great French Restaurants* (Sphere Books, 1975).

Béziat, Marc, *Recettes au pain perdu* (Rodez, Les Éditions du Curieux, 2009).

——, *Recettes paysannes du Gard* (Rodez, Les Éditions du Curieux 2008).

——, *Recettes paysannes de l'Hérault* (Rodez, Les Éditions du Curieux 2007).

Bini, Georgio, *Catalogue of Names of Fishes, Molluscs and Crustaceans of Commercial Importance in the Mediterranean* (Rome, Food and Agriculture Organization of the United Nations, 1965).

Bonnadier, Jacques, *Petit traité amoureux de l'aïoli* (Quercy, Librairie Contemporaine, 2007).

Bonnaure, André, *À table, petit précis de cuisine occitane* (Portet-sur-Garonne, 1999).

Braudel, Fernand, trans. Sîan Reynolds, *The Mediterranean in the Ancient World* (Penguin Books, 2001).

Casas, Penelope, *The Foods and Wines of Spain* (Knopf, 1982).

Centelles, Jacques, *De la Méditerranée aux étangs et marécages* (Perpignan, Sofreix, 1981).

Chalendar, Pierrette, *Cuisine héraultaise d'autrefois* (Nîmes, Éditions Lacour, 2009).

——, *La Cuisine de l'Aude* (Nîmes, Éditions Lacour, 2001).

Chaudron, Maud, *La Cuisine de nos chères mamans* (Nîmes, Éditions Lacour, 1999).

Clément, Pierre-Albert, *Foires ets marchés d'Occitanie de l'Antiquité à l'an 2000* (Montpellier, Nouvelles Presses du Languedoc, 1999).

Collège du Sigean, *Recettes traditionelles de l'Aude et d'ailleurs* (Nîmes, Lacour, 2001).

Cristol, Denis, *Recettes d'un petit village en Languedoc* (Villefranche-de-Rouergue, Fleurines, 2010).

Couplan, François and Styner, Eva, *Guide des plantes sauvages comestibles et toxiques* (Delachaux et Niestlé, 2009).

Davidson, Alan, *Mediterranean Seafood* (Prospect Books, 2012).

Davis, Irving, *A Catalan Cookbook* (Prospect Books, 1999).

Delsol, Alain, *Lo Sofregit, recettes de cuisine d'hier et d'aujourd'hui des grands-mères gruissanaises* (Gruissan, Nuances-formes-langage, 2009).

Delteil, Joseph, *La Cuisine paléolithique* (Gap, Les Éditions de Paris, 2007).

Duby, Georges, trans. Juliet Vale, *France in the Middle Ages 987–1460* (Oxford, Blackwell, 2000).

Ezgulian, Sonia, *Cuisinière Catalane* (Lyon, Éditions Stéphane Bachès, 2006).

Fabre-Vassas, Claudine, trans. Carol Volk, *The Singular Beast* (New York, Columbia University Press, 1997).

Favand, Marie-Agnès, *Mes recettes du Languedoc et des Cévennes* (Saint-Étienne, Christine Bonneton, 2005).

Fébus [Phoebus], Gaston, *Le livre de la chasse* (1387, facsimile ed. Akademische Druck- u. Verlagsanstalt, Graz, Austria, 1994).

Hours, Yves, Hours, Monique and Veyrun, Monique, *La Cuisine de nos mamées* (Nîmes, Lacour/Rediviva, 1994).

Hussin, René and Galmiche, Philippe, *Recettes en Aveyron* (Aveyron, Éditions Fleurines, 2008).

Kurlansky, Mark, *Salt* (Jonathan Cape, 2002).

Lambert, Max, *L'Olivier et la préparation des olives* (Provence, Éditions Campanile, 1993).

Lebey, Claude, *Languedoc-Roussillon, produits du terroir et recettes traditionelles* (Paris, Albin Michel, 1998).

Ledrole, Robert, *Cuisine du Languedoc* (Aix-en-Provence, Édisud, 2005).

Le Masson, Jean-Claude, *La Cuisine littorale de nos aïeules* (Nîmes, Éditions Lacour, 2001).

Le Roy Ladurie, Emmanuel, trans. Barbara Bray, *Montaillou, Cathars and Catholics in a French Village 1294–1324* (Penguin, 2002).

——, trans. Arthur Goldhammer, *The Beggar and the Professor: A Sixteenth Century Family Saga* (University of Chicago Press, 1997).

Loohuizen, Ria, *On Chestnuts, The Trees and Their Seeds* (Prospect Books, 2006).

Lorfeuvre-Audabram, Régine, *Cuisinière camarguaise* (Lyon, Éditions Stéphane Bachès, 2011).

Lovell, L.S., *The Edible Molluscs of Great Britain and Ireland, With Recipes for Cooking Them* (Reeve & Co, 1867).

Maguelone, *Beautés et Saveurs de l'Hérault* (Roquebrun, Les Éditions Aubéron, 2002).

Marco, Claude, et al., *Les salades sauvages: L'Ensalada champanèla* (Prades de Lez, Ecologistes de l'Euzière, 2003).

Marty, Albin, *Fourmiguetto: Souvenirs, contes et recettes du Languedoc* (Nonette, Éditions Créer, 1978).

Montagné, Prosper, *Le Trésor de la cuisine du bassin méditerranéen de France* (Chartres, Lainé et Tantet, 1937).

Montier, Natalie, *Identification et caractérisation des varietés d'olivier cultivées en France* (Turriers, Naturalia Publications, 2004).

Olney, Richard, *Lulu's Provençal Table* (Harper Collins, 1994).

O'Shea, Stephen, *The Perfect Heresy, The Life and Death of the Cathars* (Profile Books, 2001).

Pousson, Vincent, *Cassoulets, haricots, mongets & Cie. Légumineuses réflexions* (Portet-sur-Garonne, Loubatières, 1997).

Richardin, Edmond, *La Cuisine française. L'art du bienmanger* (Paris, Librairie Nilsonn, 1910).

Robb, Graham, *The Discovery of France* (Picador, 2007).

Rouanet, Marie, *Petit traité romanesque de cuisine* (Paris, Éditions J'Ai Lu, 1999).

Rouquette, Francine, *Les Cuisines du Languedoc-Roussillon, mer et montagne* (Provence, Éditions Campanile, 2007).

Rouré, Jacques, *Table mise en pays Catalan* (Barbentane, Éditions Equinoxe, 1997).

Thibaud-Comelade, Eliane, *Cuisine Catalane et vins de Roussillon* (Portet-sur-Garonne, Loubatières, 1995).

——, *La Cuisine catalane* (Cahors, Éditions Jacques Lanore, 2006).

—— [as Comelade], *Les coques catalanes* (Portet-sur-Garonne, Nouvelles Éditions Loubatières, 1991).

Trutter, Marion ed., *Culinaria Spain – Spanish Specialities* (Cologne, Könemann, 1998).

Valeri, Renée, *Le Confit et son rôle dans l'alimentation traditionelle du sud-ouest de la France* (Kristianstad, Sweden, LiberLäromedel Lund, 1977).

Vidal, Jean-Claude ed., *Mémoires du pays d'Orb – contes, légendes, recettes de nos grands-parents* (Presses du Languedoc, 1999).

Vidaud, Jacques, *Le Figuier* (Centre Technique Interprofessionel des Fruits et Légumes, 1997).

Wolfert, Paula, *Mediterranean Grains and Greens* (Harper Collins, 1998).

Wright, Rupert, *Notes from the Languedoc* (Pézenas, Domens, 2003).

Index